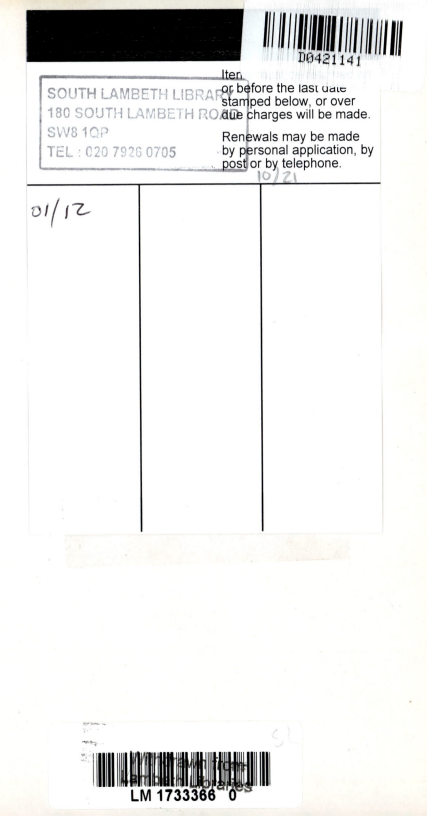

THE WAR FOR GAUL

A New Translation

JULIUS CAESAR

TRANSLATED BY JAMES J. O'DONNELL

PRINCETON UNIVERSITY PRESS
PRINCETON AND OXFORD

Published by Princeton University Press
41 William Street, Princeton, New Jersey 08540
6 Oxford Street, Woodstock, Oxfordshire OX20 1TR

press.princeton.edu

LCCN 2018948731
First paperback printing, 2021
Paperback ISBN 9780691216690
Cloth ISBN 9780691174921

British Library Cataloging-in-Publication Data is available

Editorial: Rob Tempio and Matt Rohal
Production Editorial: Debbie Tegarden
Text Design: C. Alvarez-Gaffin
Cover Design: Matt Avery/ Monograph Studio
Cover image is copyright © Shutterstock
Production: Erin Suydam
Publicity: Jodi Price
Copyeditor: Emma Arrington Stone Young

This book has been composed in ScalaOT

Printed in the United States of America

Contents

Introduction

Caesar deserves to be compared with Alexander the Great. No one before or since comes close. Command, conquest, and a lasting legacy set them apart from the likes of mere strivers like Napoleon or Hitler. And the war in Gaul was the making of Caesar.

Have I said that right? Isn't that what you would expect a translator of Caesar to say? It's all entirely true and many have said as much before. But saying *just* that makes you admire him without understanding him, makes you complicit in his ill-doing as well. This translation of his account of the war in Gaul will try to restore *your* objectivity and freedom of judgment. Make of him what you will.

* * * *

Cormac McCarthy should be the one to write the story of Caesar in Gaul. As insensitive and brutal as McCarthy's Americans afoot in a land of native and Spanish peoples they wrongly took for uncivilized, Caesar's armies had little excuse for what they did and they preferred not to remember it once done. But Caesar told their story coolly. Though people die in droves, horribly, on these pages, the Latin word for "blood" appears only twice, near the end.

The facts of the story must be made clear. A general with something to prove, a career to make, and plunder to be harvested for financial gain was handed an army and a province and a guarantee he would have both for long enough to make serious mischief. He spent nine years battering his way through his province and the rich and promising lands beyond, bullying allies and brutalizing the resistant. By the time he was through, the lands and peoples that obeyed his commands—and those of his successors for another half millennium—had been vastly increased, and he was poised to make himself master of the world, or at least the world that stretched from the English Channel to Damascus.

He had no business doing any of this. His colleagues admired his chutzpah, knowing that he went far beyond every reasonable moral or legal boundary. His excesses were possible because he was in competition with two other monsters, one of whom fell in battle at the opposite end of the world while Caesar was in Gaul, the other of whom let Caesar go too long, then fought him, then fled, and ended up hacked to death by the minions of a king who thought it prudent to curry favor with Caesar.

But the book Caesar wrote is magnificent: amoral, certainly, but clear, vivid, and dramatic, a thing to be remembered and read for the ages. Books about war often make us sympathize with the wretchedness of the victims. This one forces us to be Romans of the kind its author wanted to be. We read it nervously, cheering for a bullfight we didn't want to attend and don't approve of, admiring the grace of the awesome minuet that floods the sand with blood. There is no denying that this is a great work of literature, one of the greatest, and at the same time, there should be no denying that it is a bad man's book about his own bad deeds. I think it is the best bad man's book ever written.

But many will resist my saying the plain fact. Because his carven prose depends on a deliberately restrained vocabulary and a terse, correct style, the book has been thought suitable for schoolboys for many generations, until about the time Latin schoolmasters discovered finally that women can read too. Now the book is in disfavor, for the wrong reasons: because it is about war, and because it is too easy. But we all need to read books about war if we are to avoid dying in one, and this book is anything but easy.

The best reasons for not teaching this book to the young are that it gets war exactly right and morals exactly wrong, and that it achieves a crystalline purity of style that looks easy from every angle but proves to be sternly difficult and demanding when faced flat on. This is a book for the middle-aged and sober, for those who know that the world is not run according to their tastes and never will be, for those who listen best to the author who has truly mastered his language, whatever he has to say—and who think that such an author must indeed have something important to say and hear.

The book pretends to be a set of notebooks, *commentarii*, the sort of official memos generals sent home to inform their masters of their deeds, the sort historians could come along and use to construct genial and politically agreeable accounts of great events. The style is meant to look simple and to seduce. When we read it, we are meant to think we are getting the plain facts, direct and unvarnished. The old maxim is *ars est celare artem*—"never let 'em see you sweat" captures the sense of that shopworn Latin phrase. Nobody ever saw Caesar sweat.

Translators of Caesar have always been helpful—much too helpful. Surely, they think, the reader just wants to know what really happened. Caesar would be pleased to think that's what we think he's offering. The effect of this connivance with the general is not only to be found in the maps and diagrams and illustrations that go with the best translations but in the expansiveness and preemptively explanatory construction of every sentence. The translations I've looked at in English generally add almost as many words again as Caesar needed in the original, so that he becomes downright chatty and helpful. No. This book is fiercely austere, for brave and attentive readers, ready to march twenty-five miles a day under full pack and be ready for more tomorrow.

GAUL

Caesar has us imagine that he has invaded a land of Wild West instability and aggressiveness and tamed it for civilization. No.

Where and what was Gaul? The province Caesar was formally assigned included the Roman territories of Illyricum (the east coast of the Adriatic), Cisalpine Gaul (what is now Italy north of the Apennines and south of the Alps, running from Turin to Venice), and the old Roman "province," both what is now called Provence and the strip of further Roman territory along the Mediterranean coast linking to Spain. The Roman proconsul normally sat at Modena, halfway between Rimini and Piacenza along the "Emilian Way" (the marching road already plotted out by the Romans in 187 BCE). Caesar would grant citizenship to Cisalpine Gaul's residents in 49, and Octavian would formally dissolve that province and fold all Italy into a single jurisdiction in 42.

That province of Transalpine Gaul was what the Romans had claimed after the Punic Wars, to secure the coast and a path to Spain. The modern cities of Aix-en-Provence and Narbonne descend from settlements designed to secure the eastern and western segments of their holdings. Strictly speaking, Cisalpine Gaul and that province were the Gaul Caesar was assigned to govern and protect.

But the Gaul of Caesar's book is all the Gaul Rome didn't rule when he arrived, Real Gaul for us is approximately modern France, bounded by Alps, Rhine, Atlantic, Pyrenees, and Mediterranean. Caesar created that Gaul, most notably in his pithy opening sentence about "all Gaul" and "three parts." What he says there is, like much in this book, moderately true and entirely self-serving. Gaul for him was what he wanted it to be.

The leading nations among the Gauls were the Sequani, Haedui, Arverni, and Bituriges. They were all to be found in central Gaul. Aquitaine and Brittany were home to smaller, poorer peoples. Between the Seine and the Loire was the hotbed of a certain Gallic spirit, among the Carnutes and Senones. Modern Chartres was the site of the annual festival of Gallic religious observation, led by the druids who fascinated Caesar. It was there that Vercingetorix, himself from the Auvergne, found resonance for his call to arms in 52 BCE.

Well on in the commentaries (at 6.12), Caesar tells a story of old rivalry between the Haedui and the Sequani in which the Haedui had been worsted and subjected to their neighbors. But at the very beginning (see 1.31) he names both the Haedui and the Sequani as the leading peoples of the Gaul. In fact, readers should pay particular attention to the Haedui throughout, just as readers of Thucydides should always keep an eye on the Corinthians. They were almost always loyal to Rome and Caesar, but they were adept at playing Caesar and Rome to their own ends. Watch as you read how often they are the ones to alert Caesar to a supposed threat and how often Caesar's actions wind up confirming the Haedui in their place of power and prestige, both among Gauls and with Romans. They loom very large in the years 58–57, disappear from the narrative in 56 and 55, then return to view when Vercingetorix does, in the first pages of the seventh commentary on the year 52. Might not a Haeduan aristocrat after Vercingetorix's fall be pleased with a Gaul that had been reshaped for Haeduan benefit by the great general?

And beyond Gaul lay Germany. Gaul was Caesar's to conquer, Germany was the other threatening world that lay beyond. His Germany (colorfully described in his sixth commentary) is as much a place of his imagination as his Gaul is.[1] Great rivers bind people together more than they separate them and it's clear that people moved back and forth across the Rhine with ease. But the river made a convenient tactical boundary for Caesar, so that's where he divides his worlds. (He came to rely on "German" troops to support his own.)

In the heartland, a Gallic nation was a tiny community of oligarchs, big men with land and influence, lording it over a population limited in means and cultural capacity. The Gallic nations were smaller, less urbanized, less literate, less monetized, and therefore less imperial and less able to trade to their advantage than Rome was, but in many other ways very similar to Rome.

The peoples of the Roman province, stretched along the Mediterranean coast from the Alps to the Pyrenees, were far further advanced as measured by Rome. Nonetheless, it would be fully a century from the end of Caesar's time in Gaul before the emperor Claudius made his famous speech in 48 CE to extend the possibility of membership in the Senate to citizens from the three Gauls. Till then, Roman presence in Gaul was a Roman army facing in

---

[1] The first paragraph of Caesar's first commentary contains the first Roman mention of "Germans." The polymath Greek geographer Posidonius, who died at a great age at about this time, is the other earliest writer to mention a people by that name. Cicero picks up the word in his oration toadying to Caesar on consular provincial assignments in 56. The Germans qualify as what we now call an "imagined community" after Benedict Anderson's work.

two directions, keeping out Germans and policing mostly compla-
cent Gauls.

We get a snapshot of Gaul just before Caesar in the career of
Marcus Fonteius, proconsul in the 70s. He worked in the shadow of
Pompey, who was fighting rebels in Spain and drawing on Gaul as
a source of supplies. Fonteius laid heavy taxes on the Gauls, which
they paid by borrowing money from Romans, landing heavily in
debt to Roman loan sharks. Fonteius was also accused of taking a
cut himself. Cicero in a speech defending Fonteius against well-
founded accusations of corruption speaks of Gaul (by which he
means the province) as chock-full of Roman citizens and Roman
businessmen.

The Transalpine province was an afterthought added to Caesar's
responsibilities when he had already been assigned Illyricum and
Cisalpine Gaul. The natural expectation would have been that he
might have to police the Sequani just outside the province's boundaries. The planned migration of the Helvetians at the beginning of
his time in Gaul was a godsend to Caesar, offering the pretext for a
wider war.

From out of the past, the Cimbri and the Teutones played a helpful role as bogey men, looming in the minds of senators at Rome,
readily invoked by Caesar to justify his bold actions. Their rampage
through Gaul and into Italy, lasting from 113–101 BCE, had been the
crowning success of the general and consul Marius and the making
of his younger rival Sulla. Rome successfully defended itself against
an enemy of uncertain scale and ambitions; Marius and Sulla created the autocratic national security state that Caesar would finally
command alone. The "new model army" that Marius created was
larger (and capable of being made larger still), more professional,
and more loyal to its generalissimo than the armies of old.

The Roman story of that war did not emphasize how much Rome
had earned hostility by its own actions in southern Gaul leading to
the establishment of the province. The bloody scale of the ultimate
victory and the destruction of the Cimbri and Teutones as peoples
were certain to have both terrified and enraged the Gauls who
observed it. The culminating battle of Vercelli (between Turin and

Milan) in 101 ended with Sulla victorious and reports of 140,000 enemy killed and another 60,000 captives destined for slavery at best.

Caesar's own creation of "Gaul" was a long-, long-lasting achievement. His Gaul is roughly today's France, his Germania roughly today's Germany. Like Menachem Begin, he created facts, facts we still deal with.

WAR

War is a mad, unnatural thing. Killing is hard work and dangerous; the life surrounding the few days of actual battle is arduous. Romans feared "barbarians"—but what did the barbarians think of Romans? "Watch out, watch out, the civilized people are coming, and you know how appalling *they* can be!" Reading Caesar is good for us if we are appalled and slightly stunned by the spectacle and by the way we are expected to take the spectacle in stride, as though it's the sort of thing good, smart people engage in, the sort of thing that's morally and culturally superior to mere barbarism.

But what actually happens in warfare? A war is outwardly a collection of battles, but the battles are not where the real action is. A real victory doesn't take place on the day of the battle, but the next day or the next week. The victory is won when the defeated commander decides not to risk another battle. He may be short on manpower or food, or perhaps he is not confident that his men will have the will to respond well if he commands them. Or is it won when a community decides not to muster forces and fight but to pay protection money instead and settle for subservience?

Caesar did not overwhelm Gaul. He was at a significant numerical disadvantage in facing his opponents. At his maximum strength, he had perhaps 60,000 men in arms with him, to fight up and down a country of populous and prosperous communities extending some 500 × 300 miles. Even if he could fight successfully, he could never garrison every town and every river crossing adequately to defeat all comers—unless he broke their spirit, unless he made their commanders see that resistance was futile. Yet by the time he left he was sure that he had pacified *all* of his Gaul, and in an important way he had.[2]

In the first weeks of 49 BCE, Caesar left Gaul to pursue his glory back in Italy and moved on to the civil wars he would fight in Greece, in Egypt, in Africa, and in Spain. He would return to Gaul himself only briefly in 49, to see to the subjugation of rebelling Marseilles, part of Rome's settled domains for decades. But the huge, fractious, unhappy new territories that he bludgeoned into submission from 58 to 50—all throughout the civil war, none rebelled. They were beaten, and stayed beaten. They had been persuaded that Rome could and would muster the troops to face any uprising and that when successful Rome would be pitiless. The atrocities of war that we will review in these years were strategically vital to Rome's success. They showed the Gauls that a civilized people would stop at nothing to secure their conquest of the barbarians. The conquest remained secure for four hundred years at least, about the length of time separating us from Shakespeare's last plays and the settlement of Jamestown in Virginia. War is good for some things.

And war is good for generals in particular. Among the many important things Caesar doesn't talk about in his commentaries is the astonishing wealth that bled from Gaul into his own pockets during these few years. Any attempt to quantify the riches Caesar garnered will fail, but Cicero's estimate of what the next governor of Gaul might expect after Caesar's death was *pecunia infinita*—money beyond measure. Plutarch said that Caesar sacked 800 towns in Gaul; one of his modern students can only count eight mentioned in these pages. His bag men had to be busy travelers.

Even if 800 exaggerates, Caesar was busy in ways he does not tell us. Already by 54, he was using the proceeds of conquest to begin work on what would become his grand forum in Rome, with his friends Oppius and (for that moment) Cicero leading the development work, buying up land at very high prices. It remained a prior-

[2] Well, he says repeatedly that he's done it. *De bello Gallico* 2.1 (early 57), 3.7 (early 56), 6.5 (early 53), 7.1 (early 52, just before all hell broke loose) and (Hirtius saying it for him) 8.24 and 8.46 (end of 51).

ity and preoccupation for the rest of Caesar's life. The dedication in 46 BCE of the temple in that forum of Venus Genetrix embedded Caesar's ancestry legend in the cityscape on a grand scale, as good a moment as any to select as the beginning of the serial dynasties of Caesars that would last many centuries. There were friends to be rewarded as well, potential friends to be bribed, enemies to be bought off, troops to be rewarded and equipped. There was no end to the money to be spent. War is good for some things.

What did Caesar leave behind in Gaul when he went off to his great war with Pompey and the Senate? We should first not ignore the small colony of ex-soldiers settled at Nyon on Lake Geneva a few miles above Geneva itself—a watchpost to keep an eye on Helvetians and Germans, but also the nose of the camel of military settlements that would soon enough be a primary vehicle of the Romanization of Gaul under Caesar's successors.

Caesar's successor was *intended* to be Lucius Domitius Ahenobarbus, from a powerful family with longstanding ties (probably including economic ties) with Gaul—not a bad choice, but fiercely opposed to Caesar. (His great-great grandson would be the emperor Nero.) On his march south into central Italy, Caesar confronted and captured Ahenobarbus at Corfinium, in the mountains east of Rome, where he was on his way toward Gaul. Caesar grandly released his prisoner; Ahenobarbus fought against him again at Marseilles a few months later and died on the battle field of Pharsalus, brave, resourceful, and unlucky.

After Ahenobarbus was out of the picture and until his own death, Caesar named all the successors we know of. During that period, a rebellion among the Bellovaci had to be squashed in 47–46, but had little consequence. In 39, we see Octavian's closest colleague, Agrippa, serving as proconsul and campaigning in both Aquitaine and the Rhineland, but we know of no other governors over the area in the troubled time before the battle of Actium resolved Rome's wars in favor of Octavian in 31 BCE. In his turn, Octavian regularized organization of the provinces on more settled lines with only occasional small outbursts of resentment. Perhaps the only substantial concern after Octavian's death was an uprising Tiberius faced in 21 CE.

Patience and persistence prevailed, and Gaul was effectively a part of Rome, without any major insurgency, until Roman inattention left it to shape a new identity under the Franks in the fifth century CE. This great and surprising fact is a measure of Caesar's success. His decision not to punish the Arverni and the Haedui after Vercingetorix undoubtedly helped: he could have been short-sighted and vindictive, but for all the blood that was shed at his behest, Caesar always knew that generosity was a powerful weapon as well. The settlement Caesar imposed was sufficiently generous and sufficiently respectful of the existing powers in Gaul to be apt for stability.

$$* * * *$$

A word about the mostly faceless. To be Caesar's soldier in Gaul was no walk in the park. There was, first of all, the walking itself, hundreds of miles of it. Then there was the sleeping in camp facilities (at best) as a way of life. Roman camps were well designed and executed and summer nights in Burgundy and Alsace were not all that unpleasant, but a soldier's life was a desirable one mainly if grinding rural or urban poverty was your alternative. Then there was the fighting. On average, Caesar had his forces in Gaul, or some of them, engage the enemy half a dozen times a year, two or three of those times in concerted pitched battles with much risk to life and limb. Much like the American military in its recent adventures, Caesar reported huge numbers of enemy losses and few on his own side, and given his advantages of discipline, tactics, and weaponry, this is not implausible. But still there were wounds sustained, injuries from breaks and falls and sprains, and colleagues to bury.

On the other hand, there were opportunities. At various points, we see Caesar sharing the prizes of conquest with his soldiers. After Vercingetorix's defeat, Caesar even tells us (7.89) that he parceled out one slave apiece to every one of his soldiers. Some of them will have stayed with their new owners, milling in with the traders and other camp followers that accompanied and supported the army. And some of those camp followers were slave-traders, happy to take surplus human stock off a soldier's hands for cash, to take away for resale lucratively elsewhere. (Caesar regularly speaks of the army's "baggage," the collection of necessary and personal belongings that had to be wrangled from one place to another, a source of risk when men in crisis thought of saving their skins first and their packs a close second.) A Roman soldier was not so unlike a Keralese construction worker in the Persian Gulf today, enduring challenging circumstances for the relatively sound assurance that after his service was over, he would be able to settle somewhere to farm and marry on better terms than would ever have been possible for him without his time in service. It was a tough life, but better than many of the alternatives.

The Roman army was now a mainly professional force, with relative amateurs in the most senior officer ranks. The majority of the soldiers who marched with Caesar came from his recruiting ground in northern Italy. The legion was the largest unit he managed, made up of cohorts; it was the cohort that gave soldiers their comrades and their command structure. Cavalry were never as formally organized, and non-Roman soldiers, called auxiliaries, would be organized as best they could. (See "Caesar's Implicatures" below for a brief overview of the technicalities of the Roman army.)

And there were victims. Caesar regularly demanded that a defeated nation supply him not only with tribute but also with hostages of suitably high rank as pledges of good behavior. The curious fact of Roman history, to which Caesar is no exception, is that hostage-taking very, very rarely led to any harm befalling the hostages. They were humiliated and discommoded, to be sure, by degrading removal from their communities, but Caesar seems to have parked them all in Haeduan country at the town of Noviodunum (modern Nevers: BG 7.55) and ignored them. At the time of the great insurrection of 52, the Haedui, Caesar's allies and enablers and unreliable subjects, are said (BG 7.63) to have executed the hostages there—why?

And then there were still other victims. Observe how each year Caesar selects places for his troops to quarter for the winter. In doing so, he guaranteed that the communities on which he foisted them would eat less, suffer abuse, especially for women, and endure petty and grand assaults on their peace and dignity until spring put the soldiers on the road again. War's victims aren't all found on the battlefield.[3]

BARBARIANS AND GODS

The Latin word *barbarus* echoes Greek βάρβαρος, supposedly onomatopoetic for the inarticulate babbling of the uncivilized. Riggsby 151–52 has cataloged its use in the BG with a surprising result. Hostile or negative use of the term is almost entirely confined to a handful of passages placed in the mouths of Gallic speakers (first: Diviciacus the Haeduan at 1.31). Indeed, the *only* passage in Caesar's narrating voice that Riggsby categorizes as similarly hostile is 4.10, a paragraph that I have for other reasons deleted as a likely later interpolation. For Caesar in the remainder of the work, the word is a neutral descriptor for people living far from the benefits of civilization—often Germans.

Caesar consistently refers to each named Gallic people as a *civitas*, which modern translators often render as "tribe," a word whose English resonance is one or two steps culturally lower than *civitas*. Its root in *civis*, "citizen," the abstract *civitas* denotes a body of citizens and becomes in modern languages the primary word for an urban community: *città, cité, ciudad, city*. With the best recent translators I regularly use "nation," offering the same merited respect that is now shown to native American peoples.[4] Caesar's Gaul, on his own showing, is a civilized place.

[3] The almost completely invisible place of women in the *Gallic War* rarely earns even a footnote. No woman is named in its pages, though one paragraph mentions marriage politics. For the rest, women are seen in numbers beseeching, grieving, and/or being slaughtered.

[4] As best I can tell, naming Gallic and native American communities "tribes" goes back no further than the nineteenth century.

Caesar's landscapes are singularly lacking in divine presence. In the sixth commentary, his account of Gallic customs makes frequent reference to their gods in comparison to Roman deities, but apart from that the pickings are slim. I count half a dozen incidental mentions of gods and religion in action and the closest thing to a religious action is the prayer of a dauntless standard-bearer of the tenth legion about to leap into the waves and wade ashore in Britain. Whatever Caesar's own views and practices (as *pontifex maximus:* see below), his soldiers assuredly invoked divine protection and support however they could—as did his enemies. We hear nothing of that.

CAESAR

Who was Caesar? He told us himself, in a speech he gave for an aunt's funeral in 69 BCE, when he was a pushing young man on the make from a has-been family.

> My aunt Julia's family on the mother's side went back to the kings, on the father's side to the gods. Her own mother was of the Marcius Rex family that began with Ancus Marcius [fourth of the seven kings of Rome in the legendary age 753–509 BCE], while the Julii, *our* family, sprang from the goddess Venus. The family is marked by the holiness of the kings, who were rulers among men, and reverence toward the gods, by whom even kings are ruled.[5]

Kings and gods—not bad ancestry. The claims of course are humbug. But Caesar became Rome's highest priest in 63 BCE, was nearly a king when he died, and was venerated as a god thereafter.

To be sure, Caesar's Julii were an old family of the good sort, faded away into mere respectability. None of his real ancestors had done anything noteworthy in a couple of hundred years. Technically they counted as "patrician," superior to the mere "plebeian," but real dignity and influence was won in other ways. There were plenty

---

[5] Suetonius, *Julius* 6.1. Suetonius wrote Caesar's life about 150 years after his death. I quote him not as gospel truth, but he surely had accurate information lost to us and at least represents a view from within the Roman establishment.

of nobodies of good family about. Though Caesar could boast ten consuls in his family, eight of them were no more recent than the fifth century BCE. His chance for advancement lay in whom else he knew and was related to. (If Cicero was the quintessential "new man" from a family that had never known power, we should think of Caesar as new-from-recycled-materials.) That had to do with how the world had changed in his time.

As late as the time of the Scipios and the Gracchi in the second century BCE, prominent leaders could emerge from the pack of oligarchs at Rome and make spectacular careers or meet violent ends, but short terms of office and constitutional checks and balances ensured a reversion to norm after meteors flared. Two new consuls were elected every year, from a group of families small enough to be envied but large enough to be at odds with each other as often as not. It was only with the rise of the great general Marius (consul, fabulously and unprecedentedly, seven times, between 107 and 86 BCE) that we see the future start to emerge.

That future depended on individual leaders who secured their own power outside the ordinary channels and sustained themselves on the public stage for decades, sometimes even living to retire sumptuously. Marius created this type when he reinvented the Roman army. No longer would it suffice to have prosperous citizens enter the military for limited terms—Rome's ambitions needed more army than that and more "sword fodder" who could easily be squandered in battle.[6] Marius let anyone serve and be paid, as long as he was a citizen, and this made for armies big enough for a Rome with imperial reach. Marius won wars in Africa and, tellingly for Caesar's future, in Gaul, then stepped aside as virtual civil war followed in the 90s, returning for his last consulship in 86 in the midst of real civil war between himself and the next claimant to a glorious future, the dictator Sulla.

---

[6] Drew Faust, *The Republic of Suffering* (2008), recounts how expendable ordinary American soldiers were up to the time of the Civil War, when they began to earn the dignity of individual burial and tombstones; as late as World War II, this American respect for mere soldiers baffled Soviet generals still lacking such scruples.

Sulla advanced Marius' strategy for self-aggrandizement by inventing the practice of offering his troops the prospect of land ownership (most of them now were too poor to own anything) if they served him long enough and well enough. A Roman general who returned successfully from war was acclaimed with the title *imperator*. From Sulla forward, *imperatores* mattered increasingly more than consuls.

Sulla was a ruthless brute, who survived Marius (who died of natural causes in 86) and through a spectacularly bloody reign of terror forced Rome into a new political and social normalcy. Then he retired after his second consulship in 80, dying two years later and leaving the senators in the city to take their turns in the consulship and make their hash of things.

Caesar was born in 102 or 100 BCE, just as Marius was completing his series of victories over the Teutones and Cimbri. He began thinking of public life in the age of speciously restored republicanism after Sulla. When barely of an age to wear the toga of manhood, he was marked by ambition. People spoke of him as a candidate for the prestigious priesthood of Jupiter called *flamen dialis* in perhaps 84–83 BCE. He made a patrician marriage to Cornelia, the daughter of the consul Cinna, but Sulla, at the peak of his power, did not like the family alliance and ordered a divorce. Caesar bravely and dangerously refused and had to light out for the territories—in this case, Sabine mountain country east of Rome, where he contracted malaria while hiding out but survived, and survived again by buying off bounty hunters with cash. On pleas from the college of Vestal Virgins and distinguished relatives who would soon hold the consulate, Sulla forgave Caesar. In after years he was conveniently said to have said that there were a lot of Mariuses in that boy.

The 70s and 60s BCE were a time when Rome was not so much stable as stunned, its politicians unimaginative and mainly inert. The next generalissimo was making his way forward in the person of Pompey, but it took him till the year 70 to attain consulship at age 36 (even that was precocious). Caesar's military career began then, as a junior officer in several of the campaigns of the time, perhaps even the war against Spartacus and his rebellious fellow slaves in

Italy. He won the "civic crown" awarded for saving a citizen's life fighting on enemy ground. (The crown was an oak leaf assemblage and this may have been the first time when Caesar noticed that such distinctively honorable headgear offered a good cover for the thinning hair about which he was said to be hypersensitive.) The great story told from those days was how he was captured by pirates and ransomed by family, then raised a force to go after the pirates. When he captured them, he was kind enough to order their throats slit before having them crucified.

Caesar also spent some of the decade on military service in Roman police actions in the near east, and he passed some time with king Nicomedes in Bithynia—mainland Anatolia a little east of what would become Constantinople, rather the frontier of Roman reach in those days but a perfectly civilized place to be a king's guest. That visit spawned rumors that the king had been smitten with the young Roman and made him his sexual favorite. Thirty years later, Roman soldiers marching in Caesar's great triumph in 46 BCE would sing bawdy songs about his time with Nicomedes, but they also sang with cruel envy of the enthusiasm with which he spread his attentions among the women of Gaul, a topic unmentioned in these commentaries.

Caesar's own military achievements at this stage, though, were no more grandly important than the "whaling voyage by one Ishmael" that inserts itself among the headlines in opening chapter of *Moby-Dick*. The great news of the decade was the final settling of the hash of king Mithridates of Pontus, the "poison king" who proved to be Rome's last great adversary in the extension of empire. Pompey's greatness was secured by defeating him in 66, though Mithridates escaped and remained a marginal force to reckon with until he lost his last battle on a Crimean promontory in 63. With his defeat, the income from Rome's provinces was doubled. Perhaps six years Caesar's senior, Pompey would now have the presumptive right of greatest precedence until Caesar could build an army and make some money. It's important to realize that in Pompey's decade and a half Caesar was always the rising star. He never had any military achievement to match that of Pompey, not even his defeat of Vercingetorix in 52—a defeat the book you are about to read rather magnifies, undoubtedly to ensure that Caesar's greatness would equal Pompey's. (Their other rival, Crassus, was sure he could make his name with vast conquest on the eastern frontier—and so that is where he died.)

Caesar's speech about his sainted aunt Julia took place in 69 BCE. It was important not because of kings and gods, but because of Marius, because aunt Julia had been Marius' wife. Her funeral was a sort of coming-out party for Marius' followers, who had been in subdued abeyance since Sulla's victories and Marius' death a decade and a half earlier. Caesar making that speech associated him not with the hereditary patrician aristocracy but with the ambitious plebeians on the make whom Marius had exemplified.

If Caesar had genuinely useful connections, they came from his mother's side of the house. Her uncle had been consul a few years before she married Caesar's father, as her grandfather had been consul before that. Those family connections and the remaining partisans of Marius were the people Caesar could start with as he made his way toward the greased pole of Roman political advancement. Caesar's wife Cornelia had died in 69, so when back in Rome, he married Pompey's daughter in 67 ("hold your friends close, your enemies closer"). Sober traditional men like the younger Cato and the rising Cicero (from Marius' home town, but otherwise a nobody himself) counted on the stunned old order remaining what it was. Not so Caesar. He was more imaginative and he took chances.

In these shabby years, the two most important bad boy mighthave-beens of Caesar's age both came to bad ends, Catiline and Clodius. Caesar was astute enough to use them, in some ways even support them, but to escape their fate. They roused the rabble, each in their own way, and contributed to making "the people" a more considerable, if volatile, force in politics. Caesar's generosity made them *his* volatile force. He served as curator of the Appian Way and then as curule aedile in the mid-60s, spending lavishly on public spectacles and public buildings, without worrying too much about where the funds would come from. Caesar was always an astute politician, a brave soldier, and a successful orator and writer, but the way in which he excelled every other Roman of his time and times before was in his ability to spend money to the benefit of his reputation in the eyes of the Roman people. Now, if not before, everyone knew who he was and paid attention.

Catiline could have been a somebody in Roman politics, but he was headstrong and impatient. When it became clear that the way to consulship was not opening for him, he aspired to power by other means. Just whether and how there was a "first Catilinarian conspiracy" in 66 BCE, as some claimed, is dubious, but the allegations Cicero made about two years later tell us at least that Catiline was already pushing and maneuvering then. He was a candidate for consul in 64 to serve for the year 63, campaigning on what now seems a wild program of debt cancellation; he lost to Cicero. Cicero's move to crush him in the fall of 63, ending in Catiline's exile and death and the military suppression of his allies, is all too famous. What Catiline really aimed at and with what plausibility may be debated—an outright coup?—, but his fall was the making and the unmaking of Cicero at least. Cicero was proud to have rescued the republic and puzzled that doing so won him so many enemies—so many that he was sent into exile five years later for having put Roman citizens to death without due process. He returned a few months later (we'll follow his story while Caesar is in Gaul) and had another fifteen years to perform the role of senior statesman, but he was never an independent force and ended badly himself when the triumvirs who succeeded Caesar decided he was no longer useful. His head and hands were nailed up to public ridicule in the forum.

But Caesar, Caesar slipped through the Catilinarian moment adroitly and unscathed. It's hard to know exactly how he did this because our best source, Sallust's famous little book on Catiline, dates from twenty years later, after Caesar and Cicero were dead, and Sallust had axes to grind.[7] What is clear is that Caesar came closer than any other senator to supporting Catiline, speaking up, in Cicero's hour of histrionics, for moderation and restraint, speaking

---

[7] The position Caesar is seen to take in Sallust is diametrically opposed to the position his heirs the triumvirs were taking at the moment when Sallust wrote.

against the death penalty. But by the time Cicero stood up for his first Catilinarian oration, the fix was in and Catiline was doomed. Caesar's speech for moderation came after Cicero had given three of his four great orations and is paired by Sallust at least with a counterproposal of great strictness from the ever-austere, ever-unrealistic Cato. If that's really how it went, Caesar could not have been happier with the chance to show himself on the side of "the people" without having to pay a price for doing so. Some were certainly irritated by his position, but few if any were angered, and he lived to rise further.

And Caesar had something else on his mind in 63, for that was the year in which he seized the opportunity to put himself forward, still not quite forty years old, for the grave and reverend office of *pontifex maximus*, an office we could call "high priest" of Roman religion were it not that the words "priest" and "religion" are both highly misleading in such a context. "Chairman of the board of governors of Roman ritual practices" might be a better title, and it was a job with much patronage to dispense—perfect for the man making his way by shows of generosity. Getting this job cost him a fortune in, well, bribes would be the word for it, and it was a near-run thing. Suetonius tells us that when he left the family home for the critical vote, he told his mother that if he came home at all that evening, he would be *pontifex maximus*—otherwise he would need to go into exile. He came home. And Suetonius' account says that though his two opponents were much older and more distinguished, he got more votes from *their* voting districts than they got from all the voting districts together.

So the brilliant career continued. In 62, Caesar served as praetor, departing for Spain in 61. As he was in that transition, the great comedy of Rome's other might-have-been, Publius Clodius, erupted. Clodius was another crowd-pleaser with poor impulse control. In December 62, enamored of Caesar's wife (Pompey's daughter), he tricked himself out in drag and slipped into Caesar's house during the festival of the Good Goddess (*Bona Dea*), which was a ladies-only event. A serving girl detected him and raised an alarm. This was the opportunity for Caesar to divorce his wife with the famous remark that Caesar's wife should be above suspicion. Tried for impiety but not for adultery (which would carry a severe penalty), Clodius was acquitted after Caesar left for Spain. Caesar never let an opportunity slide past: now he was quit of Pompey's daughter and Clodius was grateful to him for not prosecuting the adultery. The upshot was that Clodius was now willing to front for Caesar in pleasing the mob without Caesar needing to take responsibility for Clodius' acts.

In 60, Caesar returned to Rome mid-year for the consular elections. He prevailed, in tandem with an unsympathetic colleague, Bibulus, and prepared for his year by coming to a meeting of the minds with Pompey and Crassus, the only two serious rivals for power. Ducks in a row, he moved quickly in office to make his mark, most notably with a land law that gave state land to Pompey's veterans, on the view that the teeming city would be better served if an appreciable number of destitute trained killers were relocated and put to work farming. In the end, Caesar forced through a law approving the resettlement and including the public land in Campania that had been held by the city of Rome since Capua was destroyed in 211 during Hannibal's war. He also made sure that Pompey's acts in Asia in preceding years were formally approved and he promised recognition of the throne of king Ptolemy XII in Egypt as a faithful Roman client. The prospective client showed his gratitude in advance with promises of a vast bribe to support Pompey and Caesar. (By the next year, that deal frayed badly, as we shall see.) These measures were steamrolled past the other consul, Bibulus, who tried in every way to obstruct them, then in the spring withdrew to his home and avoided public appearances for the rest of his year. Others lay low as well.

In March of 59, meanwhile, the deplorable Clodius requested and received a transfer from patrician to plebeian status as a step toward winning election as a tribune of the people in December, a role in which he could win favor with the populace and, now, serve Caesar's ends. The balance of the year for Caesar was contentious, but he got his one important prize in May: confirmation of a five-year appointment as proconsul, that is to say, governor for the provinces of Illyricum and Gaul, with four legions and the right to appoint his own legates. Gaul was much on people's minds in 60 and 59, as when Cicero reported to Atticus[8] the senate's concern that the Helvetians looked like trouble and would need stern preventive measures. An arranged marriage between Pompey and Caesar's daughter sealed his security as he prepared to leave the city for what would turn out to be nine years.

One gnat that needed swatting was Cicero, always concerned to show himself to be his own man, at least until he found someone else to curry favor with. In 59, Cicero, in a speech defending his former co-consul Gaius Antonius on a charge of misconduct during his governorship in Macedonia, chose to bewail some aspects of the political situation. Or that's how Cicero put it, while others took his words as "a most bitter attack upon Caesar, whom he held responsible for the suit against [Antonius]," and "even went so far as to heap abuse on him." Whatever the facts, Cicero could claim after his exile that it was within three hours of the speech that Clodius had been legally adopted into a plebeian family, thereby giving him the status he wanted.[9] If we view Cicero not from his point of view but from Caesar's, the sequence of Caesar's acts amounted to excellent management—that is to say, defanging—of Cicero and his possibility for serious mischief. To believe Cicero, moreover, Caesar even offered him a post as a legate on his staff in Gaul, with the immunity from prosecution that military service would bring. If Cicero had gone along, there is little doubt he would have returned as Caesar's man—a wealthy man, but not his own. (At the same moment, Pompey was encouraging Cicero to stay and tough it out. Neither Pompey nor Caesar cared what Cicero actually did.)

The future was adumbrated in August 59 when the German king Ariovistus was recognized as a friend of the Roman people. He had resettled into northern Gaul from Germany three years before. In 58, Caesar would fight him in Gaul, unsure just how much treacherous communication his enemies back in Rome had

[8] Cicero Epp. Att. 1.19.2.

[9] Cassius Dio 38.11 reports the politics; Cicero *de domo* 41 offers his spin. Dio's excellent history of Rome extends to 229 CE, and has good but not impeccable sources.

with their supposed ally. Was there really a plot against Pompey's life in the summer of 59? Who might have been behind it? Caesar? Cicero? The man who brought the accusation was found dead in prison. And in August 59, Clodius took office as tribune. His year in that role significantly exacerbated the air of barely controlled violence that marked Roman public life, but his considerable achievement was the establishment of a program of grain distribution for the Roman people. There would be a third of a million people getting free bread before Caesar died.

The year ended ugly, when Clodius as tribune intervened to prevent the outgoing consul Bibulus, seeking one last moment of recrimination, from delivering a speech on his last day as consul.

* * * *

So at the conclusion of his consulship, beneficiary of an uneasy bargain with his elders and betters Pompey and Crassus, Caesar went off to Gaul as proconsul with a remarkable five-year mandate. His enemies wanted him prosecuted for what he had done as consul, but he eluded them long enough to take up command and the immunity that came with it. The threat would hang over his head and play a part in the way his Gallic time ended.

There were several possible outcomes for a proconsul's adventure.

The most probable was simply: nothing. Plenty of Roman senators went out to take nominal command of armies and govern provinces in those days. Their main goal was to enrich themselves with some discreet show of military victories allowing a little plunder, plus some less discreet milking of the locals. A governor named Verres in Sicily just about the time Caesar was making his name was a good example of what was possible in the line of enrichment, but we know of it because Cicero used the hapless Verres to make his own career by attacking the corruption in a series of speeches for the prosecution. Verres may have gone a bit far, but one should sympathize with him a little as he went off into post-Cicero exile. Wasn't it unfair to single out one among many practitioners of normal Roman governance?

The second most probable outcome of such an assignment was more stark: the governor would come back dead. As soon as Caesar indicated that he would take active command and pursue an ambitious military strategy, a grisly end rose sharply in his prospects. What was he thinking of?

The least likely outcome people would have thought of was the one that did in fact—almost—occur. That would mean military success, plunder with enrichment, and then return to a political environment that would eat him up alive. Prosecution, jealousy, infighting, conspiracy: all perfectly normal. When Caesar's time in Gaul did finish, he was threatened with prosecution immediately on his return, prosecution that should have ended his career. His rational strategy was to safeguard his new wealth and make his way to a safe and luxurious exile.

What Caesar actually did—win battle after battle, enrich himself improbably, build a strong network of political allies, and return to chase all his rivals—literally—from the city—was just too improbable to imagine. But he did it. And in doing it, he made himself the Caesar of history. If any of the other more probable things had happened, we would remember him as a nonentity. One well-placed arrow or axe-stroke in Gaul would have sealed his fate as a nobody.

We know him because he prevailed, and we know him so well because he wrote about it so well.

The introduction to each commentary below will review the political and military situation of each year and the accompanying footnotes will fill in the details. But what was it like for Caesar to go off to fight in Gaul at this point?

He would remain in his assigned province north of the Rubicon river for fully nine years, with his base of operations either Modena or Ravenna. He would be in that region almost every winter, usually to hear legal cases that had sprung up across the province.[10] In the

---

[10] He tells us explicitly he did this at the end of 58 (1.54), 57 (2.35), 55 (5.1), and 53 (6.4); he remained with the troops in Gaul for the winter of 54/53 to stabilize the mili-

spring of each year, he would make his way up to Gaul for the year's campaigning, on the standard ancient practice of avoiding military activity during the wet winter months when food supplies were limited and travel soggy and impeded. From his headquarters, four hundred miles would take him comfortably into Gaul, a distance he could cover in horse-drawn carriage in a few days at a pinch, but a week perhaps was a more normal journey. If he crossed the Alps heading northwest and came to Geneva or Lyon, it was another four hundred miles to Normandy, the English Channel, or the Rhine— again, another week or so of travel with some urgency. Troops, afoot, moved much more slowly, hence his practice of positioning them as carefully forward as he could when they went into winter quarters, a practice that repaid his care until the ambushes of late 54.

He commanded his troops through legates and sometimes praetors who led the actual legions, while he had his own staff of secretaries around him. Montaigne, writing of Caesar, observed that the great Albanian general of the fifteenth century Scanderbeg thought that ten to twelve thousand men was the right size for an army— thus a little less than three Roman legions. That professional judgment deserves respect inasmuch as Scanderbeg still had a sense for the span of control that was *possible* for a general who depended on rumor, runners, and range of vision to know what was before him and offer timely direction.

Caesar was a general who lived and fought with his troops, though his way of living was considerably more comfortable than theirs. He shows us vignettes of himself engaged at some risk in battle and Suetonius tells a particularly delightful if suspicious story of Caesar learning that his men were being surrounded in their camp in Germany and venturing in to take up active command by dressing in Gallic clothes—presumably the distinctive *bracae* (English: "britches") that toga-bearing Romans found so exotic.[11]

---

tary situation that had deteriorated sharply with the assaults on his camps and deaths of his legates that year. In 52 and 51, he was back in Gaul, and at the end of 50 was back in northern Italy monitoring the situation at Rome and preparing to make his way back to Rome.

[11] Suet. *Jul.* 58.1.

Caesar kept in close touch with affairs back at his provincial headquarters when he was in farthest Gaul, and with affairs at Rome. Three or four secretaries or agents waited on him at all times and we get the story that he dictated letters while on horseback, sometimes several at once. He was always fully informed about Roman affairs and always acting with a view to the effect on his Roman audience, but he rarely mentions such concerns in the commentaries.

He was in the main successful. Suetonius[12] assessed his work and saw only three real reverses that he faced in his nine years: almost losing his ships in a storm off Britain, the losses of the legates Sabinus and Cotta and many of their troops in the ambushes of 54, and the loss of a legion in battle at Gergovia during the great uprising of 52, followed by the great victory at Alesia that brought the insurgency of Vercingetorix to an end.

Do those successes mean he was a "great general"? If we judge a general by the success of his troops on the battlefield—setting aside the inevitable costs of war in blood and treasure, setting aside all the ethical constraints that we regard as essential to civilization, and setting aside any consideration as to whether to be a "great general" it is necessary to have met even the minimal standards of fighting a just war—then if you force me to answer the question I will say, yes, he was. But then I will insist you allow me to ask you how one can be a "great general" without being at the same time a war criminal.

* * * *

The Caesar we meet in his *commentarii* is a fighting machine, a general who thinks only of strategy and tactics. If you read *only* Caesar's account, you are watching a very artificial performance. In the pages that follow, I will be at pains to present that story in a context that lets you see Caesar the man and politician, not just the general he wanted you to see. Inevitably, some will feel disappointed by the deflation that results.

---

[12] Suet. *Jul.* 25.

So this is a good place to be fair, even kind, to Caesar, so as not to mislead. It will be clear from what follows that for ambition, ruthlessness, and blood-curdling amorality, he is hard to rival. True, he is no Hitler and no Stalin, though he did not need to be in order to reach his goals.

But he was first of all amazingly intelligent and amazingly fortunate in his judgments. He was, for example, surprisingly learned and sophisticated in his intellectual interests. In the midst of wartime in Gaul, he found time to write and publish a combative, original, and substantial work of scholarship, his book *On Analogy*, which contributed aggressively and well to the liveliest current debates about language and culture (see below, page xxxix). In his time as dictator, he knew enough to make calendar reform a priority and to find the people who could do it right.[13] With just one tweak since (in 1582), seven billion people know how to, and mostly do, reckon the month, day, and year the way he ordered. He held his own with the philosophers and poets of a remarkably creative and exciting time in Roman life.

But his temperament was even more astonishing. Some old sage—Oliver Wendell Holmes Jr.?—is said to have said of Franklin Roosevelt that he had a second-class intellect but a first-class temperament. Caesar was undoubtedly first-class on both counts. He gambled repeatedly with his life and fortune and repeatedly won. He knew or at least intuited what Rome needed if it was to be successful in making its way from a city-state with a regional dominion over neighboring peoples to a stable empire with many subject populations and vast expanses of territory. We are trained to lament the decline of old "republican" ways, but those ways had gone obsolete fifty years and more before Caesar. A tiny oligarchy of short-term

---

[13] He had the right to do that in his role as *pontifex maximus*, and the problem was urgent and the calendar far out of whack because Caesar had spent almost two decades neglecting his pontifical duty and had failed to order insertion of the "intercalary" ("leap-year") periods, averaging 22–23 days every other year, often enough to keep calendar and seasons in line with each other. So for example, in the year 55 BCE (Caesar crosses the Rhine and goes to Britain the first time) ended astronomically on about 20 November, so the days of summer had begun shortening in early May and the equinox fell in mid-August.

amateur rulers could not hold together a Mediterranean-wide enterprise. If the "Roman empire" had not succeeded the late, lamented republic, then Rome would have seen its domains wither and shrink and collapse and would doubtless have been itself conquered by others. (My guess is that whoever ruled Alexandria in Egypt would have won the day—as indeed almost happened at the battle of Actium in 31 BCE, between Octavian and Antony, Caesar's heirs both of them. Suetonius reports that Caesar himself was thought to have been planning to move the capital to Alexandria.)

And Caesar knew, arguably, when to die. When the Ides of March came round in 44 BCE, Caesar's work was done. The 13 years of civil war that followed would have disappointed but not surprised him. He probably thought the struggle wouldn't take that long; he probably thought Antony would prevail; but he would have been happily surprised to see what became of the nephew he hardly knew, who turned into Caesar Augustus. Scholars will argue this, but as he stood on the verge of what would have been a grand, Alexander-like expedition to the east, he was genuinely indifferent to his own future. There is something sublime and enviable about that.

But we must remember then above all that this was still a very bad man. It's perilously easy to fall into talking about Rome and its fortunes as if empires are intrinsically good things when they are demonstrably not. Once you have one, it has its uses and getting rid of it is dangerous, no question, but the bloody, ruthless work of making one remains inexcusable. Killing people is wrong, even on the rare occasion when it is unavoidable. Caesar's character comprised his learning, his courage, and his heartlessness. If a modern therapist got him on the couch, he would have to address the paradox of voracious appetite, especially sexual and probably bisexual, but also relentless self-discipline to the point of ascetic austerity. I suspect his eventual diagnosis would include the word "sociopath," but diagnosis is inevitably comparative, and a few genuinely incomparable individuals make even diagnosis almost irrelevant.

And in the end, Caesar's Rome prevailed. On the most conservative estimate, his consolidation saw Rome through two hundred and fifty years of political, economic, and military success, until the

disorder of invasions, coups, and economic collapse in the third
century. On the most generous estimate, the Mediterranean empire
he created lasted, with various upheavals, until the deposition of
the last sultan in 1922. The war whose aftermath cost the sultan his
title was remarkably rooted in national ideologies attaching themselves to Roman pedigrees. It had pitted against each other the sultan, a czar, two Kaisers ("czar" and "Kaiser" are just the word Caesar
in Slavic and German dress), a Roman king, and a British empire
whose mythology took its roots in the descendants of Aeneas, along
with the French who had spent the previous century deciding
whether to be a republic or an empire. And of course, a truly generous estimate would claim that the European Union reincarnates
Caesar's world in its own way, even as his successor as, one might
say with tongue in cheek, senior manager of rituals, the bearer of
the title *pontifex maximus*, presides in the Vatican to this day.

What did Caesar really want? Cicero says Caesar always had a
couplet of Euripides' *Phoenissae* in mind, which he renders roughly
"if you must break the law, break it for the sake of being a king: otherwise behave yourself."[14] What did Caesar really want?

CAESAR'S MONEY

It was Cassius Dio (42.49) who called Caesar a money-getter (almost
"money-grubber": χρηματοποιός) and quoted Caesar to the effect
that strong regimes needed soldiers and money, but everyone had
always known his propensity. His spending had become *notably* lavish in his year as aedile, when he sponsored the two great spectacles
of games and shows, the Ludi Romani and the Megalesia. One
source has him in debt by a vast amount by the beginning of 61—in
other words, he badly needed a consulship and a lucrative procon-
sulship. Fourteen years later, in the middle of the civil war, with all
the plunder of Gaul behind him, he was still deep in debt. But generous he had been to those who supported him and those he needed.
The only people he seems not to have been able to buy were Cato

---

[14] *De officiis* 3.82, quoted already by Suet. *Jul.* 30.

and his circle. Equally noticeable are the people (like Memmius, Cicero, and Curio) who had been openly hostile or at least reserved and who turned their coats and tuned their supportive voices when his generosity intervened. Cicero found this an embarrassment in 51/50 when, still in debt to Caesar from a loan in probably 54, he tried to give the money back and Caesar wouldn't have it—keeping him on the string. And in 50 Cicero hesitated to speak up against Caesar for fear that Caesar's man of affairs Balbus would turn up shortly after to call the debt at an unsustainable moment.

The best measure of Caesar's success in all this is simple: twenty-four legates served him as general officers in Gaul; of the twenty-one still living during the crisis of 49, only two went with Pompey—Titus Labienus and Quintus Cicero. Labienus was the most senior, professional, and independent of his officers, while young Cicero was the most political and least impressive. The rest stayed bought.

"In Gaul, he rifled the chapels and temples of the gods, which were filled with rich offerings, and demolished cities oftener for the sake of their spoil, than for any ill they had done."[15] He so flooded Italy and the provinces with gold that its value in other coinage went down some 30 percent. Suetonius also accuses him of flat-out stealing three thousand pounds of gold from the Capitoline during his first consulship and substituting an equal weight of gilt brass. Cicero, into whose hands a fair amount of Caesarean money fell, was censorious in his *On Duties* (*De officiis*), written a few months after the Ides of March, saying that generosity was one thing, but distribution of ill-gotten gains had nothing generous about it.

COMMENTARIES

Because the Latin term "commentarius" has a long later history in English, we usually leave the word to be rendered by its cognate, but in its time the word came closer in sense to "memorandum" or "notebook," in the sense of an informal document recording factual material. Among others, generals wrote them, as reports of their

[15] Suet. *Jul.* 54.

activities sent home to governments and citizens. Sulla wrote ὑπομνήματα ("memoranda") after all his fighting was done. Pompey had his campaigns written up for him by a Greek and by a Roman freedman. There are several cases from minor figures of the age of Marius. For Caesar's time in Gaul, there were verse accounts. A poet named Varro from Gallia Narbonensis wrote on Caesar's war with the Sequani, and there was perhaps another poem by one Furius Bibaculus. Cicero said he planned one.

But all agree that Caesar's work is unique and at least a little evasive. Presented as *commentarii*, his memoranda ostensibly offered the unvarnished facts for others to embroider into epics and histories. In fact, they were immediately recognized as highly wrought works in their own right, likely to defeat all attempts to make something more of them. Cicero said as much, praising them with some reservations as "splendid: bare, straight, and handsome, stripped of rhetorical ornament like an athlete of his clothes."[16] They were also praised by Caesar's continuator, Aulus Hirtius, in the preface to his appended account of the years 51–50 (the eighth commentary here). On the other hand, the historian (and sometime general) Asinius Pollio, a follower of Caesar a generation younger, thought they were neither careful nor truthful enough, accusing Caesar of too readily believing others' accounts of events he had not witnessed and of writing of his own deeds in a way that fell short of accuracy, hinting at deliberate misrepresentation.[17]

The least that must be said is that the *commentarii* are highly selective and narrowly focused. They account for military events only; they account for them in an almost entirely sequential narrative, with neither retrospect nor foreshadowing to fill in a story, beyond occasional "as he learned from captives . . ." remarks. They include digressive chapters on the local mores and customs of Gauls and Germans, containing some accurate material but also some embroidery added later by Caesar or others. At the same time, they give little flavor of the military life and little of military logistics. Forag-

[16] Cicero, *Brutus* 262, written in 46; here trans. T. P. Wiseman.
[17] Suet. *Jul.* 56.4.

ing to feed animals and troops will be noticed, but not other acquisition of supplies (at 3.5 his troops are running out of throwing weapons: how did they resupply?). We get no sense of the size of the unmilitary band of camp followers (blacksmiths, clothiers, whores), none of any modes of transport save shank's mare, nothing of sanitation, disease, sex, or commercial and other relations with the "natives." The consequent austerity of the narrative is striking.

The most famous feature of the book, of course, is the third-person narrative.[18] Despite a handful of exceptions, the narrating Caesar and the acting Caesar are rigidly kept apart. It's only speculation to say that this was meant to facilitate a Caesar-centric reading back home, in public readings designed to keep the heroic author's name on the reading slave's lips at every turn. The success of the rhetorical move is that it never becomes wearying or artificial.

Almost as important but generally unremarked is his management of time. His narrative runs smoothly along from event to event in a timeless present. His past tenses often indeed shift into what we call the "historical present" for a more vivid sense of presence.[19] So the narrative has no future—no anticipation of his plans beyond the tactics of a single battle, no hint of future events that at the time of writing he already certainly knew. We are meant to feel that we are there in Gaul, with the troops, amid the events of the moment, as blind to the future as the army was.

So when were they written? Scholarly wars on the scale of Caesar and the Nervii can be fought over this subject. There are partisans for annual publication and for all-at-once production. Either Caesar

[18] Caesar names himself about 380 times in the seven commentaries he wrote, about once every 125 words. Hirtius *needs* to use the name and uses it slightly more frequently, about once every 100 words.

[19] E.g., "I see this student reading my book and I say to her, how are you liking it, and she says, not bad but I wish I could figure out what he really thinks about Caesar, and so I leave her there and come back here to write down what she said." Caesar's frequency of employment of the device goes up sharply in the last three commentaries he wrote (5, 6, 7), peaking in the tense and dramatic episode of 6.36–41, where Quintus Cicero's troops are trapped and endangered. Caesar clearly wanted to do this, and so I have let him. Most translators render him almost entirely into the past tense.

sat in winter quarters each year, writing up the last year and sending
the result on to Rome for public consumption (except that he did the
fifth and sixth commentaries together at the end of 53 BCE, not having dared to try during the bad winter of 54–53 after the gruesome
attacks on his camps) *or* he wrote up the whole account, perhaps
using his earlier reports to the senate, in the winter of 52–51, after
Vercingetorix had been defeated and captured. Argument can be
made both ways, with various qualifications. (The annual composi-
tion school is likely to admit that some retouching was possible
when the seven Caesarean *commentarii* were joined up, while the
all-at-once partisans allow for some variation dependent on the original individual annual reports.) What is remarkable, however, is
how equably the work accepts both hypotheses. There are only a
very few inconsistencies (in 2.28, he tells us he destroyed the Nervii
utterly, while in 5.49 he finds himself facing 60,000 soldiers in
the Nervii homeland), evidence, however we conclude, of a stern
self-discipline.[20]

For purposes of this translation, I have chosen to privilege my
own partisan position on this question and assume annual production. That assumption underlies what I say, but also the way in
which I present the work. Each year's *commentarius* is presented
with a prefatory essay designed to put the reader in the position of a
Roman citizen at the time of the events recounted. Each essay out-
lines the events of the year to come, both at Rome and in Gaul, so
the reader can read it as a Roman at the end of that year might have
heard it. These introductions will help keep close to the forefront of
the reader's mind the things that were in Caesar's mind that he
doesn't talk about. As will be clear, his actions in Gaul were strongly
influenced by the political requisites for enhancing his position
back home—so I think I can add at least one reason to the ones he
gives for going to Germany and Britain in 55, for example. Readers
of the all-at-once school may still be grateful to me for the story I am
thus enabled to tell.

[20] In favor of annual production, we observe besides the increase of the historical
present that the amount of quoted direct speech grows from book to book and there
are more words found only once in Caesar's writings in the later books.

The quality of the work is less surprising when we consider the variety, nature, and sophistication of Caesar's other works. We already mentioned the *de analogia*, *On Analogy*, in two books. We believe that he wrote that work in the spring of 54,[21] between the summers of his campaigns in Britain, and we take it to be a rejoinder to Cicero's *de oratore* (*On the Orator*), which was finished in November 55. Think of the elaborateness of Cicero's prose and the conciseness of Caesar's and you can surmise something of the differences between them at a theoretical level, differences Caesar set out to heighten. His book is dedicated, to be sure, to Cicero, and the rejoinder is therefore friendly if firm. (The dedication, which Cicero carefully quotes,[22] is mildly ambivalent—praising Cicero for being the great innovator of brilliant speaking while claiming with false modesty a place for "easy and everyday speech"—for all that Caesar's own carefully crafted prose gets its simplicity and lucidity by being anything but easy and everyday in character.) A later writer and friend of an emperor, the African sophist Fronto, described Caesar as writing while weapons flew about him—surely an exaggeration, but a way of suggesting that the *de analogia* was remarkable nonetheless.

CAESAR'S IMPLICATURES

Rather than embed verbose explanations in the translation, I will supply keys here to Caesar's commonest shorthand language about places and armies and the things they do, keys to explain things his contemporaries knew perfectly well.

When Caesar speaks of the land he travels over, he will mention Illyricum (the east coast of the Adriatic roughly matching former Yugoslavia, down from Trieste to Albania), Cisalpine Gaul ("Gaul this side the Alps," what we might call Lombardy or northern Italy), and "the province" (Rome's established territory in southeastern Gaul—whence the name "Provence"). Those territories were his

---

[21] Suetonius *Jul.* 56.5 says he wrote it while going from Cisalpine Gaul back to Transalpine in the spring.

[22] *Brutus* 253.

assignment as proconsul. But he also speaks when in Gaul of "Italy," by which he always means the same thing as Cisalpine Gaul; Hirtius in the eighth commentary speaks of "Gaul of the togas," meaning the same territory again, land where there were Roman citizens to wear the distinctive garment.

Caesar marched through these lands during the six or so warmer, drier months of the year, taking his troops into winter quarters when the weather deteriorated and the days shortened. (October to April, especially October and November, are the wet months at Rome, for example, and ancient armies marched and slept poorly on muddy roads and wet ground.) His months were roughly our months, but the kalends marked the first of the month and the ides fell about halfway through (in March, July, October, May, corresponding to our 15th of the month, otherwise the 13th). Daylight was divided into twelve hours year-round, nighttime likewise. That meant that the length of an hour shortened in winter, lengthened in summer. The sixth hour fell at noon.[23] Night maneuvers were rare and risky.

The fundamental army unit was the legion, of about 4,500 soldiers. A legion was divided into ten cohorts, each of which in turn was divided into six centuries of about eighty men. Centurions were the lowest-ranking leaders, but the "first spear" was the senior centurion in the legion, an important rank for which brave men competed. The legion as a whole was commanded by a legate or, slightly lower ranking, a quaestor. Other mid-rank officers included tribunes and prefects. All those men were citizens. The armed force was supplemented by cavalry units with their own prefects and by "auxiliaries"—non-citizen forces accompanying the legions, not so highly trained or disciplined—but archery was generally supplied by the auxiliaries. Caesar mentions all these people, but not the train of followers, hangers-on, and profiteers who were drawn to armies like his. They were not his concern, but they presumably prospered when the army succeeded and ran for

---

[23] The accordionization of hours was less noticeable at Rome, where a summer daylight hour would be about 1:15 long and a winter hour 0:45; by contrast at London the spread is 1:25/0:35 and winter daylight in the fog runs from just after 8:00 a.m. to just before 4:00 p.m.

their lives when the army failed, blending into the scenery as persuasively as possible.

The normal equipment of a soldier was whatever armor was possible (helmet and breastplate at least), a shield, a spear, and a sword. If there were such a thing as a normal battle, advancing soldiers threw their spears to disrupt the enemy's formation, then charged with swords, hacking, stabbing, and chopping as best they could. Weapons others had dropped were seized to reuse often enough. But when the army found itself facing a walled town, other tools were needed and the Romans were masters of the technology. (Though at one point we do hear of a Gallic nation that fought the Romans often enough to learn from their techniques.) To approach a wall in safety, soldiers would form a "tortoise" by a horizontal arrangement of shields locked together to create the equivalent of an amphibian's shell, under which men could advance. Slightly more elaborate and less portable/mobile were "sheds," good to build at the foot of a town's walls to provide protection for tunneling or—a favorite technique—building a ramp to lessen the height advantage of the wall or even reach to its top. Protected small towers, atop a wall or facing it, also gave protection. Other hardware was available, like grappling hooks. Sometimes Caesar speaks of "hurdles," meaning in this case a wood or wicker frame that could be deployed to make marshy ground walkable or propped and advanced for various defensive uses.

When an army had been very successful, its general was voted a "supplication" back at Rome, lasting a certain number of days. Originally and notionally a day for religious observances of thanksgiving, it had become by Caesar's time at least as much a holiday. Pompey was the first general to be voted a supplication lasting as long as ten days, Caesar the first to be awarded twenty. In after times, the number inflated further to keep pace with commanders' egos.

TRANSLATION

Caesar's book is a favorite of war buffs, and rightly so. The greatest of them was Napoleon III, who "wrote" a two-volume biography in 1865 drawing heavily on the researches of Colonel Eugène Stoffel, who scoured the battlefields and mapped the mappable. Editions since are generally full of maps of fragments of Gaul with the bars and arrows of military units and maneuvers. The great bridge over the Rhine in the fourth commentary generally gets a special page or two of diagrams. Translation follows suit, carefully adjusting to the topography and making all things clear. The reader of such a handsome and well-illustrated translation runs a grave risk of being misled into thinking the work a transparent objective account of a determinate and complete set of historical events surrounding Caesar's time in Gaul. One of my main purposes in this translation is to avoid leading the reader into such error.

So here are a few assumptions. Caesar's audience did not know the geography of Gaul in any meaningful way. It had no access to anything we would call maps. No one other than Caesar and his legates had walked the battlefields and knew how they lay or even where they were.

I will go further. Caesar did not set out to write lucid, comprehensive, accurate battle reports. He did not mind being accurate and indeed seems generally so, and he is even sometimes fairly comprehensive. But his purpose was to tell a good story, his story, his way, and to do so in a distinctive and peculiarly potent style. The modern reader who wants to know just where on the hillside at Alesia the ramparts were located is doing Caesar a disservice and missing his point.

I do provide an orienting map and links to some other geographic help, but I draw the line at providing a picture of a bridge that probably couldn't actually have been built the way he says it was and manage to stay erect. My translation, moreover, seeks to be equally helpful to Caesar and to the reader. I think I help Caesar when I translate what he actually said and translate it in a way that brings over into English the force, effectiveness, and conciseness of what he said. Caesar was never chatty or helpful, and I've tried to emulate him. A measure of that success is possible.

The modern translations of Caesar's *De bello Gallico* that I have examined regularly use between 1.5 and 2 English words (and sometimes more) of translation for every 1 word of Caesar's Latin. *Wortreich, Weitschweifig* ("word-rich, far-wandering," i.e., prolix) the Germans would say.[24] My translation comes in at 1.247, or 15–40 percent below average. Translating that way can become a bit of a game, but I think it gave me a useful discipline. Have I really captured him in the fewest words possible? (An earlier draft had him down to 1.19. It has oozed a couple of thousand words longer in the name of accuracy and clarity.)

I have had a ghostly colleague in all this whom I must praise, gone though he is these hundred years. Heinrich Meusel (1844–1916) was a butcher's son who took his doctorate at Halle and became a Gymnasium-teacher in Berlin, Kreuzberg, and Cologne. His substantial scholarly achievement reached its peak in the construction of his *Lexicon Caesarianum* and in the thorough revisions he made to the standard commentaries on Caesar's works (both had been begun by Friedrich Kraner and revised by Wilhelm Dittenberger). Meusel has his quirks, but he is Caesar's closest reader and cares deeply about what the words mean and how they mean it. When I came to work on Hirtius' eighth commentary, where Caesar's lucidity gives way to something the consistency of mud, it was a pleasure to have Meusel's spluttering companionship in figuring out what Hirtius was doing. *Ungeschickt* ("clumsy") was Meusel's favorite word for Hirtius' style. In one way I follow Meusel more than is the fashion now, in accepting his identification and deletion of passages helpfully interpolated into Caesar's text, to make explicit or clarify what he said, especially in matters of geography. Meusel has persuaded me that such passages are often geographically inaccurate and grammatically or at least stylistically un-Caesarean. (I identify the deletions of more than a few words in my notes.) If I have erred in following him, it is with the purpose of letting the taut and clear prose of Caesar keep up its relentless pace.

I have used Caesar's Latin names wherever possible for places and people, but let Mark Antony have his familiar Anglicized spelling.

---

[24] Full disclosure and perhaps not uninteresting. English uses more words to say the same thing than Latin, but our words are shorter on average (think of a/an/the), so if I let my computer count not words but characters, my translation is actually a little shorter than Caesar's Latin, 367,000 characters to 375,000, a saving of about 2%.

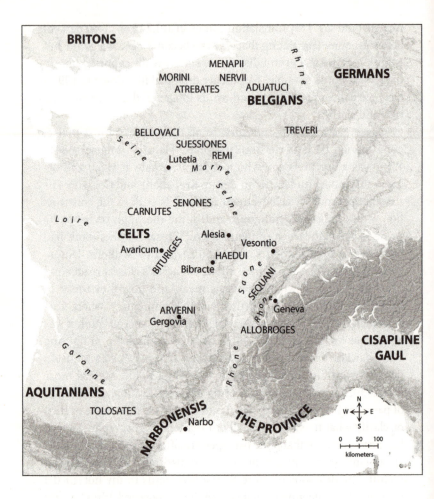

MAP OF GAUL

The wonderfully helpful modern maps that scholars have drawn over the last two centuries create a world nothing like the one Caesar and his contemporaries could have known. This map is intentionally drawn to approximate the knowledge that a Roman reader might have or have drawn from reading Caesar. It is still much too accurate for its purpose, showing the land masses, mountains, rivers, and seas as accurately as moderns know how to represent them. To make a mental adjustment for that, remember perhaps that the ancients believed that if you proceeded from Gaul to Britain to Ireland, the next land west to which you came was Spain. The best place to go further for a collection of online maps specific to Caesar is the splendid Dickinson College Commentaries site created by Professor Christopher Francese; the Caesar-in-Gaul maps page there is http://dcc.dickinson.edu/subjects/gallic-war-maps. The reader who wishes to explore the spaces and places of this book in more detail can also go to https://drive.google.com/open?id=1uSO QsaxXjm4BXxTUlzAJZv5JW4Fokug_&usp=sharing or, more compendiously for the same thing, https://tinyurl.com/y8mgfp5g. On that map, I have marked with push pins every ancient place named in this volume with at least short explanatory notes. The map is searchable using either ancient or modern place names.

The best comprehensive atlas of the classical world is R. J. Talbert, ed., *The Barrington Atlas of the Greek and Roman World* (Princeton University Press, 2001).

THE WAR FOR GAUL

FIRST COMMENTARY

58 BCE

Caesar departed for Gaul in early 58 BCE, leaving behind a newly enriched imperial city stumbling into what would be the worst decade of its history—until the decade that followed it. Caesar would enrich himself and Rome even more, while the governability of the whole was in free fall toward ruin. For three of the nine years Caesar would spend with his army, Rome did not manage to conduct consular elections until the new consular year had already begun. The three generalissimos dandling the empire on their knees would all die violently—Crassus with his army in 53, Pompey on the run from Caesar in 49, and Caesar at the base of a statue of Pompey in 44. Rome's chance for stable government lay hidden at this moment thirty miles south of Rome in the person of a four-year-old boy whose father had just died.

The consuls in 58 were Lucius Calpurnius Piso Caesoninus and Aulus Gabinius. Piso was Caesar's father-in-law and also earned a different fame by being the likely builder of the Villa dei Papiri in Herculaneum, where he was the patron of the Epicurean philosopher Philodemus. We benefit from that patronage because his villa had the good luck to be inundated with the ash of Vesuvius in 79 CE, and a considerable trove of literature, including works of Philodemus, remained there to await modern technology's ability to recover them, an effort still in progress.

But the tribune Clodius was the lawmaker in evidence as the year began and passed his precedent-setting grain law in January, along with a law removing a ban on *collegia*. In theory they were beneficial burial societies organized by likeminded businessmen, tradesmen, or neighbors, but they had been banned because they also became a vehicle for thugs and groups engaged in more or less organized crime. Clodius used them as his own private militia.

Caesar crossed the *pomerium*, the sacred narrowly-drawn boundary of the city, to take up his command (a general had always to leave his army outside that *pomerium*) but lingered close to the city to watch the political situation. He knew the praetors Ahenobarbus and Memmius would attack his consular acts of the year before on grounds that he had gone against the auspices. (Caesar's intransigent colleague Bibulus had made sure there were always negative auspices to ignore!) Caesar published three speeches against the two praetors, while keeping a wary eye on Cicero, who he thought might join the attack. Clodius hated Cicero, so Caesar was glad in these weeks to join the rising outrage that the demagogue was whipping up against the orator, notionally for putting Roman citizens to death without full due process at the end of the Catilinarian insurgency four years earlier.

In the third month of the year, Clodius organized an assembly (*contio*) outside the *pomerium* in the Circus Flaminius for a debate on Cicero's case. Caesar and the consuls spoke in terms that made it clear to Cicero that he could not withstand the forces against him, and so he fled the city for the safety of exile in mid-March. Clodius spent a month proposing and revising a formal ban, which was approved on April 24 by the *concilium plebis*, the people's assembly over which the tribune held sway. (Exile was enforced by a law saying the condemned could be killed at will if he did not withdraw a certain distance, usually hundreds of miles, from the city. An exile who kept his distance could live quite comfortably.)

When Caesar saw that nothing would come of the challenges to his consular acts and that Cicero was taken care of, he left in late March, traveling rapidly toward Geneva, covering some five hundred miles in about eight days. (In haste, a carriage could take him something like seventy-five miles a day if needed.) If he were ever to return to Rome and avoid the destructive rage of his rivals for power, he would have to come back with undeniable success, strong military support, and a lot of money. Failing that trifecta, he still needed money—to set himself up in protected obscurity on a Greek island somewhere. Gaul was a means to an end.

What did he find when he arrived there?

First of all, he had hurried past a good part of what he was responsible for. Cisalpine Gaul was the heart of his responsibility, and he was charged as well with maintaining Roman rule in Illyricum, the eastern coast of the Adriatic. He had veered north to the outermost edge of his domains, to Geneva, where the lake narrows to become the beginning of the Rhone river that flows west to Lyon, then south to the Mediterranean. The Gallic nation on Rome's side of the Rhone there was the Allobroges, mainly peaceable enough apart from a flurry of rumors of insurgency two years earlier. A very good luxury hotel now stands on the first few yards of territory that then lay outside Rome's rule facing the narrow channel of water that is the nascent Rhone.

Caesar knew as he made this journey that he had an army, at least. He was authorized one legion (about 5,000 soldiers) for Transalpine Gaul and three for northern Italy and Illyricum. Not long after his arrival, he recruited two more legions, paying for them himself. In 57, he would recruit two more.

At a distance of two hundred years, a historian could describe the military situation calmly: "While this was going on in the city, Caesar found no hostility in Gaul, but everything was absolutely quiet. The state of peace, however, did not continue, but first one war broke out against him of its own accord, and then another was added, so that his greatest wish was fulfilled of waging war and winning success for the whole."[1]

"Of its own accord" rather stretches a point. Caesar very consciously *chose* to be alarmed and take action when he heard that the Helvetians (a name we never translate, though we very reasonably could, as "Swiss") were restless in their lands north of lake Geneva and were packing up to move to the west of Gaul, quite a bit further out of Roman way than where they already lived. They presented

---

[1] Cassius Dio 38.31.

themselves to the new proconsul very respectably, with no more than
a bit of attitude, and asked his kind permission to make their way
west just inside the boundaries of his province, crossing that narrow
channel at Geneva and then making their way down the narrow and
sometimes steep valley of the rising Rhone toward Lyon, where they
would bend a bit northwards and continue toward the open, or at
least seizable, land in the far west, around and north of Toulouse. In
response, Caesar mildly requested a two weeks' delay to consider the
issue. What he actually meant was that he needed time to move his
troops into place and force the Helvetians to take a more difficult and
more northerly route through the lands of the Sequani.

Of the many reasons Caesar had for opposing the Helvetians (e.g.,
ambition and greed), the one he chose to emphasize then and after
was a crudely simple one: wild and wicked invaders had come toward
Rome from Gaul fifty years earlier, so he had to act to make sure
history did not repeat itself.

This first commentary tells the story of what happened next.
Things don't go well for the Helvetians. A people in mass migration,
young and old, male and female, moving at oxcart speed, are ambushed twice and quickly tamed and sent back where they came
from. Even Caesar can't make this victory look challenging. Once
defeated, the Helvetians, perhaps 100,000 in number, trudge wretch-
edly home, on short rations, to remake their lives in the ruins
they had left behind. They disappear from Caesar's story until they
supply a few troops to the great revolt recounted in the seventh
commentary.

Beyond the Helvetians lay another enemy, conveniently queued
up and almost waiting for Caesar—on his telling. Led by Ariovistus,
whom Caesar had recognized the year earlier in his consulship as a
friend of the Roman people, this was a warband that had elbowed
across the Rhine to pillage and intrude upon the Sequani along the
river south of Strasbourg. There are problems with that story, exacerbated by our hearing from Caesar that Ariovistus' friendship with
the Roman people went so far as to put him in communication with
Caesar's enemies back in Rome. To be sure, the speech that Caesar
attributes to Ariovistus in 1.44 is a pretty fair rendition of an anti-

Caesar position that has a lot to be said for it. On Caesar's telling, Ariovistus was the wicked German enemy of Gallic peace, but we can see that he was also a player in a very domestic Roman political story. We could believe it if he thought that he had been led off on this expedition precisely so that a convenient barbarian could do him in. Of course, by the time Caesar's commentary tells this story for him back at Rome a few months later, Caesar's victory is a shot across the bow for those enemies, to know what they must reckon with. What is ostensibly a story about Germans is also a story about domestic Roman politics.

This battle story does not go quite as easily as the first with the Helvetians. Caesar's troops are not now chasing a people in migration but directly facing a serious army. Whatever actually happened, Caesar the writer takes the opportunity to present Caesar the dauntless commander, rallying his troops from sluggardly cowardice to the peak of combat energy with a dramatic speech. Well, he says, if you lot can't be counted on, at least the tenth legion will support me! (This is the first of four moments for the tenth legion in the commentaries where they appear as the favorite child.[2]) The troops rally; they win a decisive victory; and the dastardly Germans run pell-mell for the Rhine, tails between legs, just as one might hope. (This is the first place in the commentaries to observe that Caesar's ostensible knowledge sometimes runs a *little* further than perhaps it might reasonably have been expected to. Just who Ariovistus' followers really were and where they went to ground should be open to doubt.)

While Caesar made his way into Gaul, Rome remained a snakepit. The question of Egypt—how it would subserve Rome best—flared up again. The most lucrative solution was for king Ptolemy to be accepted as Rome's ruler of his own land and for him to pay substantial tribute. That was the deal that had been cut in Caesar's consulship, but a difficulty lay in Ptolemy's ability to produce the tribute. The simple Roman solution was enacted by Clodius, passing a bill to annex Cyprus to Roman authority, then sending everyone's enemy, Cato the Younger, as plenipotentiary to implement the subjugation.

[2] Tenth legion: 1.40–42, 2.21–25, 4.25 (Britain), 7.47–51.

Trapped by his citizenly loyalty, Cato departed on the mission. The purpose of the annexation was to seize Cyprus' resources to pay the king's promissory note.

With Caesar safely on his Gallic campaigns, Cicero was no longer really a threat. He could come back, tamed and harmless, could he not? Pompey began floating this idea during the summer. Ten years later, in the midst of civil war, Pompey would tell Cicero that it was Caesar's doing, strings pulled from Gaul, that made the movement for return go so slowly. Clodius, feeling the ground cut out from under him, sent his toughs into the streets and there was even talk that there had been an assassination plot against Pompey. Pompey wisely withdrew from public life and remained in his house—"mansion" or "compound" might be better words—for the rest of the year.

And so Caesar's first year in Gaul drew to a close. Probably in late September, he set his troops to winter among the Sequani, the people he had just supposedly rescued from Ariovistus' depredations, while he himself returned to Cisalpine Gaul. The Sequani will not be so much as mentioned again until the sixth commentary for the year 53, but they play their part here. By settling his troops among them, outside the official boundaries of the Roman province, Caesar indicated most clearly his expansionist aims. With Helvetian and German hash settled, there was no excuse for that choice except imperialism.

Observe now Caesar's dealings with the Haedui, powerful and influential in central Gaul, with a capital city called Bibracte not far from modern Autun in Burgundy. They had "friended" (as we now say) the Helvetians, but washed their hands of them as they went down to disaster. Then most importantly it was they who put Caesar on the warpath against Ariovistus. The story of the threat to Gallic stability by the German wild men is all theirs. When all is done for Caesar, after many vicissitudes, the Haedui will prove to be doing just fine. Caesar never lets on that he knows their game.

On October 29, Pompey arranged for eight tribunes to bring forward a vote on Cicero's recall, but it was vetoed by one of the other two. Pompey then sent Sestius to Caesar to get his approval for the recall, but he still replied carefully, observing that it wouldn't help relations between Pompey and Caesar for Cicero to come back on fire for vindication. The matter would string on for most of another year.

IN THE CONSULSHIP OF
PISO AND GABINIUS

1. Gaul is divided, all in three parts: Belgians live in one, Aquitanians in another, and people called Celts in a third (we call them Gauls). They all differ from one another in languages, customs, and laws. The river Garonne separates Gauls from Aquitanians, the Marne and the Seine from Belgians. The toughest of all are the Belgians, because they are farthest from our province, its culture, and its manners, and because merchants reach them least often bringing things that make men womanly. And they're closest to the Germans living across the Rhine and are constantly at war with them. That's also why the Helvetians outdo other Gauls in courage. They fight almost daily battles with Germans, either keeping them out of their own land or taking the war right to them.[3]

2. By far the noblest and richest Helvetian was Orgetorix. In the consulship of Messalla and Piso (61 BCE), drawn by thirst for rule, he raised a conspiracy among the nobles and convinced the nation to gather all their possessions and leave

---

[3] The medieval manuscripts supplement C.'s geography with this addition: "One region, which we said the Gauls hold, starts from the river Rhone and is bounded by the Garonne river, the ocean, and the borders of the Belgae, reaching the Rhine river in the territory of the Sequani and Helvetians, and it faces the north. The Belgae start from the furthest boundaries of Gaul, reach the lower part of the Rhine river, and look to the north and the rising sun. Aquitaine reaches from the Garonne river to the Pyrenees mountains and that part of the Ocean facing Spain. It faces the setting sun and the north."

their land. They could easily—they were stronger than all the others—seize control of all Gaul.

He persuaded them easily because the Helvetians were hemmed in on all sides by geography: on one side by the Rhine, broad and deep, separating Helvetian territory from German; on another, by the high Jura mountains between the Helvetians and the Sequani; on the third by Lake Geneva and the Rhone separating them from our province. This all kept them from roving very far and made it hard to make war on their neighbors, and so these men who loved to fight were very unhappy. They thought their land too small for so many people so brave and so good at warmaking. It extended 220 miles in one direction, 80 in another.[4]

3. And so, persuaded and heartened by Orgetorix's authority, they decided to gather what they needed for setting out, buying up as many pack animals and carts as possible,[5] sowing fields full (to have enough grain along the way), and ensuring peace and friendship with the nations closest to them. They judged two years would suffice for accomplishing this. By decree, they set the third year for their departure.

Orgetorix took upon himself to go as ambassador to the neighbors. Making the rounds, he convinced Casticus of the Sequani—son of Catamantaloedes, who had been king for many years and was named Friend of the Roman People by the senate—to take the throne in his country. Likewise he persuaded Dumnorix of the Haedui, brother of Diviciacus—just then the leading man there and well regarded among the people[6]—to try the same thing, giving Dumnorix his own

---

[4] Caesar's manuscripts give 180 Roman miles (CLXXX) for the breadth NW—SE of what is now Switzerland, but that is likely an error for LXXX (just under 75 English miles).

[5] Napoleon III estimated 8,500 carts and 34,000 draft animals to pull them.

[6] Diviciacus was Cicero's houseguest at Rome in 63 BCE, the year of Cicero's

daughter as a wife. He convinced them it would be easy to succeed if they tried, and besides, he was about to take command in his own nation. The Helvetians were easily the strongest in all Gaul, and he with all his resources and his army would guarantee them their thrones.

They were persuaded by what he said and swore faith and loyalty among themselves, hoping that when they had taken their thrones, three immensely powerful and resolute peoples could control all of Gaul.

4. This business was divulged to the Helvetians by an informer. After their custom, they made Orgetorix plead for himself in chains; if condemned, his penalty was to be burned alive. On the day set for making his case, Orgetorix dragged his whole retinue to court, some ten thousand people, and gathered all his clients and debtors as well—he had a lot of them. In that way he kept himself from having to plead his case. People were upset by this and sought to protect the law by force of arms. While the magistrates were bringing a mass of men in from the countryside, Orgetorix died, not without suspicion, so the Helvetians think, that he had done himself in.

5. After his death, the Helvetians still undertook to carry out their decision to leave their own country. When they thought they were ready, they set fire to all their towns (a dozen of them), their villages (some 400), and all their private farmhouses. They burned up all their grain except what they would take with them, to make them readier to face every danger for knowing there was no hope of returning home. They ordered everyone to take three months' worth of ground grain from home. They convinced their neighbors, the Rauraci and Tulingi and Latobrigi, to join the plan, burn their towns and vil-

---

consulship. Cicero is our source for knowing D. was a druid, the only such figure whose name we know.

lages, and set out with them. They also took as allies the Boii, who used to live across the Rhine and had crossed to Noricum and besieged Noreia.[7]

6. There were just two routes they could take from home: one through the Sequani, narrow and hard, running between the Jura and the Rhone, where carts could barely pass single file and a steep mountain loomed, making it easy for a few men to block passage; the other through our province, much easier and unimpeded, especially because the Rhone, easily forded at places, flows between the Helvetians and the recently pacified Allobroges.[8] The Allobrogan town closest to the Helvetians is Geneva, where a bridge reaches to the Helvetians. The Helvetians were sure they could either persuade or force Allobroges still not well disposed to the Roman people to let them pass through their land. Everything was ready for departure and they set the day to meet at the Rhone banks: five days before the Kalends of April (28 March), in the consulship of Piso and Gabinius (58 BCE).

7. Caesar, when told they would try their way through our province, hastened his departure from Rome and headed for farther Gaul with long days on the road and so reached Geneva. He ordered up as many soldiers as possible from the whole province (there was just one legion in further Gaul), and ordered the bridge at Geneva be torn down.

When the Helvetians learned of his arrival, they sent high-ranking ambassadors to see him. Nammeius and Verucloetius led the embassy, saying they would make their way through the province with no harmful intention, because they had no

[7] The Rauraci lived south and west of the Rhine, the Tulingi north and east of it, and the Latobrigi beyond them, about where the Rhine passes out of modern Switzerland. The Boii were in motion from seats along the Danube; Noreia is possibly modern Neumarkt in Styria, Austria.

[8] The Romans had suppressed an Allobrogan rebellion in 61 BCE.

other route. They asked it be allowed with his permission. Caesar, remembering how the consul Cassius had been killed by the Helvetians and his army routed and sent under the yoke (107 BCE), had no intention of agreeing, thinking that men as hostile as these, given the chance to pass through the province, could not keep from harm and mischief. But so a little time could elapse until the soldiers he had summoned would gather, he told the legates he would take time to think. If they wanted an answer, they should return on the the Ides of April (13 April).

8. Meanwhile, he used the legion he had with him and soldiers gathered from the province to extend a rampart from Lake Geneva, which flows into the Rhone, seventeen miles to the Jura mountains, which separate Sequani and Helvetians.[9] The wall was sixteen feet high with a ditch in front of it. When they finished, he arranged guardposts and fortified strong points, to be able to stop them easily if they tried to cross against his will.

When the day that was set with the ambassadors came and they returned to him, he said that by custom and tradition of the Roman people he could allow no one to pass through the province. He would stop them if they tried to force their way. Thwarted in this hope, the Helvetians roped together boats and made numerous rafts, while others tried to break through at the Rhone's fords where the river was shallowest, sometimes by day, but usually by night. Repelled by the wall and by soldiers coming and hurling spears, they gave up the attempt.

9. The one way left led through the Sequani, too narrow to pass if the Sequani opposed them. Unable to persuade them on their own, they sent messengers to Dumnorix the Hae-

---

[9] The rampart ran along the left (south) bank of the Rhone, to prevent a Helvetian crossing into the *provincia*.

duan, to prevail with the Sequani through his pleading. Dumnorix had influence with the Sequani for his well-regarded
generosity and was a friend of the Helvetians as well, because
he had married the daughter of Orgetorix from there. Craving
a throne, he sought revolution and wanted as many nations as
possible indebted to his kindness. So he took on the task and
won from the Sequani permission for the Helvetians to go
through their land and made the two sides exchange hostages:
The Sequani were not to block the Helvetian route; the Helvetians, to pass through without harm or injury.

10. Caesar heard the Helvetians were planning to go through
Sequani and Haedui territory to the land of the Santones, not
far from the Tolosates,[10] a nation in our province. If that happened, he knew it would be a great danger for the province to
have warlike men, enemies of the Roman people, close to us
on open plains rich in grain. So he put the legate Labienus in
charge of the fortification he had ordered. He headed for Italy
by long marches and enrolled two legions there and brought
three more, wintering around Aquileia, out of winter camp.
These five headed back to further Gaul through the Alps by the
shortest route.

There the Ceutrones and Graioceli and Caturiges took the
high ground and tried to stop the army. They were beaten off
in repeated skirmishes and on the seventh day from Ocelum—
the last town of the nearer province—he reached the land of
the Vocontii in the farther province. From there he took the
army through the Allobroges to the Segusiavi, the first people
across the Rhone, outside our province.[11]

[10] The Santones lived along and inland from the coast north of Bordeaux, about
160 miles northwest of the Tolosates.

[11] C. exceeds his formal authority, leaving the province for the first time. Ocelum
is probably modern Usseglio, a tiny town northwest of Turin.

11. The Helvetians had brought their forces through the narrows and the Sequanian land and reached Haedui territory, plundering the countryside. The Haedui, unable to defend themselves, sent representatives to Caesar to ask for help: for their long service to the Roman people they should not see their land devastated, their children enslaved, and their towns besieged almost in plain view of our army. At the same time, the Ambarri, close relatives of the Haedui, let Caesar know that their own land was being ravaged: they could barely keep the enemy out of their towns. So too the Allobroges, who had villages and property across the Rhone, fled to Caesar and showed him they had nothing left but their land. All this made Caesar decide not to wait for the Helvetians to reach the Santones—by then they would have devoured our allies' wealth.

12. There is a river Saône, flowing through the land of the Haedui and Sequani into the Rhone so unbelievably slowly that the eye can't tell which way it flows. The Helvetians crossed it, tying boats and rafts together. When Caesar's scouts reported that three-fourths of them had crossed and a fourth part remained this side of the Saône, he left camp after midnight with three legions and came to the group that hadn't yet crossed the river. He caught them burdened and unawares and hacked most of them down. The rest fled and hid in the nearby woods.

This canton was called "Tigurinus"—for the whole Helvetian nation is divided in four cantons. This one had gone out in the days of our fathers and killed the consul Lucius Cassius and sent his army under the yoke (107 BCE). So by chance or by the plan of the deathless gods, the Helvetian canton that had brought great calamity on the Roman people was first to pay the price. Caesar avenged not only public but even private losses, because the Tigurini had killed, in the same battle as

Cassius, the legate Lucius Piso, grandfather of his own father-in-law Lucius Piso.

13. After that battle, he had a bridge made across the Saône to pursue the rest of the Helvetians and brought the army across. The Helvetians, startled by his sudden arrival, realized he had accomplished in one day what they had barely done in twenty—cross the river—and sent representatives to him. Divico led the embassy: he had been the Helvetian leader in the war with Cassius.

He addressed Caesar this way: If the Roman people made peace with the Helvetians, they would go and stay where Caesar determined and wanted. But if he went on prosecuting the war, he would come to recall the old loss the Roman people had suffered and the strength of the Helvetians then. Just because he had confronted one canton unawares, when those who had crossed the river could not help them, he should not credit that to his own strength or look down on them. They had learned from their fathers and forefathers to fight from strength not trickery and not to rely on ambushes. He should take care that the place where they stood shouldn't take its name from and preserve for history a disaster for the Roman people.

14. Caesar's answer: He did not hesitate, precisely because he remembered the events the Helvetian legates retold. He took them more seriously because the Roman people had so little deserved what happened. If he had known of some injury of his own doing, it wouldn't have been hard to watch out, but he was confused just because he knew he had done nothing to cause himself anxiety nor was he a man for baseless fear. Even if he could overlook the old insult, could he put aside memory of recent assaults, such as the attempt to force their way through the province against his will? Such as their

harassment of the Haedui, Ambarri, and Allobroges? Their vulgar boasting of their victory and their marveling that their attacks had gone unpunished so long both led to the same conclusion. For the immortal gods regularly allow prosperity and continuing impunity to those they will punish for their crimes—to make them feel more keenly their change of fortunes.

For all that, if they would give hostages even now (so he would know they would do what they promised) and if they made up to the Haedui and likewise the Allobroges for the injuries done them and their allies, he would make peace with them.

Divico answered: The Helvetians had been trained by their forebears to take hostages, not give them, and the Roman people had seen that. That was the answer he gave, and he left.

15. Next day they broke camp. Caesar did the same and sent all his cavalry on ahead—four thousand of them, gathered from throughout the province and from the Haedui and their allies—to watch where the enemy went. Pressing the rear guard too eagerly, they skirmished with Helvetian cavalry and some few of our men fell. The Helvetians were elated that five hundred horse had repelled so many of ours and began to hang back, harassing our forces now and then with their rear guard. Caesar held his men back from fighting and judged it enough for now to keep the enemy from plunder and destruction. So they went forward for about two weeks with no more than four or five miles between their rear guard and our front line.

16. Daily all the while Caesar demanded the Haedui supply the grain they had officially promised. Because of the cold the grain in the field was not yet ripe nor was there even enough fodder. The grain they had brought down the Saône in boats was less useful because the Helvetians had turned course away

from the river, and Caesar did not want to break off pursuit. The Haedui strung him on day by day: they said it was being gathered, shipped—it was just coming. When Caesar realized he was being led on and the date when grain must be rationed to the soldiers was pressing, he called the Haedui leaders together (there were many of them in camp). Most notable were Diviciacus and Liscus—he held the highest office, which Haedui call *vergobret*, appointed annually with power of life and death over them. Caesar rebuked them severely for not supporting him at such a critical moment, with the enemy so near at hand, when grain could be neither bought not harvested. He took it specially badly because he had taken on the war so much at their instigation.

17. At last Liscus, drawn by Caesar's words, set out what he had kept quiet before. There were men of great influence with the people who as individuals had more power than the magistrates. Their rebellious and wicked words kept the people from gathering the grain they owed. If they could not be first in Gaul, better to endure Gallic commands than Roman ones. If the Romans defeated the Helvetians, they would doubtless snatch liberty from the Haedui and all the rest of Gaul. These men reported our plans and what went on in our camp to the enemy. He could not stop them. He knew how dangerous it was for him to tell Caesar what he was now forced to. That was why he had kept quiet so long.

18. Caesar guessed Liscus' words pointed to Dumnorix, Diviciacus' brother, but quickly dismissed the meeting to keep the matter from discussion in a large group. Liscus he kept back, asking him about what he had said in the meeting. Liscus spoke freely and boldly. Caesar asked others the same privately and found the truth: Dumnorix, full of daring, was hugely popular with the people for his generosity and wanted

revolution. For many years he had bought up all the tolls and taxes of the Haedui cheaply, because no one dared bid against him. So he had increased his wealth and his capacity to be very generous. He maintained a large cavalry troop around him at his own expense. His wealth made him powerful at home and among neighboring nations. To extend his power, he married his own mother to a noble and powerful man among the Bituriges, he had a Helvetian wife himself, and he married off his half-sister and other women relatives to other nations.

Dumnorix favored and supported the Helvetians because of that connection, but hated Caesar and the Romans on his own, because their coming reduced his power and his brother Diviciacus had been restored to his former influence and honor. If anything happened to the Romans, his best chance of gaining the throne would come through Helvetian influence. The rule of the Roman people made him despair not only for the throne but for all his influence. Caesar found by his inquiries that in the cavalry skirmish gone bad a few days earlier, Dumnorix and his horsemen had been the first to flee (Dumnorix led the cavalry the Haedui had sent Caesar), spooking the rest of the cavalry by their flight.

19. When Caesar found this out, other facts appeared confirming his suspicions. Dumnorix had brought the Helvetians through the Sequani, arranging hostages between them, doing what he did without Caesar or his own people approving or even knowing, and so he was being brought up on charges before a Haedui judge. Caesar thought he had reason to act against him or else order the Haedui to do so. There was one reason not to act: Caesar's awareness of his brother Diviciacus' good will toward the Roman people, support for himself, and remarkable loyalty, fairness, and good judgment. He feared insulting the one by punishing the other.

Before trying anything, he summoned Diviciacus and sent away the usual interpreters. He spoke with him with the help of Valerius Troucillus, chief citizen of the Gallic province, a friend in whom he had utmost confidence. He reminded Diviciacus what was said in front of them about Dumnorix in the open meeting and reported what people had told him privately. He asked and encouraged him to take no offense but either to hear the case and judge for himself or direct the Haedui to judge.

20. Diviciacus, awash in tears, embraced Caesar and begged him not to judge his brother harshly. It was all true: no one was sorrier than he was. He once had broad influence at home and in the rest of Gaul, when his brother was too young to do much and depended on Diviciacus for his advance, but then he used wealth and strength to undermine Diviciacus' influence and almost to destroy him. But Diviciacus was still swayed by brotherly love and public opinion. If anything bad happened to Dumnorix at Caesar's hand while Diviciacus stood high in his friendship, no one would believe it hadn't been done with his consent. That would turn all Gaul against him in future.

When he had pleaded at length in tears, Caesar took his hand and comforted him, asking him to end his pleading. Diviciacus' influence was so great with him that in response to his wish and request Caesar could excuse harm to the republic and his own unhappiness. He called in Dumnorix with the brother present. He said what he had against him, telling him what he knew and what the Haedui complained of. He warned him to avoid all suspicion in future and said he would forgive bygones at Diviciacus' request. He set guards on Dumnorix so he would know what he did and with whom he spoke.[12]

---

[12] Dumnorix will reappear in the fifth commentary.

21. The same day Caesar was alerted by scouts that the enemy had camped at the foot of a mountain about seven miles from his camp. He sent them to describe the mountain and what the climb was like around it. They reported back it was easy. At midnight, he ordered Titus Labienus, legate with rank of praetor, to take two legions and guides who knew the way and go to the mountaintop. He told him what he was thinking. A couple of hours later, he went out himself the same way the enemy had gone and sent the cavalry on ahead. Publius Considius, a well-regarded old soldier who had fought with Sulla and later Crassus, he sent on with scouts.

22. At dawn, when Labienus had taken the summit, Caesar was a bit over a mile from the enemy camp and—he learned later from captives—neither approach had been detected. Considius raced up on horseback to tell him that the mountain he wanted Labienus to take was in enemy hands: he knew it from the Gallic weapons and insignia. Caesar took his own force up on a nearby hill and put them in battle order. Labienus, since he'd been told by Caesar not to engage until Caesar's forces were seen approaching the enemy camp—so they could attack the enemy at one time from all sides—, held the mountain and waited for our forces, holding off battle. Much later in the day, Caesar learned from scouts that the mountain was in our hands and the Helvetians had decamped. Considius in his terror had reported seeing something he hadn't seen. Caesar followed the enemy that day at the usual distance and pitched camp three miles from theirs.

23. Next day, with only two days until the army needed grain allotments and with Bibracte, much the biggest and richest Haedui town, no more than seventeen miles away, he decided he should look after his grain supply.[13] He turned from the

---

[13] Bibracte, a fortified town west of modern Autun, lies about 150 miles WNW of Geneva.

Helvetians and headed for Bibracte. Runaway slaves from decurion Lucius Aemilius' Gallic cavalry alerted the enemy. The Helvetians changed plan—perhaps thinking the Romans had withdrawn out of fear (especially because the day before we had not joined battle when we held the high ground) or else they thought we could be cut off from our grain supply. They reversed course to follow and then harass our men in the rear guard.

24. When he noticed this, Caesar took his troops up the next hill and sent cavalry to fend off enemy attacks. He set a triple line of four veteran legions halfway up the hill, then put the two legions he had just enrolled in northern Italy and all his support troops on the hilltop, thus filling the whole height above him with troops. He put baggage and packs in one place, ordering it guarded by the formation above. The Helvetians followed with all their wagons and put their baggage in one place, brushed off our cavalry, and moved in a tight phalanx toward our front line.

25. Caesar first removed his own horse, then those of other officers from sight, equalizing the risk by removing hope of flight. Encouraging his men, he joined battle. The troops on higher ground easily broke the enemy phalanx with throwing spears; then they drew swords and attacked. The Gauls were greatly hindered in fighting because several of their shields would get pierced and pinned by one spear. When the iron bent they could not pull it out or fight well enough with their left hand entangled. Many then, after flailing their arms a while, preferred to throw shields aside and fight with bodies bared. Wearied eventually by wounds, they pulled back and started to regroup on a hill almost a mile away, taking it with our men in pursuit. The Boii and Tulingi, who brought up the rear and guarded it for the enemy with about 15,000 men, attacked and surrounded our men on their unprotected flank.

Seeing this, the Helvetians who had taken the hill surged back and renewed battle. The Romans moved their standards in two directions: the first and second lines to oppose the beaten and retreating, the third line to take on the newcomers.

26. So they fought a two-front battle, long and hard. When they could resist our men's attack no longer, some retreated to the hill again as they had begun, others gathered by the baggage and carts. In this whole battle, fought from the early afternoon until evening, no one saw an enemy turn his back. Even late into the night they fought by the baggage, because they made a rampart of the carts and hurled spears from higher up at our men coming on. Some put pikes and javelins between the carts and wheels to injure our men. After a long fight, we took the baggage and the camp. The daughter of Orgetorix and one of his sons were captured there. Some 130,000 people survived that battle and journeyed all night long. Not breaking the journey at night at all, on the fourth day they reached the territory of the Lingones, while our men could not keep up with them, because of the casualties and taking three days to bury our dead. Caesar sent messengers with a letter to the Lingones, asking them not to help the Helvetians with grain or anything else. If they helped them, he would treat them as he did the Helvetians. After three days' break, he began to pursue the Helvetians with all his forces.

27. The Helvetians, short of everything, sent an embassy to discuss surrender with him. Some met him on the road and threw themselves at his feet and begged for peace, weeping as they spoke; he ordered them to await his arrival, and they obeyed. When Caesar arrived, he demanded hostages, arms, and slaves who had fled to the other side. While these things were being found and collected, about 6,000 men of the canton called Verbigenus—perhaps afraid they would be punished

after handing over their weapons or just hoping to be safe—thought that in such a mob of captives they could conceal their flight or just be overlooked, left the Helvetian camp at night-fall, and headed for the Rhine and German lands.

28. When Caesar found this out, he ordered the nations whose lands they crossed to chase them down and bring them back if they wanted to clear themselves. He treated the returned refugees as enemies.[14] He accepted the surrender of the others when they handed over hostages, weapons, and runaways. He ordered Helvetians, Tulingi, and Latobrigi to go back where they came from; since with their crops lost they had nothing at home for their hunger, he ordered the Allogbroges to supply them grain. He insisted they restore the towns and villages they had burned. He did this mainly because he wanted the place the Helvetians had left not to lie empty, or the Germans living across the Rhine would cross to Helvetian territory for the good land and they would then neighbor the Allobroges and the Gallic province. The Haedui asked to let the Boii, known for great strength, live on their land, and he agreed. The Haedui gave them land and afterwards legal status and liberty the same as their own.

29. Tablets written in Greek characters[15] were found in the Helvetian camp and taken to Caesar. They recorded by name how many had left home who could bear arms, and likewise how many children, old men, and women. There were 263,000 Helvetians, 36,000 Tulingi, 14,000 Latobrigi, 23,000 Rauraci, 32,000 Boii; of these, 92,000 could bear arms. The total of all came to 368,000. When a census Caesar ordered was held after they returned home, the number was found to be 110,000.

[14] They would be killed or enslaved.
[15] Marseilles had been founded by Greeks c. 600 BCE, hence the Greek alphabet was known: see 6.14; in 5.48, Greek letters are used in a code.

30. When the Helvetian war was done, ambassadors from almost all of Gaul, leaders of nations, gathered to congratulate Caesar. They understood that if the Romans had punished the Helvetians in war to avenge old injuries, the result stood as much in Gallic as Roman tradition. The Helvetians had planned to leave their homes in good times to wage war on all Gaul and seize power. They would choose whatever place to live in all Gaul they judged most convenient and fertile and make the other nations pay them tribute. The Gallic leaders sought to call a council of all Gaul on a set day and to do so with Caesar's permission and approval. They would have some requests to make of him by general agreement. Permission granted, they set a date for the council and on oath swore among themselves that no one would speak of it unless directed by common agreement.

31. When the meeting broke up, the same leaders as before returned to Caesar and asked to discuss their own and everyone's safety secretly, in private. Granted this, they threw themselves at his feet in tears: they were working and struggling as much to make sure what they said did not get out as to get what they wanted, for if it got out, they foresaw the worst tortures for themselves.

The Haeduan Diviciacus spoke for them: There were two factions in all Gaul, one led by the Haedui, one by the Arverni. After they struggled so much for supremacy over many years, it happened that the Germans were brought in and paid by the Arverni and Sequani. About 15,000 crossed the Rhine; when these fierce barbarians fell in love with the land, life, and riches of Gaul, more crossed; now about 120,000 of them were in Gaul. The Haedui and their supporters had taken arms against them once and again; beaten, they endured great disaster, and lost all their nobles, all their senate, all their knights. Broken

by battles and disasters, the people once most powerful in Gaul
for its own strength and for the support and friendship of the
Roman people was driven to give as hostages to the Sequani
its most noble citizens and to bind the nation on oath neither
to ask the hostages be returned nor to beseech the Roman
people for help nor to resist remaining under the sway and
command of the Sequani forever.

He alone of the Haedui could not be brought to swear the
oath or give his children as hostages. So he fled his nation and
came to Rome to ask the senate for help, because he was the
only one not bound by oath or hostages. But worse had come
to the victorious Sequani than to the defeated Haedui, because
Ariovistus, the German king, had settled in their territory, taking a third of Sequani land, the best in all Gaul, and now he
was ordering the Sequani to abandon another third: a few
months earlier 24,000 Harudes[16] had come to him, for whom
he needed a place to live. In a few years everyone would be
driven out of Gaul and all the Germans would cross the Rhine.
German land couldn't compare to the Gallic, nor their diet with
the Gallic standard. But Ariovistus, once he had beaten Gauls
in battle, a battle at Magetobriga,[17] arrogantly and cruelly demanded hostages, insisting on the children of every noble
house and practicing every kind of torture upon them if anything were not done just at his whim and will. He was a barbarian, angry and impetuous. They could not endure his rule
much longer. Without help from Caesar and the Roman people, then all Gauls would have to do what the Helvetians did,
leave home to look for another, a new residence far from the
Germans, and try their fortune however it fell out.

---

[16] Later sources place the (C)harudes on the Baltic coast just east of Denmark.

[17] Amage, near Luxeuil, well north of the territory we have seen so far.

If this were reported to Ariovistus, Diviciacus didn't doubt he would exact the harshest punishment on all the hostages he held. Caesar, by reputation (his own and the army's), by fresh victory, and in the name of the Roman people, could keep a greater mass of Germans from being brought across the Rhine and could protect all Gaul from Ariovistus' depredations.

32. When Diviciacus had spoken, everyone present began weeping and begging help from Caesar. Caesar noticed the Sequani alone of all did none of what the others did but looked sadly down, heads bowed. Struck by this, he asked them why. The Sequani gave no answer, but remained sad and silent. When he asked them repeatedly and they couldn't utter a word, Diviciacus the Haeduan answered: The Sequani's fate was worse and weightier than the rest, in that they alone did not dare complain or seek help even secretly. They feared the cruelty of the absent Ariovistus as though he were right there, because the others were able to flee, but the Sequani, who had welcomed Ariovistus into their land, whose towns were all under his control, would have to suffer every cruelty.

33. Learning this, Caesar heartened Gallic spirits with words and promised to make the matter his own concern: he had great hope that his deeds and reputation would make Ariovistus stop his depredations. Giving this speech, he dismissed the meeting. Afterwards, many reasons made him think he should consider and undertake the business. First, because he saw the Haedui, often called brothers and relations by the senate, enslaved and subjected to the Germans, with hostages held by Ariovistus and the Sequani. To have this under the great authority of the Roman people was exceedingly embarrassing to himself and to the republic. He saw the danger of Germans growing gradually accustomed to crossing the Rhine and a great mass of them coming to Gaul. He did not

think fierce barbarians would hold back, once in control of Gaul, from entering the Roman province and then heading for Italy, as the Cimbri and Teutones had done before. This he thought he had to oppose as quickly as possible. Ariovistus had clothed himself in insufferable chutzpah and arrogance such as not to be endured.

34. So he decided to send messengers to Ariovistus to ask he pick some middle ground for a meeting: he wanted to discuss public affairs of the highest importance for both. To that embassy Ariovistus replied: If he needed anything from Caesar, he would go to him; if Caesar wanted anything, he should come to him. He certainly would not dare go without his army to the parts of Gaul Caesar had now taken, and he could not gather his army in one place without great logistical effort. He was surprised that Caesar or indeed the Roman people should have any business in *his* Gaul, which he had won in combat.

35. When this answer reached Caesar, again Caesar sent messengers with this commission: so indebted was Ariovistus to the kindness of Caesar and the Roman people (for during Caesar's consulate he had been named king and friend by the senate), then if these were his thanks to Caesar and the Roman people—grumbling at an invitation to conversation and thinking it not worthwhile to discuss and understand their common concerns—, here is what Caesar demanded: first, he should bring no further groups of people across the Rhine into Gaul; then he should give back the hostages he had from the Haedui and allow the Sequani to give back the ones they had taken at his direction; he should not harm the Haedui nor make war on them or their allies. If he complied, he would have permanent influence and friendship with Caesar and the Roman people; if Caesar did not get what he asked, then, since the senate had decreed in the consulship of Messala and Piso (61

BCE) that whoever governed the Gallic province should for the republic's sake defend the Haedui and the other friends of the Roman people, Caesar would not overlook the harm done to the Haedui.

36. Ariovistus replied: It was the law of war that conquerors command the conquered as they wish. The Roman people was equally accustomed to commanding their vanquished as they chose, not as others prescribed. If Ariovistus did not tell the Roman people how to use its authority, he should not be kept from exercising authority by the Roman people. The Haedui had risked war, clashed at arms, and been overcome, so now they were his tributaries. Caesar would do great harm if his arrival made Ariovistus' revenue decline. He would neither return hostages to the Haedui nor do harm of war to them or their allies, if they abided by their agreement and paid annual tribute. If they did not, the "brotherly" Roman people would be far away. And Caesar trumpeted that he would not overlook harm done to the Haedui—no one fought with Ariovistus without being destroyed. If Caesar wished, let him join battle, but he should know what strength unbeaten Germans possessed, a people tested in arms, now living in the open fourteen years.

37. This message came to Caesar just as legates from the Haedui and also from the Treveri arrived. The Haedui complained that the Harudes, lately crossing into Gaul, were ravaging their land: they couldn't buy peace from Ariovistus even with hostages. The Treveri complained that a hundred cantons of Suebi had camped on the Rhine, trying to cross, led by the brothers Nasua and Cimberius. Greatly upset by this news, Caesar thought he must hurry, for if the new band of Suebi joined up with the old forces of Ariovistus, they would be

harder to fight off. So with grain collected as quickly as possible, he headed against Ariovistus in long marches.

38. When he had gone three days, he had report that Ariovistus with all his troops was heading to Vesontio,[18] the largest town of the Sequani, to occupy it. Caesar thought he should take great care that this not happen. Everything useful for war could be found there, and nature fortified the place to make it good for conducting warfare. The Dubis river surrounded almost the whole town as if drawn by compasses. The remaining space, about 600 feet, where the river left off, was closed in by a high hill, whose base reached the riverbank on each side. A wall around the hill made it a citadel joined to the town. Marching there by long nights and days Caesar took the town and posted his guard.

39. While he stayed at Vesontio a few days to gather grain and supplies, our men inquired and heard Gauls and merchants describing the Germans' huge bodies, their incredible strength, and their experience in arms. They had often encountered them and could not stand the sight of them or endure their gaze. Great fear suddenly seized our whole army and upset their minds greatly. It started from the military tribunes, the prefects, and the others who followed Caesar out of friendship from Rome without much military experience. One and another suggested reasons why they had to leave and asked his permission to go. Some remained out of shame, wanting not to be suspected of fear. These could not make sham faces or hold back tears, so hid in their tents, complaining of fate and lamenting with friends their common danger. All over camp, wills were signed and sealed.

[18] Besançon was a hundred miles NE of where C. left the Helvetians.

The fear they voiced gradually upset the ones with long experience in camp, the soldiers and centurions and cavalry commanders. They wanted to be thought less fearful and said it wasn't the enemy they were worried about, but the narrow road and deep woods between them and Ariovistus, or else they said grain could not easily enough be supplied. Some even told Caesar that when he ordered camp broken and the standards forward the soldiers would not obey or move the standards, out of fear.

40. Realizing this, he called a council bringing together the centurions from all units, rebuking them strongly: mainly for thinking that where or how they were led was theirs to discuss and consider. Ariovistus had eagerly sought the friendship of the Roman people during his consulship; why would anyone think he would abandon his responsibility so rashly? Caesar was sure that when Ariovistus heard his demands and saw the fairness of his proposals he would not reject the favor he and the Roman people showed. But if fury and madness drove him to make war, what then to fear? Why should they despair of their own strength or his prudence? That enemy threat came in the times of our fathers when the Cimbri and Teutones were beaten back by Marius, earning fame for the army no less than the general; the threat came again lately in Italy in the uprising of slaves who had the advantage of a certain amount of experience and training gotten from us.[19] So one can judge how important bravery is, particularly because we see how people who had been baselessly feared when unarmed were overcome when they were later armed and victorious. These are the same people the Helvetians often fought and generally beat on both sides of the river, but the Helvetians were no match for our army.

[19] The slave revolt led by Spartacus occurred in 73–71 BCE.

Ariovistus defeating the Gauls[20] and their ensuing flight should not trouble anyone, knowing that he was lucky to find the Gauls wearied by war, then held himself in camp amid swamps for many months, giving battle no chance. When the Gauls gave up and began to scatter he suddenly attacked, defeating them by strategy and planning more than strength. That plan could work against inexperienced barbarians, but our troops he could scarcely hope to take in this way. If they supposedly feared for grain and for the narrows ahead, they were arrogant, showing no confidence in their general and trying to tell him his job. He was taking care: the Sequani, Leuci, and Lingones were supplying grain, with more ripening in the fields. They could see the road for themselves soon enough. If rumor said some would not obey or move the standards, he was unworried: he knew whose orders an army wouldn't follow, someone either abandoned by luck or proven to be greedy. His whole life testified his innocence, while his luck was shown by the Helvetian campaign. So what he had been putting off for another day he would do immediately, breaking camp that night at the fourth watch, to find out at once whether shame and duty were stronger with them than fear. If no one followed, then he would go with the tenth legion alone, of which he had no doubts. They would be his praetorian guard.

41. That speech ended, their minds veered round wonderfully and became eager and ready for fighting. The tenth legion expressed thanks first through the military tribunes because he regarded them so highly, assuring him they were right ready for war. Then the other legions through the military tribunes and first rank centurions made amends with Caesar:

[20] At Magetobriga (1.31 above).

they never hesitated or feared or preferred their view of the war over the general's. Accepting their assurances and taking directions from Diviciacus, in whom he had the greatest confidence, he set out before dawn, as he had said, to take the army by a circuitous route of almost fifty miles through open country. On the seventh day, not breaking the journey, he was told by scouts that Ariovistus' force was no more than twenty-two miles away from ours.

42. Hearing of Caesar's arrival, Ariovistus sent legates to him. The conversation he had sought before was now acceptable to him, since Caesar had come near and Ariovistus thought he could engage without danger. Caesar did not reject the proposal and thought Ariovistus was finally coming to his senses, since he volunteered what before he had refused to concede. He had great hope, for the kindnesses he and the Roman people had shown him before, that he would climb down from his stubbornness when he knew what Caesar wanted. The fifth day was set for the conference. Meanwhile with legates going back and forth regularly, Ariovistus insisted Caesar bring no infantry to the conference, fearing he would be surrounded and ambushed. Both should come with cavalry: otherwise he would not come. Caesar, since he wanted nothing to get in the way and disrupt the conference and didn't trust his safety to Gallic cavalry, thought it best to unmount all the Gallic horsemen and place on horse legionary soldiers of the tenth legion, in whom he had the highest confidence, to have the friendliest guards if need arose. When he did this, one of the soldiers of the tenth not unfacetiously said Caesar had done more than he promised. He promised to make the tenth his praetorian guard, but enrolled it among the knights instead.[21]

---

[21] A joke no less: the so-called *knights* (*equites*) were the second-ranking class of Roman citizens after the senators, and in many cases outshone the senators in wealth.

43. There was a large open plain and on it a substantial earthen mound: a place equally spaced from the camps of both. They came there as agreed to confer. Caesar posted the legion he had brought on horse 200 paces from the mound, so Ariovistus posted cavalry at like distance. Ariovistus demanded they confer on horseback, bringing ten others each with them. When they got there, Caesar began speaking by recalling his own and the senate's generosity toward Ariovistus: he had been called king and friend by the senate, with gifts abundantly sent. This happened to few and was usually granted for the highest services. Ariovistus, who had no special entrée or legitimate reason for asking, won these awards by the generosity and kindness of Caesar and the senate. Caesar described the old and sound reasons for the connection with the Haedui, how often and how honorably the senate had named them in its decrees, how the Haedui had been leaders of all Gaul before ever they sought our friendship. The Roman people habitually wanted their allies and friends to suffer no losses, but to advance in influence, dignity, and honor. Who could stand it if what they brought to their friendship with the Roman people could be snatched away? He ended by demanding what he had given the legates to demand: Ariovistus should wage no war on the Haedui or their allies, he should return hostages, and if none of the Germans could be sent home, no more at least should be allowed across the Rhine.

44. Ariovistus replied briefly to Caesar's demands, then spoke at length of his own strength. He had crossed the Rhine not on his own but on invitation and request from Gauls. With great hope for great rewards he had left home and family. They had homes given to them in Gaul by Gauls, hostages given them voluntarily. By right of war he took tribute, which victors regularly impose on the vanquished. He had not attacked the Gauls, but the Gauls him. All the nations of Gaul had come to

attack him and range camps against him. All their forces had
been driven back and beaten by him in one battle. If they
wanted to try again, he was ready to fight again; if they wanted
peace, it was unfair to refuse him the tribute they had paid
voluntarily till then. The friendship of the Roman people
should be an ornament and protection for him, not a disadvantage—that's why he sought it. If tribute were forgiven and
his prisoners taken away because of the Roman people, he
would no less easily reject the friendship of the Roman people
than he had sought it. Bringing many Germans into Gaul: he
did it to protect himself, not to attack Gaul, as you could see
because he had come only when asked and fought not to attack
but to defend. He had come to Gaul before the Roman people
did. Never before this time had the army of the Roman people
gone beyond their Gallic province. What did Caesar want? why
had he come into Ariovistus' territory?

This Gaul was his province as the other was ours. He should
not be forgiven if he attacked our territory, and so we were
unfair to hinder him in exercise of his rights. As for Caesar
calling the Haedui "friends," he was not such a simple barbarian that he didn't know that in the last Allobroges war the
Haedui had not helped the Romans and in the quarrels the
Haedui had with the Sequani they had not used the help of the
Roman people. He had every right to be suspicious of pre-
tended friendship—Caesar had an army in Gaul to oppress
him with. If Caesar did not leave and take his army out of this
part of the country, Ariovistus would treat him not as friend
but as enemy. If Ariovistus killed him, he would do a favor for
many nobles and leaders of the Roman people—he'd been told
this directly by their own messengers. He could win their
friendship and influence by killing Caesar. But if Caesar departed and handed him free possession of Gaul, Ariovistus

would reward him with a great prize and fight whatever wars Caesar wished with no effort or risk on Caesar's part.

45. Much was said by Caesar making his point: He could not abandon the matter, for neither he nor the Roman people were used to abandoning allies of great merit, nor did he think Gaul belonged more to Ariovistus than to the Roman people. The Arverni and Ruteni, overcome in war by Fabius Maximus (121 BCE), were pardoned by the Roman people, making no province of them and exacting no tribute. However far back we look, Rome's dominion in Gaul was always fair. Gaul deserves to be free, left by the senate's judgment to use its own laws even when defeated in war.

46. While the conversation went on, Caesar was told that Ariovistus' cavalry was approaching the hill, riding up to our troops, hurling stones and spears against them. Caesar ended the parley and returned to his men, ordering them to throw no spears at all back against the enemy. Even if his chosen legion could safely fight the horsemen, he did not want beaten enemies to be able to say they were surrounded by him when they had trusted in the parleying. After it got abroad among the soldiers how arrogantly Ariovistus had banned Romans from all Gaul while his cavalry attacked our side and disrupted the meeting, they were filled with much greater enthusiasm and energy for fighting.

47. Two days later, Ariovistus sent spokesmen to Caesar. He wanted to deal with him on the things they had started to talk about and left unfinished. They could set a day for renewing the parley or, if he didn't want that, he could send a legate to Ariovistus. Caesar saw nothing to talk about, especially because the Germans on that day before could not be kept from throwing spears at our side. He thought it would be dangerous to send a legate from our side and expose him to these wild

men. He thought best to send Ariovistus a brave and polished young man, Valerius Procillus, son of Valerius Caburius (the father won citizenship from Valerius Flaccus[22]). Procillus was reliable and knew the Gallic language well, which Ariovistus had long used himself, and the Germans had no reason to harm him. He sent along Metius as well, who had been Ariovistus' guest. He ordered them to find out and report what Ariovistus was saying. When Ariovistus saw them in his camp, he exclaimed in front of his army, why have they come to him? To spy on him? He kept them from speaking and threw them in chains.[23]

48. That day he moved camp forward and settled at the foot of a hill five or so miles from Caesar's camp. The next day he brought his troops past Caesar's camp and made camp almost two miles beyond him, the better to cut Caesar off from the grain and supplies brought in by the Sequani and Haedui. For the next five days, Caesar brought his forces out and kept them in battle order so Ariovistus could fight if he wished. Ariovistus kept his army in camp all these days, skirmishing daily with cavalry.

This was the way of fighting the German practiced: he had 6,000 cavalry and the same number of swift and fierce infantrymen, each selected by a horseman to protect him. During these fights, the cavalry returned to them, and they came into the fight if things got tougher. If a badly wounded rider fell, they swarmed round. If they had to go out farther or pull back faster, their swiftness was so practiced that they could keep up with the horses, clinging to their manes.

[22] Proconsul for Gaul in 83 BCE.
[23] Ariovistus had every right to do this; C. has A. appear arbitrary and cruel in doing exactly what C. would do himself.

49. When Caesar saw Ariovistus holding to camp, he didn't want to be kept from his supplies, so he picked a good place about 600 yards past where the Germans were settled and marched there in triple line. He kept the first and second lines in arms, ordering the third to fortify camp. Ariovistus sent some 16,000 men in arms with the whole cavalry to frighten our men and keep them from fortifying camp. Nevertheless Caesar, as he had decided, ordered two lines to repel the enemy, the third to complete the work. When camp was fortified, he left two legions there and some of the auxiliaries, taking the other four legions back to the main camp.

50. Next day, following his plan, Caesar took troops out of both camps and, going a little way from the main camp, drew up his line to give the enemy a chance to fight. When he saw they still didn't come out, he led the army back to camp around noon. Then Ariovistus finally sent some of his force to attack the smaller camp. Both sides fought hard till evening. At sunset, Ariovistus took his troops, who had given and taken many injuries, back to camp. When Caesar asked prisoners why Ariovistus wouldn't fight, he found out that the custom with the Germans was for the mothers to cast lots and read signs to proclaim whether it was time to engage or not. They had said the Germans would not win if they joined battle before the new moon.

51. Next day Caesar left enough guard for each camp, then set all his auxiliaries before the smaller camp for the enemy to see. His legionaries were fewer in number than the enemy, so he used auxiliaries for appearances. He himself marched in triple line up to the enemy camp. The Germans finally had to bring their forces from camp and line them up by nation evenly spaced: Harudes, Marcomani, Triboci, Vangiones, Nemetes, Eudosii, Suebi. To take away hope of escape, they

surrounded the army with carts and wagons and set upon them their women, who reached out to the soldiers going into battle, weeping and begging not to be handed over to Romans as slaves.

52. Caesar put legates (and in one case a quaestor) in charge of each legion so every soldier's bravery would have a witness. He began the fight on the right flank, noticing the enemy was weaker there. Our men answered the signal eagerly and ran at the enemy suddenly and swiftly, so there wasn't room for throwing spears at them. Abandoning their spears, they fought hand to hand with swords. The Germans quickly made their usual phalanx to resist assault from our swords. Many of our men were seen jumping up on the phalanx, ripping away shields, and inflicting wounds from above. When the enemy's left flank was beaten back and thrown into flight, they pressed hard with their larger force on their right. Young Crassus,[24] commanding the cavalry, noticed this, and since he was less bogged down than the officers on the front line, he sent the third line to help our men where they were struggling.

53. So the battle was renewed and the enemy all turned and ran, not stopping until they got to the Rhine nearly five miles away. A few were sure enough of themselves to swim or take boats and find their safety. Among them, Ariovistus found a small boat tied to the bank and fled. Our cavalry chased down and killed all the rest.[25] Ariovistus had two wives, a Suebian he had brought from home and a Norican, sister of king Voccio, whose brother sent her to marry him in Gaul. Both died trying to escape. One of his two daughters was killed, the other captured. Valerius Procillus was dragged off bound in triple chains

[24] Son of the wealthy triumvir, to fall with his father fighting the Persians at Carrhae five years later.

[25] Plutarch *Caesar* 19.5 says the victims numbered 80,000.

by his guards as they fled until Caesar, riding in pursuit with cavalry, came upon him. This pleased Caesar as much as the victory, to see this leading man of the Gallic province, his friend and often host, snatched from the enemy's hands and restored to him. Fortune had not reduced his pleasure and satisfaction by doing the prisoner serious harm. Procillus said they had cast lots over him three times in his presence, to see whether to burn him alive at once or hold him for another day, and he was saved by virtue of the lots. Metius was also found and brought back.

54. When the battle news crossed the Rhine, the Suebi who had come to the Rhine banks began to return home. When those who lived closest to the Rhine sensed their fear, they pursued and killed a great number of them. Winning two great wars in one summer, Caesar led the army to quarters among the Sequani a little earlier than the season required. He put Labienus in command of quarters while he left for nearer Gaul to hold court.

SECOND COMMENTARY

57 BCE

The consuls have almost no role in what goes on this year. Caesar spends part of his winter enrolling two additional legions while he is in Cisalpine Gaul, stretching his finances until the Senate agrees more than a year later to pay them and the other two legions recruited in 58. He is now up to eight legions, twice what he was originally authorized.

The strategy for the year that we infer was a twofold movement. Caesar and his main force would first go north from their winter quarters among the Sequani to challenge and subdue the nations he had identified at the outset as the most threatening, those he called Belgae, facing the Rhine north of Strasbourg. There he was successful.

As that campaign progressed, he would send his legate Crassus west to Normandy and Brittany to make a show of force among peoples who would never present him or his successors with a serious challenge. At the end of the year, he decided to maintain his forces in north-central Gaul, strung out mainly along the valley of the Loire.

Two of Caesar's generals loom into view in this commentary, men with futures important to Caesar. Quintus Titurius Sabinus is the lesser figure, son of a mint-master, barely mentioned here (2.5), but charged with putting down the rebellion of Viridovix in 56.[1] In 54, he

---

[1] Caesar is curiously inconsistent in referring to him, sometimes as Titurius, sometimes as Sabinus; to avoid confusion (no other person is treated this way), I always include "Sabinus" when he is mentioned.

will be attacked in winter quarters in the northeast and will be massacred with all his troops in Caesar's worst defeat in the Gallic years. Titus Labienus, on the other hand, stood higher in Roman society and had served as tribune in 63 BCE, winning the favor of both Caesar (whose election as *pontifex maximus* he enabled) and Pompey. He is with Caesar for all of the Gallic years as his most senior, reliable, and successful general. At the outbreak of civil war in 49, all sides were startled to see him change loyalty completely to Pompey, fight on his side at Pharsalus, and eventually die fighting for the anti-Caesareans at Munda in 45. They brought his head to Caesar.

This may have been the quietest year at Rome of all Caesar's time in Gaul, but no one observing the political life there would take much comfort. Gradually, gradually as the year unfolded, the tribunes Milo and Sestius, friendly to Cicero and holding office in the wake of Clodius, who had to step down in December 58, steered public opinion toward resolution. (Milo had his own street fighters, as Clodius had, and they mainly kept the peace this year.) On August 4, the centuriate assembly, a body in Rome's governance where the urban underclass (whose favor Clodius had bought with the grain dole) was outweighed by other classes, voted Cicero's return. Cicero had edged closer to Rome from his original exile haven in Thessalonica and was awaiting the news in Dyrrhachium, modern Durrës in Albania, the closest port to Bari and Brindisi on the heel of Italy. He made his way then promptly home and arrived in the city on September 4, doubtless timing his arrival for the great annual spectacle of the "Roman games" beginning on that day.

He found a city that had been enduring sporadic food riots since mid-July, when they broke out at the annual festival of Apollo. Just four days after his arrival, Cicero showed his gratitude and support by moving in the Senate that Pompey be put in charge of the grain supply. The motion was easily approved. Pompey was granted a five-year term—effectively a five-year monopoly on a role as the most visible and generous benefactor of the urban populace. By December, however, his opportunity would open a gap between him and Caesar, as Rutilius Lupus, one of Pompey's tribunes, moved to suspend settlements in Campania under Caesar's land law. The loss of revenues from public land that resulted from those settlements was straining Pompey's ability to spend money on grain.

Working hard at being Pompey's man, Cicero was still a trigger for Clodius' gangs. In early November, Cicero was concentrating on rebuilding his house on the Palatine, which had been destroyed to allow the very ground to be consecrated for a temple devoted to Liberty on Clodius' motion. Built afresh, the house would stand for Cicero's restoration to full status, a restoration he shaped with a series of orations. On at least one occasion, there were demonstrations around the site, to keep Cicero aware of the hostility he still faced. Clodius wasn't going away. As the year wound down, the generalissimos could look forward to a mixed year in 56 with consuls not to their liking.

And the Egyptian comedy continued. King Ptolemy was still unwilling to return home until his status was assured, while the philosopher who had led Ptolemy's opponents from Alexandria to Rome was murdered at the senator's house where he had been staying.

This is the setting in which the first of Caesar's commentaries were being read in Rome, to dramatic effect. And Caesar's war against Ariovistus was separately made the subject of a poem, the *Bellum Sequanicum*, by Varro, a young poet on the make from Narbonne in Caesar's province, happy to be thought well of by the general and his supporters.

After Caesar headed north in June, his first campaign in northern Gaul stumbled through some confusion, but the battle of the Sambre was his first aggressive victory that went beyond the psychodramas of his relationships with old partners and rivals. If he could prevail in the north, he was now clearly a force to be reckoned with. Despite the victory, it was his first experience in taking significant casualties.

His time in the west was even more successful, where he clearly outclassed the collection of smaller nations he set out to awe and subdue. These people had done nothing to earn Caesar's attentions and were clearly looking only to defend themselves in an asymmetrical conflict. Subjection at a price was their best option.

At the very end of the season, Caesar had one last demonstration of his power and relentlessness to make back in the north, subduing the Aduatuci. In full control, he decided to make an example of his victims and rounded up, at his count, 53,000 captives and sold them into slavery, an act as lucrative as it was brutal.

This is one of very few places in Caesar's account where he lets us see him turning his campaign into significant financial advantage for himself. He needed the money to pay those legions and for more besides. To make this sale, he needed cash-rich slave traders in the pack of salesmen and whores who collected around the army. They needed reliable followers who could bring many thousands of people under control, keep them from escaping, keep them fed, and move them in suitable detachments to where they could be resold. Some may have had to go hundreds of miles on a trail of tears. (Slaves were a safer investment when they were far from any chance of reconnecting with their former lives.) Even if we were to discount the number 53,000 by 50 or 80 percent as a mental exercise, managing such a mob on its path to immiseration was a considerable logistical effort, one that made its own impression on all those who saw the trains of the recently enslaved trudging past.

Caesar was ready to take the troops into winter quarters by October. When his report that all Gaul had been pacified arrived, his management of public opinion at a distance won him a formal thanksgiving decreed by the Senate amounting to fifteen days' holiday, three times the usual number. (The city's working class must have been pleased!) The stories coming back were making a difference. Cassius Dio reports that Pompey, however, was heard to opine that it would be time for Caesar to come back soon, if all was really settled. Caesar would make the claim of total pacification several more times, unembarrassed then when the next uprising broke out. The thanksgiving decree effectively put a seal of approval on the whole of Caesar's unlicensed escapades.

IN THE CONSULSHIP OF
LENTULUS SPINTHER AND
METELLUS NEPOS

1. While Caesar was in nearer Gaul, various stories and then a letter from Labienus came to him telling how the Belgae were plotting against the Roman people and exchanging hostages with each other. They were plotting because they feared that when Gaul was subdued our army would be turned on them next, and because they were being encouraged by some of the Gauls. Some hadn't liked seeing Germans linger in Gaul, taking it even worse to see the Roman army winter there and grow accustomed to the place. Others were just frivolous and excitable, eager for new regimes, which would be harder to attain under our rule.

2. Concerned by these reports, Caesar enrolled two new legions in nearer Gaul and sent Quintus Pedius the legate[2] to take them to central Gaul at the beginning of summer. As soon as fodder was available, he came to the army himself. He assigned the Senones and the other Gauls near the Belgae to find out what was going on with them and inform him. They all consistently reported that troops were being gathered and an army brought together in one place. With that Caesar had no doubt about setting out in that direction. When he had an as-

[2] Son of Caesar's older sister, to be consul in 43 BCE.

sured supply of grain he broke camp and came to the borders of the Belgae in about two weeks.

3. When he arrived unexpectedly, faster than anyone thought, the Remi, closest in Gaul to the Belgae, sent two leading men, Iccius and Andecombogius, as representatives to say they gave themselves and their followers loyally into Roman hands. They had not allied themselves with the Belgae or conspired against the Roman people and they were ready to give hostages and do what we commanded, taking us into their towns and helping with grain and other supplies. All the other Belgae were up in arms, and the Germans living this side of the Rhine had joined them. The furor was so great that the Remi could not even keep the Suessiones, who have the same laws as they, the same customs, and the same regime in war and peace, from joining the Belgae.

4. He asked them which nations were in arms, how large they were and what they could do in war. This he learned: many Belgae came from Germany, crossing the Rhine long ago to settle because the land was fertile. They drove out the Gauls who lived there and were the only ones, when all Gaul was in uproar in our fathers' times, to keep the Teutones and Cimbri from entering their land. Memory of this gave them great prestige and high spirits in battle. The Remi said they had thoroughly ascertained their numbers because as near relatives they knew how many troops each nation had promised for this war in a general council of the Belgae. The Bellovaci were particularly well thought of for their strength and standing and numbers of men: they could bring together 100,000 armed men and promised 60,000 of them, insisting on having command of the whole campaign. The Suessiones, their neighbors, had the largest, most fertile territory. In recent

memory, their king had been Diviciacus,[3] the most powerful man in Gaul, who held sway over a great part of this country and Britain as well. Galba was now king. His justice and judgment earned him leadership of the whole war by common consent. With twelve towns, he promised 50,000 armed men. The Nervii, thought to be the fiercest among them and farthest distant, promised the same. The Atrebates were reckoned at 15,000, the Ambiani 10,000, the Morini 25,000, the Menapii 9,000, the Caletes 10,000, the Veliocasses and Viromandui the same, the Aduatuci 19,000, and the Condrusi, Eburones, Caerosi, and Paemani, who are all just called Germans, were reckoned at 40,000.[4]

5. Caesar encouraged the Remi and spoke to them generously, summoning their senate to come to him and bring their leaders' children as hostages. All this they did, right on the assigned day. He encouraged Diviciacus the Haeduan, showing him how much it mattered to the republic and their common safety for enemy forces to be kept apart so he wouldn't have to fight with so many at one time. This was possible if the Haedui would lead their forces into the land of the Bellovaci and start to plunder their fields. He sent him away with these orders. When he learned from the scouts he had sent and from the Remi that all the Belgic forces brought together were coming toward him and were now not far off, he hurried to take his troops across the Aisne river in the farther parts of Remi territory. He made camp there. This action protected one side of the camp with the riverbank and made the rear secure from enemy attack, allowing safe transport of supplies from the Remi and other nations. There was a bridge at the river. He set

---

[3] Not the Haeduan Diviciacus we saw in the first commentary.

[4] 308,000 in all, against Caesar's eight legions totaling about 40,000 (a level he mostly maintains from now on).

guard there and left the legate Titurius Sabinus on the other side with six cohorts.[5] He ordered camp fortified with a wall twelve feet high and a ditch eighteen feet wide.

6. The Remi town of Bibrax[6] was seven miles from this camp. Marching straight in, the Belgae launched a major siege there. Bibrax barely survived the day. Gauls and Belgae use the same siege technique: surrounding the fortifications with men, they began by hurling stones from all sides, stripping the ramparts of defenders. They made a tortoise,[7] approaching the gates and undermining the walls. They did this easily, for with so many throwing stones and spears, no one could stay on the wall. When night ended the assault, Iccius from the Remi, high-ranking and influential there and one of the legates making peace with Caesar, sent him a message that unless help were sent them they could hold out no longer.

7. At midnight Caesar sent Numidian and Cretan archers and Balearic slingers (using Iccius' messengers as guides) to support the townsfolk. When they arrived, the Remi took hope for defense and grew eager to fight, while the enemy similarly lost hope of taking the town. Lingering near the town a while, they plundered the fields of the Remi and burned all the villages and farmhouses they could reach. They headed then with all force for Caesar's camp and made their camp less than two miles away. This camp, marked out by smoke and fires, stretched across more than seven miles in breadth.

8. Caesar chose at first, seeing how many and how strong the enemy were, to refrain from battle. He risked daily cavalry skirmishes to see what the enemy's strength could do and how

[5] A legion normally comprised ten cohorts of about 500 fighters each.

[6] Location uncertain: in the vicinity of modern Reims.

[7] The Romans had the advantage in armament that wealth and technology bring, but their opponents were often able to emulate (or learn) their tactics very well indeed.

bold our men were. He found that ours were none the weaker and that the place before the camp was suited for setting up a battle line. The hill they camped on rose slightly above the plain, as broad as his battle line would be, with steep declines on both sides and a gently sloping front from the crest to reach the plain again. On each side of the hill he stretched a trench crossways about 400 feet long and at the end of the trenches put small forts and catapults, thus to keep the enemy, when lines were drawn, from doing what it could do with great numbers, that is, surround Caesar from the sides as they fought. Then he left the two newly-drafted legions in camp to bring out for support if needed and set the other six in battle line before camp. The enemy similarly led their troops from camp and drew them up.

9. A little swampy ground lay between the armies. The enemy waited to see if ours would cross, while ours were in arms and ready to attack them if they started to cross in full kit. Cavalry skirmishes meanwhile broke out between the lines. When neither made a start at crossing, Caesar took our troops back to camp, while the cavalry fight favored our side. The enemy headed straight from there for the Aisne, which we said lay behind our camp. They found fords and tried to bring part of their force across, thinking they might be able to win the fort the legate Sabinus protected and destroy the bridge. If they couldn't, they would ravage the fields of the Remi, which were immensely useful for our fighting, and keep our men from resupply.

10. Alerted by Sabinus, Caesar sent all his cavalry and light-armed Numidians, slingers, and archers across the bridge and went to join them. There was a hard fight there. As they crossed the river in full kit, our men attacked them and killed many.

We drove back with a shower of spears the ones who bravely tried to make their way through the corpses and the first ones to get across we surrounded with cavalry and slaughtered. The enemy saw they had been wrong about taking the town and crossing the river and that our forces wouldn't advance to fight on uneven ground. Grain supplies were beginning to fail them so they called a council and decided they would all return home. To whatever land the Romans next took their forces, they would gather there in defense from everywhere, preferring to fight on their own land than elsewhere and to use their own grain supplies. Among other reasons, they were led to this conclusion by knowing that Diviciacus and the Haedui were approaching the land of the Bellovaci. These last could not be persuaded to stay any longer and thus be unable to offer support to their own people.

11. With that plan, at the second watch, with great noise and hubbub, they left their camp pell-mell, under no command, everyone crowding to the front in a hurry to get home—it made the departure look like a rout. Caesar's scouts reported this immediately, but he feared ambush, not yet understanding why they were leaving, so he kept army and cavalry in camp. At dawn, reassured by the scouts, he sent his whole cavalry on to delay the enemy's rear guard. He put the legates Pedius and Aurunculeius Cotta in charge; he ordered the legate Labienus to follow with three legions. These attacked the rear guard, following them for many miles and hacking down a great number of the enemy in flight. When that rear line was caught and took a stand and resisted the attack of our soldiers bravely, the advance guard, seemingly out of danger, uncoerced and uncommanded, heard the shouting, abandoned any semblance of discipline, and found safety, all of them, in flight. So

without any danger our forces killed as many of them as the day was long, abandoning pursuit at sunset and returning to camp as ordered.

12. Next day, Caesar, before the enemy could recover from fear and flight, led his army to the Suessiones' land, close to the Remi, and by a long march quickly reached the town of Noviodunum.[8] Trying to take the town on the march, because he heard it was undefended, he was unable to prevail even against a handful of defenders because the ditch was broad and the wall high. Preparing camp, he started bringing up sheds and other siege engines. Meanwhile all the fleeing Suessiones came that night into town. Quickly moving up the sheds, he erected ramps and placed towers on them—a mass of siege works swiftly raised such as Gauls had never seen or heard of before. Startled, they sent negotiators for surrender to Caesar and, supported by the Remi, obtained their safety.

13. Caesar accepted leaders of the nation and two sons of king Galba himself as hostages and all weapons were given up from the town. He accepted the Suessiones' surrender and led the army to the Bellovaci, who had all gathered in the town of Bratuspantium.[9] When Caesar was four or five miles away, the elders of the town all came forth, holding out hands to Caesar and proclaiming themselves willing to trust in his power, promising they would not go in arms against the Roman people. When he reached the town and pitched camp there, boys and women similarly reached out their hands to Caesar from the walls, seeking peace from the Romans in their fashion.

14. Diviciacus spoke for them (after the Belgae retreated, he sent the Haedui forces home and returned to Caesar): the Bel-

---

[8] Soissons, one of several Gallic towns of the name Noviodunum that he will mention. C.'s Roman readers had no such helpful footnotes as this.
[9] Bretueil.

lovaci, always true friends of the Haedui, had been driven to abandon the Haedui and make war on the Roman people by their leaders, who claimed the Haedui were enslaved by Caesar and were suffering every indignity and insult. The leaders of that scheme, seeing what ruin they had brought to their nation, had fled to Britain. Not only the Bellovaci but also the Haedui on their behalf were asking he employ his mercy and kindness. Doing so would extend the influence of the Haedui among all the Belgae, whose help and support they used whenever war came to them.

15. Caesar agreed to trust and receive them out of respect for Diviciacus and the Haedui. Because they were great among the Belgae for their influence and their numbers, he insisted on taking 600 hostages. When these were handed over and all the weapons of the town were collected, he went from there to the land of the Ambiani, who surrendered all they had without delay.

The Nervii bordered their land. When Caesar asked about them and their ways, he found that merchants had no approach to them and they allowed import of no wine or other luxury goods, because they thought these things weakened spirits and diminished courage. They were fierce and very brave, criticizing and accusing the other Belgae for surrendering to the Roman people and throwing away their ancestral courage. They insisted they would send no ambassadors and accept no terms of peace.

16. After three days' journey through their land, he learned from captives the Sambre river was no more than ten miles from his camp. Camped across the river, waiting for the Romans, were all the Nervii, along with the Atrebates and Viromandui, their neighbors whom they had persuaded to take the same chance on war. They were waiting for the forces of the

Aduatuci en route. They had put women and others of ages unsuitable for battle in a place where marshes made approach difficult for an army.

17. Knowing this, he sent out scouts and centurions to choose a good place for camp. Many Belgae and Gauls surrendered, obeyed Caesar, and traveled with him. Some of them, he later learned from prisoners, seeing how our army traveled those days, came to the Nervii at night and told them how large baggage trains came between individual legions. When the first legion reached camp and the others were still a great distance away, there would be no problem attacking them with their baggage. When they were beaten and their baggage plundered, the others would not dare stand against them. It helped the informers' plan that the Nervii of old, with no cavalry power—even now, they pay no attention to it, but whatever they accomplish they do with foot soldiers—, in order to fend off cavalry from neighbors coming their way for plunder, cut into and bent down young trees so that with their branches growing horizontally and bushes and brambles planted between them, these hedges offered the protection of a wall, making it hard not just to pass but even to see through them. Since this would slow the progress of our line, the Nervii thought the plan worth trying.

18. The place our men had chosen for camp was like this. A hill sloping down evenly reached the Sambre (which we mentioned above). Across the river with a similar slope a hill rose opposite them, open below for about two hundred paces, wooded on top, making it hard to see through. The enemy kept themselves hidden in these woods, but a few cavalry units were to be seen in the open space along the river. The river was about three feet deep.

19. Caesar sent cavalry ahead and followed in force, but his order of march differed from what the Belgae had told the Nervii. Approaching the enemy, Caesar, as was his way, led six legions without baggage and had the whole army's baggage put behind; then the two newly-enrolled legions brought up the rear of the whole line, guarding the baggage. Our cavalry crossed the river with the slingers and archers, joining battle with enemy cavalry. While they would fall back with their force in the woods and break out again out of the woods to attack our men, we did not venture farther in following than the open ground allowed. The six first legions to arrive did their surveying and began to make camp. When those hiding in the woods saw the first of our baggage, which they had agreed was the sign for engaging battle, they settled their line and ranks in the woods and encouraged one another, then suddenly flew out in full force to attack our cavalry, who were easily driven back in disarray. They raced to the river so incredibly swiftly that they seemed to our men to be in the woods and at the river at the same moment. Just as swiftly they made for the opposing hill, our camp, and those who were working there.

20. Caesar had to do everything at once: set up the standard, call soldiers back from work, summon back those who had gone out farther for material for a rampart, draw up the line, encourage the soldiers, and give the signal. The attack left too little time for all this. Two things helped: the knowledge and experience of the soldiers (tested in earlier battles, they could tell themselves what needed to be done as easily as hear it from someone else), and Caesar's command forbidding legates to leave their legions before camp was finished. With the enemy swiftly at hand, they did not wait for Caesar's orders but took care of what seemed best themselves.

21. Caesar, giving the necessary commands, running wherever opportunity presented to encourage the soldiers, came to the tenth legion. He encouraged them with a speech just long enough to say they should recall their former courage, remain calm, and bravely resist enemy attack. When the enemy was scarcely a spear's throw away he gave the sign to fight. Going to encourage the other wing, he found it already fighting. There was so little time and enemy spirits were so ready for fight that there was no time for fitting on insignia or even for putting on helmets and removing shield covers. Whatever part of the line and whatever standards each man coming back from work chanced upon, there he stayed, not to waste time looking for his own unit.

22. He deployed the army more as the situation and the urgency allowed than by military doctrine, with different legions resisting the enemy in different places. The thick hedges, as we said, made it hard to see. Reserves couldn't be placed properly, nor arrangements for what was needed where. Not all the orders could be given by one person. With such diverse disadvantages, luck's outcomes were very various.

23. Soldiers of the ninth and tenth legions, standing on the left wing, threw their spears and quickly drove the Atrebates (that's who they faced), breathless and tired from running and done in by wounds, from higher ground into the river. Pursuing them with swords as they tried to cross weighed down, they killed most of them. Our men did not hesitate to cross the river. Advancing uphill they again joined battle and routed the enemy resistance. Elsewhere,[10] the eleventh and eighth legions, routing the Viromandui they had battled, fought down

[10] The tenth and ninth legions were on the left, the eleventh and eighth here are in the center, and the twelfth and seventh held the right. As the left and center advanced, the right was isolated.

to the riverbank from above. With just about the whole camp undefended on the front and left, when the twelfth and not far away the seventh stood firm on the right, all the Nervii in tight formation, led by Boduognatus the commander, hurried there. Half of them tried to surround the legions on the open side, while the other half tried to take the high ground of the camp itself.

24. Then as our cavalry and light-armed infantry returned to camp, driven back together in the first attack as I said,[11] they encountered the onrushing enemy and again fled in another direction. From the camp gate and hilltop, the camp followers had watched our troops crossing the river in victory, then gone out for plunder; now seeing the enemy prowling in our camp, they fled pell-mell. Then the cries of the baggage-minders went up, heading one way and another in terror. The Treveri cavalry coming from their nation to support Caesar were disturbed by all this—and their reputation for bravery is unique among the Gauls. They saw our camp full of an enemy mob, our legions under pressure and almost surrounded, and the camp follow-ers, cavalry, slingers, and Numidians scattered and fleeing in all directions. Losing hope in our cause they made for home. They told their people the Romans were beaten and overcome, their camp and baggage in enemy hands.

25. Caesar left off encouraging the tenth for the right wing, where he saw his men under pressure. The standards of the twelfth were pressed together in one place, legionaries crowded together and getting in each others' way. The centurions of the fourth cohort had all been slaughtered, the standard-bearer killed, the standard lost, and just about all the centurions of the others cohorts killed or wounded, notably first spear

---

[11] The extremely rare first person singular in Caesar; see also 4.27, 5.54, 6.24.

Sextius Baculus, bravest of men, exhausted by so many serious wounds he could barely stand.[12] The rest lagged and some from ranks behind had deserted, leaving battle and dodging arrows, while the enemy did not stop attacking from lower ground, coming up in front and pressing on both sides. He saw things were tough and there was no help to be brought up. Snatching a shield from a soldier in the rear—he'd come without one himself—he went through to the front rank, calling the centurions by name, encouraging the other soldiers, ordering standards brought up and formations loosened so they could use swords more easily.[13] His coming brought the soldiers hope and renewed spirits, each one longing to exert himself well in the general's eyes, even in direst circumstances. The enemy attack was slowed a little.

26. When Caesar saw that the seventh legion nearby was equally under enemy pressure, he ordered the military tribunes to bring the legions together gradually, turn the standards around, and attack the enemy. This they did, each of them helping one another, no longer afraid of being surrounded if they turned, and began to push back more confidently and fight more bravely. Soldiers of the two legions watching the baggage at the rear, hearing of the battle, were spotted hurrying up by the enemy on the hilltop. Labienus, taking the enemy camp and looking down from above at what went on in our camp sent the tenth to help us. When they learned from the fleeing cavalry and camp followers how things stood, how dangerous it was for camp and legions and general, they made haste every way they could.

[12] Recurs as a sturdy fellow at 3.5 and 6.38.
[13] The whole paragraph to here is one sentence in Latin, a thrilling rush of 137 words.

27. Their arrival brought such a reversal that even our fallen men, exhausted by wounds, re-entered battle leaning on their shields. Unarmed camp followers, sensing the enemy's fear, confronted armed men themselves, while the cavalry, to erase the shame of flight with their bravery, pressed out ahead of legionaries all over the field. But the enemy, with their last hope for safety, displayed great courage. As front line soldiers fell, the next stood upon them where they lay and fought from their bodies; when they were thrown down and the corpses piled up, survivors hurled things at our men as if from a hillock and threw back spears they had caught.

28. After this battle, the Nervii were almost destroyed in name and race. Their elders—we said they were hidden in valleys and swamps with the children and women—on hearing of the battle, thinking the victors would stop at nothing and the vanquished would have no safety, all agreed to send representatives to Caesar and surrender to him. Recounting the calamity to their nation, they said they were reduced from 600 to three senators, from 60,000 people to scarcely 500.[14] Caesar, to show himself merciful to wretched suppliants, looked after them carefully, ordered them to stay in their land and towns, and commanded their neighbors to abstain from all harm and ill-doing.

29. The Aduatuci we spoke of before were making their way with all force to assist the Nervii, but heard of this battle on the way and returned home. Abandoning all their towns and forts, they brought all they had together in one town splendidly protected by nature. With high rocks and cliffs on all sides around, on one side a gentle slope left an approach no more than 200

[14] In three years (5.38), they will be mustering a sizeable force.

feet wide. That they fortified with a high double wall, on which
they settled heavy rocks and sharpened sticks. They were descended from the Cimbri and Teutones. They had left the baggage they could not carry as they headed for our province and
for Italy on this side of the Rhine along with a guard of six thousand men. After the downfall of the invaders these were hounded
for many years by their neighbors, sometimes waging war
against them, sometimes defending against attacks, but then
made a peace agreement and chose this place for their home.

30. As our army arrived, they made several sorties from the
town and fought our men in skirmishes. Then, when we had
surrounded them with a rampart 12 feet high and about 14
miles around, they kept themselves to town.[15] Seeing sheds
brought up, a ramp raised, and a tower built at a distance, they
first mocked and taunted from the walls, for building such an
engine so far away. Whose hands or strength did such short
men (for the most part Gauls despise our short stature compared to their huge bodies) think would establish such a heavy
tower on the wall?

31. But when they saw it move and approach the walls, disturbed by the novel, surprising sight, they sent to Caesar ambassadors for peace, who spoke thus: They could not think the
Romans waged war without divine help, if they moved up such
tall engines so quickly. They yielded themselves and all they
had to our power. One plea they made: if his kindness and
mercy, of which they had heard from others, decided the Aduatuci should survive, he should not strip them of their weapons. Almost all their neighbors were enemies and envied their
prowess; they could not defend themselves from them if they
handed over their weapons. Better for them, if put to it, to

[15] Fourteen miles is clearly what the manuscripts say and clearly just daftly too
large a circle even for Caesar to build. Two to three miles would be more like it.

endure anything from the Roman people than be tortured to death by those whom they were used to dominating.

32. Caesar answered them thus: He would preserve their nation out of kindness, not because they deserved it, if they surrendered before a battering ram touched their wall, with no condition of acceptance except they yield their weapons. He would do what he did for the Nervii and order their neighbors to do no harm to Rome's subjects. When they had reported to their side, the Aduatuci said they would do what he commanded. They cast a great mass of weapons from the wall into the trench before the town—the heap of weapons almost equaled the height of wall and the ramp—but still hid and kept about a third of them in the town, as was after seen. They opened the gates and enjoyed peace that day.

33. Toward evening Caesar ordered the gates shut and the soldiers out of the town, so townspeople would not be harmed by soldiers in the night. They had made a plan before, as we found out, believing that after surrender we would remove our guards or at least keep watch carelessly. Some had weapons they had kept and hid, others made shields of bark or woven reeds covered hastily, for lack of time, with skins. After midnight they broke out of town suddenly with all force, where the approach to our fortifications seemed less steep. As Caesar had ordered, a fire signal was given and our men rushed from the nearby forts. The enemy fought as hard as brave men with their last hope of safety, on unfavorable ground against men who hurled weapons from rampart and towers—for all hope lay in courage alone. Four thousand men were killed, the rest forced back into town. Next day the gates were broken—no one defended them now—and our soldiers entered and Caesar sold the whole town in one auction lot. The buyers reported the number enslaved at 53,000.

34. Then he heard from Crassus, whom he had sent with one legion to the Veneti, Venelli, Osismi, Coriosolitae, Esuvii, Aulerci, and Redones, maritime nations reaching the ocean, that all of them had been brought under the authority and power of the Roman people.

35. With this, all Gaul was pacified.

The impression of this war on the barbarians was so powerful that the nations across the Rhine sent embassies to Caesar promising to give hostages and do as he ordered. Caesar was making haste for Italy and Illyricum and told these embassies to return early next summer. He settled the legions for winter among the Carnutes, Andes, Turones, and the nations close to the places where he had fought, then left for Italy. For all this, on Caesar's report, a supplication of fifteen days was decreed, which had happened to no general before.

THIRD COMMENTARY

56 BCE

"All Gaul was pacified." The year 56 would prove the limitations of Caesar's peace across the northern provinces where he had been successful in 57—but the action all takes place elsewhere.

The first half-dozen paragraphs of his account of this year really belong to the narrative of the preceding year, whose story extended into late November. They are postponed for rhetorical effect, to allow that narrative of the second commentary to conclude with victory and thanksgiving. These events occurred after the campaign year ended for Caesar with his departure for Italy, and they flow seamlessly into the story of 56. The legate Galba whose close call is here recounted would reappear as one of the conspirators against Caesar in 44.

The two consuls for 56, Cn. Cornelius Lentulus Marcellinus and L. Marcius Philippus, were both restive and obstructionist toward the influence of the three generalissimos. Marcellinus took steps to try to limit Caesar's governorship and install a successor by 54, while resisting a deal that would install Crassus and Pompey as consuls for 55. Philippus, though married to Caesar's niece and thus stepfather to the small boy who would become Caesar Augustus, supported Marcellinus. The resistant faction looked to Domitius Ahenobarbus as a prospective consul for 55 and successor to Caesar in Gaul in 54.

Caesar himself began the year with a rare visit to his provincial territory of Illyricum on the Adriatic, and then returned to Aquileia at the very head of the Adriatic, throughout Roman times the most important city at the crossroads between Italy and the Balkans, before eventually yielding that role to Venice. While at Aquileia, Caesar heard that elections for lower offices had gone badly for him and that Ahenobarbus was campaigning hard to supplant him. Cicero, meanwhile, was feeling his oats again and as late as the first of April was supporting those who still wanted to overturn Caesar's consular acts, in particular his land law, even as the Senate voted 40 million sesterces for Pompey to expend on the grain supply. Content with that for himself, Pompey dined with Cicero in early April and showed no signs of unhappiness with Cicero's alignment with the anti-Caesar faction.

What Cicero did not know when he dined with Pompey was that Pompey's departure a day or two later on a trip to Sardinia was to be detoured north along the coast to the town of Lucca just beyond Pisa. A few days before that dinner, Crassus had gone to Ravenna to meet with Caesar to begin making strategy and, incidentally, to tell Caesar that Cicero had been acting very badly. Caesar and Crassus made their way to Lucca, there to meet Pompey. The later historians Appian and Plutarch make this into a grand summit meeting, quoting numbers of 200 senators and 120 lictors supposedly in attendance. Some were there, but those numbers seem to be inflated: testimony to the high importance of the meeting and its effect on what would happen in the years to come.

The meeting was held on about the seventeenth of April and a deal was quickly done. First, the consular election for 55 must be carried successfully for Pompey and Crassus, and so Caesar would release some of his men to come down to Rome in the winter to offer their votes and their intimidating presence in support of the chosen candidates. In return, Caesar's command would be extended another five years, after which he could stand for election to be consul again in 48. Both Pompey and Crassus would have extended governorships of their own coming out of their next consular year. (Pompey took Spain, with no intention of actually going there, while Crassus accepted Syria as a base of operations for what he expected would be his own great military adventure against the Parthians.) This was likely also when Crassus prevailed on Pompey to give up his idea of a grand campaign to Egypt to establish Roman sway once for all. Ptolemy was still working to deliver a submissive puppet state; not until Caesar went to Egypt during the civil war did Rome's interests there advance. During the time in Lucca, Caesar also saw Appius Claudius Pulcher, Clodius' elder brother, on his way out to govern Sardinia, and used the opportunity to tell him to encourage Clodius to persist in his latest flip-flop to support Pompey and Caesar.

After the meeting, Caesar left immediately for Gaul (early June) to settle an uprising among the Veneti. Pompey on his way to Sardinia sent messages to Cicero by two routes (one being Cicero's brother Quintus) with strict instructions to let go of the Campanian land question.

Cicero accordingly avoided the meeting of the senate that was set to discuss that issue and soon turned his coat completely to stand in support of the generalissimos. In a letter of this period, Cicero speaks of this as singing his "palinode," the literary term for a recantation or change of heart. He supports, perhaps even proposes, the decree to give Caesar state funds to pay for his four new legions as well as the right to appoint ten legates of his own choosing to serve him instead of the usual three. In early July, he gives a substantial and elaborate speech in support of the Lucca arrangements, published as *De provinciis consularibus* (*On the Consular Provinces*). He defends the campaign as the first actively positive Roman venture in Gaul after too many efforts simply to deter invaders from there, and he plumps up hoary tales of Gallic hordes. "I see that Caesar's plan was very different. He meant to make war not only on those who took arms against Rome but to reduce all Gaul under our authority." Cicero knows in at least some detail the story of the battles with the Helvetians and Germans. "No one in his right mind about our republic, as far back as you go, thought of Gaul as anything but a great threat to our rule."

Cicero also lent his services as barrister to defending Caesar's senior staff member Balbus (so senior that he shared with Caesar and one other lieutenant a secret code for communicating with one another) on a trumped-up charge concerning his citizenship, which he in fact owed to Pompey. Cicero had finally figured out that while grave and reverend senators may have had votes, Pompey, Crassus, and Caesar had armies and that times had changed. From this moment in 56 moderns speak of the three as "triumvirs" in honor of their blatant bargain to hold and share power.

The decision to allow Caesar to pay for his legions occasioned a comedy in its own right, when a rogue tribune tried to resist supporting Caesar by summoning him for trial on accusations rooted in his actions as consul in 59. With the generalissimos aligned and Cicero now on board the effort was pointless.

So now Pompey and Crassus were free to step forward and suborn a friendly tribune into preventing the holding of consular elections at the normal time, postponing them until after the hostile consuls were out of office on the first of January. (When the year began consul-less, an *interrex*—"regent," from which we get "interregnum"—was appointed to administer affairs but on the understanding that he would not make substantive decisions.) That gave Caesar the opportunity to send some troops from Gaul to Rome on furlough to meddle in the elections.

The year ended with a modicum of control for the three generalissimos. Cicero, clearly abashed by his decision to cave in to their pressure and by the loss of his political autonomy (a loss he would partly redress only after Caesar's death, by attacking Antony) retreated to his villa outside Rome and wrote and published *De oratore* (*On the Orator*), his great work on the nature of oratory and its place in public life. It is a dialogue set almost forty years earlier in the years between the dominant periods of Marius and Sulla, a time not unlike the moment at which Cicero wrote. Cicero believed that the virtuous and educated man who could hold a crowd with his words was the ideal leader for Roman society, and he wrote this and several other books on that theme in just the years when it was becoming clear that he was completely and entirely wrong. A decade later, as Caesar was at his peak of power, Cicero retreated again, this time to write his main philosophical works with a greater air of detachment.

Caesar noticed Cicero's book and had time to think about it and to prepare his *De analogia* (*On Analogy*) by way of reply in the midst of his many other activities.

For he *was* somewhat busy in the field in the summer of 56. The nations of Brittany and Normandy that he had subdued the previous year were now back in revolt. An ancient source thinks they were eager to preserve their role as leading traders with Britain. The real action against the rebels waited for late summer, when Decimus Brutus could bring a fleet of ships to bear, after which speedy resolution was achieved.

The end of the campaigning season then saw him back to the other northern theater of operations from the previous year, now to stifle a revolt among the Menapii. One of the mild inconsistencies that encourages us to think these commentaries were written and sent off originally one at a time can be seen in the way he treats the Menapii here in the third commentary as an isolated people defending their prerogatives, then speaks of them in the fourth commentary as deeply in cahoots with other nations.

So now Caesar might well think he had done the important work. Aquitania, the third part of Gaul he identified on his opening page, still lay behind him unvisited, but it was quiet and could be reserved for another day. As he returned in November to Cisalpine Gaul and sent troops on ahead to meddle in the consular elections at the end of 56, he might well take a deep breath and think of wider horizons.

IN THE CONSULSHIP OF LENTULUS MARCELLINUS AND PHILIPPUS

1. When Caesar left for Italy, he sent Galba with the twelfth legion and some cavalry to the Nantuates, Veragri, and Seduni, who extend from the Allobroges border, lake Geneva, and the Rhone to the crest of the Alps. He wanted the road through the Alps kept open, where merchants passed at great risk, paying high tolls. He let Galba settle the legion to winter there if he thought it necessary. Galba, fighting a few good skirmishes and seizing several forts, received ambassadors and hostages from all sides and made peace. He settled on placing two cohorts among the Nantuates, while he with the other cohorts of that legion would winter in a village of the Veragri called Octodurus.[1] The village sits in a small valley with its plain hemmed in all around by high mountains. Since it was divided in two by a river, he let the Gauls have one part of the village and assigned the part they left empty to his cohorts. He fortified the site with rampart and trench.

2. When some days had passed in camp and he had ordered grain brought in, suddenly he heard from scouts that the Gauls in the part of town left to them had all departed by night and the overhanging mountains were held by a great crowd of

---

[1] Likely modern Martigny, at the head of the valley stretching SSE from the east end of Lake Geneva toward the Great Saint Bernard Pass.

Seduni and Veragri. There were several reasons for the Gauls to plot suddenly to restart war and overwhelm the legion. First, they thought little of a legion below full strength, with two cohorts removed and others absent and scattered securing provisions; second, they thought their first onrush would be unstoppable because the land was not level and they would be rushing down from mountains to valley hurling weapons. More, they were unhappy because their children had been taken as hostages and they were convinced the Romans were trying to take the Alpine summits not just for passage but to keep permanently and to join this territory to the neighboring province.

3. Galba heard the news with his winter quarters and fortifications still unfinished and nowhere near enough grain and other supplies provided, because after the surrender and hostage-taking he thought he had nothing to fear from attack. He quickly gathered his counselors and sought advice. In such sudden and unexpected danger, with armed men seen filling the high ground, no help on the way, no supplies at hand, and the roads cut off: despairing of safety, many in his council urged abandoning the baggage and breaking out along the same roads by which they had come, and struggling to safety. The majority wanted to hold that plan for the worst case and now to try their luck and defend the camps.

4. They had barely enough time to deploy and settle on a plan, when soon the enemy on a signal ran down from all sides throwing stones and Gallic javelins at the rampart from below. At first our men fought back hard with full strength and threw no weapon from the rampart that missed its mark. Whatever part of camp seemed pressed and short of defenders, others went to help. But we were outmatched: as fighting went on enemy troops wearied in battle left and others came up with their full strength, while our side could not do likewise because

we were too few. Not only could the weary not leave battle, but even the wounded had no chance to withdraw from where they had stood and fall back.

5. When the fighting had gone more than six hours straight and strength and weapons were failing our men, as the enemy pressed harder, beginning to hack the rampart and fill the trench as our side wearied, things came to a crisis. Sextius Baculus, the first spear centurion we described as exhausted by wounds when fighting the Nervii, and Volusenus, military tribune and a man of great intelligence and courage, ran to Galba and showed him that the one hope of safety, their last recourse, was to try to break out. So he gathered the centurions and quickly alerted the soldiers to break off fighting gradually, just deflecting weapons flung at them, and rest from their effort. Then when the sign was given they would break out of camp and put all their hope for safety in their courage.

6. They did as ordered, erupting suddenly from every gate, leaving the enemy no way of knowing what was happening or of regrouping. Luck changed: they cut off and cut down men who had come hoping to seize the camp. Of the more than 30,000 men—the number of barbarians known to be there—more than a third were killed and the rest were hurled terrified into flight, not even able to make a stand on the heights. When the enemy were all routed and stripped of weapons, our men withdrew into the fort. After this battle, Galba did not want to tempt fortune again. He remembered he had come to winter quarters with one idea but found a very different state of affairs. Concerned over grain shortage, next day he burned all the village farmhouses and made for the province. No enemy checked or slowed their journey, so he brought the legion safe to the Nantuates and then to the Allobroges. There they wintered.

7. After this, since Caesar thought Gaul was now at peace, he left for Illyricum in early winter to visit and get to know those peoples and lands. War broke out suddenly in Gaul: here is why. The young Crassus was wintering near the ocean among the Andes people with the seventh legion. Because there was a shortage of grain there, he sent numerous prefects and tribunes to neighboring nations to seek provisions. Among them Terrasidius was sent to the Esuvii, Trebius Gallus to the Coriosolites, and Velanius with Silius to the Veneti.

8. This nation was far the most influential on the whole seacoast in that area, for the Veneti have many ships accustomed to sailing to Britain and they excel the others in knowledge and experience of sailing. The sea spreads roughly there, while the Veneti hold the few ports, so almost all who use those waters pay them taxes. They started to detain Silius and Velanius and anyone else they could catch, thinking they could thereby recover hostages they had given Crassus.

The neighboring nations were inspired by their example—Gauls are sudden and abrupt in their strategems—to hold Trebius and Terrasidius for the same reason. Sending messengers swiftly, their leaders swear to each other to act only by common strategy and together accept fortune's outcome. They encouraged other nations to persist in the liberty they inherited from their elders rather than endure Roman slavery. The whole coast is quickly brought to agreement and they send a single embassy to Crassus: if he wants to recover his men, he should return the hostages.

9. When Caesar, while still far away, had report from Crassus, he ordered longboats be built on the Loire (which flows to the ocean), oarsmen recruited from the province, and sailors and pilots found. Settling this quickly, as soon as the season

allowed he headed for the army.[2] The Veneti and the rest heard of Caesar's coming and realizing at once how great a misdeed they had committed started to prepare for a dangerous war, beginning especially to gather things needed for ships. Their hope grew stronger because they knew the lay of the land. Land routes were interrupted by estuaries; sailing was hard for those who did not know the area, and there were few ports. They were sure our troops could not remain there long because of grain shortage. Should all go against them, they had their sea power and the Romans had no naval capacity and did not know the shoals, ports, and islands where they would fight. And of course sailing the vast and spreading ocean was very different from a narrow sea. Settling their plan, they fortified towns, brought grain from fields to towns, and brought as many boats as possible to the Veneti, where it was clear Caesar would fight first. They enlisted the Osismi, Lexovii, Namnetes, Ambiliati, Morini, Diablintes, and Menapii as allies and sent for support from Britain, which is opposite those shores.

10. We've shown how difficult fighting would be, but much still encouraged Caesar to fight that war: the offence of detaining Roman knights, rebellion after surrender, betrayal after giving hostages, so many nations plotting—and chiefly he wanted to keep other nations from thinking they could do the same if he let this pass. He knew most Gauls loved uprisings and were easily and quickly roused to fight, while all men naturally pursue liberty and hate a slave's lot, so he decided to divide and distribute his army widely before more nations could join the plot.

11. So he sent the legate Labienus with cavalry to the Treveri, near the Rhine, commanding him to approach the Remi and

[2] Caesar was likely still in northern Italy, perhaps Ravenna, perhaps Lucca. "As soon as the season allowed" veils the political reason for delay.

the rest of Belgae and keep them in line. If Germans, reportedly invited to support the Belgae, tried to force the river in
boats, he should stop them. He ordered Crassus to head for
Aquitaine with twelve legionary cohorts[3] and a large number
of cavalry, to keep them from sending help to Gaul and linking
up such nations. He sent the legate Titurius Sabinus with three
legions to the Venelli, Coriosolites, and Lexovii, to keep that
force at a distance. Young Brutus he put in charge of his fleet
and of the Gallic boats he had ordered the Pictones, Santones
and other peaceful areas to bring, and told him to set out for
the Veneti at once. Caesar made his way with foot soldiers.

12. Their towns were set mostly at the end of tongues of
land and promontories with no approach on foot when the tide
drove in from the deep, which happens every twelve hours, nor
by boat when the tide lessened and ships were driven onto
shoals. Attacking these towns either way was hindered. When
they were overcome by our huge siegeworks—pushing back
the sea with earthworks and ramps as high as the town walls—
they despaired of their chances and drew up a great many
ships, something they did superbly. Loading aboard all their
possessions they escaped to neighboring towns, there to protect themselves again with the advantages of the site. They did
this the more easily much of the summer because our boats
were held back by storms and sailing was extremely difficult
on the vast and open sea with high tides and almost no ports
at hand.

13. This is how their ships are built and armed: the bottoms
are flatter than on our ships, to take the shallows and low tides
more easily; bows and sterns are higher, to face storms and
high waves; the ships were all made of oak to handle whatever

---

[3] Twelve cohorts rather than the usual ten of a single legion.

assault and blows; crossbars of boards a foot high were fastened with iron nails as thick as a man's thumb; anchors were lashed with iron chains instead of rope; skins and lightweight leather were used for sails, whether because they had no linen and didn't know its use or more likely because they thought ocean storms and wind blasts could not be endured or such heavy ships controlled well enough by sails.

14. After taking several towns, Caesar realized the effort was going nowhere. The enemy couldn't be harmed or kept from escaping towns we captured. He decided to wait for his fleet. When it arrived[4] and the enemy saw it, some 220 of their ships, fully armed and ready, set out from port against ours. Neither Brutus, leading the fleet, nor the centurions and military tribunes piloting individual ships knew what to do or how to press the fight. They knew their prows would do no harm: platforms built on our decks were overtopped by the poops of the barbarian ships. Weapons couldn't easily be hurled from below and the ones launched by Gauls would fall heavily. Our men had one very useful device ready, sharpened hooks attached to poles, like the ones for attacking city walls. They grabbed and dragged the ropes linking masts and yards, tearing them apart when our men leaned on their oars. With the ropes cut, the yards had to fall. Since the Gauls relied heavily on sails and rigging, when those were taken away, they lost all control of the ships at once. The rest of the fight depended on courage, where our soldiers were easily better, especially when the fight was waged in sight of Caesar and the whole army. No brave act, however modest, could go unnoticed, for all the hills and high ground close by from which you could look down on the sea were held by the army.

[4] We seem to be now in the bay of Quiberon. The Roman fleet has been struggling north with the unfamiliar ocean to get there from the mouth of the Loire.

15. When the yards were down and two or three ships surrounded each of ours, our soldiers made every effort to board the enemy ships. After the barbarians realized this and many of their ships were taken, with no help to be found, they sought safety in flight. As they turned their ships with the wind, such a calm and lull set in suddenly that they could not move from where they were. This was a great chance to end the business. Our ships chased them down and defeated them one by one, with only a few of their fleet reaching land by nightfall, after fighting from the fourth hour to sunset.

16. With that battle, the war with the Veneti and the whole coast was done. They had brought all their young men, all their elders with any standing or wisdom, and all the ships they had anywhere to that one place. Losing them, the rest had nowhere to retreat and no way to defend their towns. So they surrendered themselves and all they had to Caesar. Caesar decided to punish them severely so barbarians in future would respect the rights of ambassadors. The whole of their senate was killed and the rest of them sold into slavery.

17. While this was going on among the Veneti, Titurius Sabinus and the forces he had from Caesar reached the land of the Venelli.[5] Viridovix ruled there and held supreme command of all the nations in revolt: he had raised an army from them. In a few days the Aulerci, Eburovices, and Lexovii (who put their senate to death for refusing to stand for war) closed their gates and joined Viridovix. A mass of lowlifes and brigands from all Gaul came together, hoping for booty and eager for war, fleeing the daily grind of farming. Sabinus stayed camped in a well-chosen place, while Viridovix set down against him a couple of miles away and brought his troops out ready to fight

[5] In Normandy, perhaps 150 miles ENE from the scene of Caesar's sea battle.

every day. Not only did Sabinus face enemy scorn, but criticism was heard from our own soldiers. He gave the impression of fear so strongly that the enemy ventured to come right up to the camp walls. He acted thus because with so many enemy before him, he judged he should not fight in the absence of the supreme commander unless on a fair field or if a favorable chance arose.

18. Sure the rumor of his cowardice was strong, Sabinus chose an able and clever Gaul from the support troops and convinced him with great prizes and promises to go to the enemy and told him what he wanted done. When he reached them posing as a refugee, he reported on Roman fear and how hard pressed Caesar was by the Veneti. Sabinus was all but ready that night to lead his army secretly from camp to bring help to Caesar. Hearing this, the Gauls exclaimed that this chance of accomplishing their business must not be lost—they should go for the camp. Many things encouraged them in this plan: Sabinus' hesitation the preceding days, confirmed by the refugee, shortage of foodstuffs (which they looked after too carelessly), the hope for the Venetic war—and of course men easily believe what they want to believe. Drawn in by these things, they wouldn't let Viridovix and the other generals leave council before they agreed to take up arms and make for our camp. Delighted in this agreement as if victory were assured, they gathered brush and branches to fill the Roman ditches and headed for our camp.

19. The camp was on high ground most of a mile uphill from the valley. They made a great run for this, to give the Romans too little time to arm and gather, and arrived breathless. Sabinus roused his men and gave the signal they wanted. While the enemy was slowed by the loads they carried, he ordered a sudden breakout from two gates. With the advanta-

geous position, the inexperience and fatigue of the enemy, and the courage of our soldiers and their experience in other battles, they couldn't resist even one attack from us and immediately turned tail. Our fresh soldiers pursued their burdened ones and killed many; our cavalry chased the rest, leaving few who actually escaped.

At one moment, Sabinus heard of the naval battle and Caesar heard of Sabinus' victory, as all the nations surrendered at once to Sabinus. The Gallic spirit is eager and ready to fight, but their minds are weak and unable to endure disaster.

20. When Crassus arrived then in Aquitaine, he realized he would have to fight where a few years before the legate Valerius Praeconinus was killed and the army beaten, when the proconsul Manlius had abandoned his baggage and fled.[6] So he knew he needed to move with not a little care. Looking after provisions, gathering auxiliaries and cavalry, and individually summoning proven fighters from Tolouse and Carcasonne and Narbonne, the Gallic nations closest to our province, he led his army into Sotiates territory. Hearing of their coming the Sotiates gathered a large army and cavalry (they are strong in horsemen) and attacked our line on the march. They engaged first a cavalry battle and then when their horse were beaten back and our troops were in pursuit, suddenly they revealed foot soldiers placed in ambush in a nearby valley. These attacked our men in disarray and renewed battle.

21. They fought long and hard. The Sotiates, heartened by earlier victories, thought the safety of all Aquitaine depended on their courage; our men wanted to show what they could do without a general, without other legions, with a very young commander. Wearied and wounded at last, the enemy turned

---

[6] The earlier defeat occurred in 78/77, on the periphery of the campaign to overthrow the rogue rule of Sertorius in Spain (who lasted from 82 to 70).

and ran. Killing many, Crassus turned aside to attack the Sotiates' town. Facing strong resistance, he built sheds and turrets.
They tried a breakout on one side, then on another tunneled
under our sheds and ramp. (The Aquitani are adept at this
because there are many copper mines among them.) When
they realized they could not win this way because our men
were so persistent, they sent ambassadors to Crassus to negotiate surrender.

22. When the surrender was accepted, they handed over
their weapons as ordered. While all our men were occupied
there, Adiatunnus, their supreme commander, appeared from
another part of the town with 600 loyal men they call *soldurii*.
They share life's goods with others to whom they vow their
friendship. If any violence befalls them, either they endure the
same fate together or commit suicide. In the memory of men
there has been no man who refused to die himself when someone to whose friendship he was pledged was killed. Adiatunnus tried to break out with them, when with a shout from that
part of our defenses, our men ran to arms. The fight was stren-
uous. Driven back into the town, Adiatunnus still won from
Crassus the same terms of surrender.

23. Accepting the weapons and hostages, Crassus left for
the land of the Vocates and Tarusates.[7] Hearing we had taken
a town fortified by nature and man a few days after we arrived,
the barbarians were alarmed, sending ambassadors every
which way, conspiring, exchanging hostages, gathering forces.
Ambassadors were sent to the Spanish cities nearest to Aquitaine, summoning troops and leaders, on whose arrival they set
out to wage war with a huge force and great confidence. As
leaders, men were chosen who had been with Sertorius all his

[7] This extends Crassus' intervention in Aquitaine farther to the west, away from
the peoples he knew he could count on when he came.

years and were thought to have the highest military expertise. Following Roman practice, they set out to choose their sites, fortify camps, and cut our men off from supplies. When Crassus found this out and knew his own limited forces could not easily be divided, while the enemy could roam and block roads and leave guards enough in camp, he realized that grain and provisions could not easily be supplied, while the number of enemy grew daily. He thought he should not wait to give battle. Reporting this to his council and finding that all agreed, he decided to fight the next day.

24. At dawn all our forces came out drawn up double file, auxiliaries in the middle, all waiting on the enemy's plan. They thought it safe to fight, since their force was huge, their reputation in war venerable, and our forces few, but still they thought it safer to block the passes and shut off supplies to gain victory without injuries. If the Romans began to retreat because supplies were short, they planned to attack them marching with their baggage. Their leaders approved this plan and stayed in camp when the Roman forces came out. Crassus saw this. The enemy's hesitation and reputation for cowardice made our men more eager to fight and everyone was heard saying that we must not wait longer but go for their camp, so he harangued his men and made for the enemy camp amid general enthusiasm.[8]

25. There some filled the ditches, others, hurling many spears, drove defenders from the wall and ramparts, and the auxiliaries—Crassus didn't much trust them—supplied stones and spears for fighting and brought turf for a ramp, making it look as if they were fighting. At the same time the enemy fought firmly and not fearfully and weapons thrown down from above did not miss their marks. Our cavalry reported to

---

[8] This is the only case of Caesar's forces attacking a protected Gallic encampment.

Crassus after circling the enemy camp that it was not so carefully fortified at the gate on the back: approach there was easy.

26. Crassus encouraged the cavalry prefects to arouse their
men with great prizes and promises, showing them what he
wanted. As ordered, they led out the cohorts that had been left
to guard the camp, still unwearied, and took them a long way
around so they couldn't be seen from the enemy camp with all
eyes and minds fixed on battle. Quickly reaching the rear defenses we mentioned, they pulled them down and took their
stand in the enemy camp before they could be clearly seen,
before the enemy could know what was going on. Hearing
shouts from there, our men were reinvigorated and began to
fight more fiercely, as often happens with hope of victory. The
enemy, on all sides surrounded, despairing of everything,
burst out from the ramparts and tried to find safety in flight.
Our cavalry chased them down on open field, with scarcely a
quarter left of the 50,000 that had gathered from Aquitaine and
Spain, then came back to camp late at night.

27. On news of this battle, most of Aquitaine submitted to
Crassus and sent hostages voluntarily. This included the Tar-
belli, Bigerriones, Ptianii, Vocates, Tarusates, Elusates, Gates,
Ausci, Garumni, Sibusates, and Cocosates. A few remote nations failed to do so, counting on the season, for winter was
near.

28. Summer was almost done, Gaul was all at peace—except for the Morini and Menapii, who were up in arms and
never sent Caesar ambassadors for peace. Caesar thought this
war could be quickly finished and took his army there. They
set out to wage war very differently from other Gauls. Realizing
that great nations had fought battles and been beaten and overcome, while they had spreading woods and swamps around

them,[9] that's where they took themselves and all their possessions. Caesar reached the forest edge, starting to fortify camp
and not yet seeing the enemy. While our men were scattered
at work suddenly they flew out of the woods on all sides and
attacked us. Our men snatched up arms and drove them back
into the woods. Killing many of them and following them farther into tangled places, we lost a few of our own.

29. The next days, Caesar had the woods cut down. To prevent flank attacks when his soldiers were unarmed and unwary, he placed the lumber they cut before the enemy and piled
it up as a rampart on both sides. With huge space cleared incredibly quickly in a few days, with our men holding their
cattle and the remnants of their baggage, they went deeper into
the forest. Such storms arose that we were forced to stop work:
under constant rain our soldiers could stay no longer in tents.
And so, wasting their fields and burning their villages and
farmhouses, Caesar led his army away and set them in winter
camp among the Aulerci and Lexovii and other nations that
had most recently made war on him.[10]

[9] Now we are at the other end of Gaul, in the region of Dunkirk and Bruges, indeed swampy until the seventeenth century.

[10] He moves now west into Normandy, wintering there to be readier for the next
year's expedition to Britain.

FOURTH COMMENTARY

55 BCE

The consular year of Pompey and Crassus should have been Pompey's great year for undivided glory.

It certainly began well, when Crassus' son Publius, one of Caesar's legates, brought a thousand legionaries over the Alps and down to Rome to offer whatever muscle was deemed necessary to get the right election result. Crassus was still at his father's house in Rome in February when he met Cicero there. The soldiers were well-trained and obedient, making the winter march of nearly 2,000 miles roundtrip—many weeks on the march. Clearly the generalissimos thought them important and useful.

The most remarkable event of the year at Rome was the dedication of the senior consul's great contribution to the cityscape, known as the Theater of Pompey. A stone theater was unprecedented at Rome, where performances had always relied instead on jerry-built wooden structures dismantled after the shows. Pompey had seen better on his eastern expeditions and correctly intuited an opportunity. The resulting building, just outside the ancient city's *pomerium* in the Campus Martius near today's Campo de' Fiori, was a theater and more. It offered spacious gardens, shaded colonnades for the display of sculpture and other works of art, a meeting hall for the Senate's occasional use, the immense theater itself (the stage front facing the house was about 100 yards long, and the distance from the stage to the farthest and highest seat was about 175 yards, leaving seats for perhaps 10,000 people, perhaps twice that), and finally, perched high atop the seats of the theater, a temple to the goddess Venus Victrix ("the victorious"), Pompey's favorite. Given old prejudices about theaters, actors, and immorality, the temple's presence in the complex mitigated the presence of a permanent theater in the eyes of traditionalists.

In sum, the building was a monument to Pompey and arguably the grandest construction in the city at that date. Caesar in a few years rejoined, as we shall see, by constructing the first of the "imperial forums," an extension to the old forum on its northeast side, but Pompey had made his mark. The dedication was accompanied by shows and celebrations enough to mark this as a year to be remembered. Cicero heralded the event by anticipating the most elaborate and magnificent games in living memory, such as had never been seen before and could not be imagined to be seen again. When it came to the event, a performance of Accius' play about Clytemnestra featured 600 mules on the stage, Naevius' play about the Trojan Horse had 3,000 wine bowls on view, and all the battle scenes had soldiers fabulously armed.

The Senate would meet in its hall at Pompey's theater complex on the Ides of March in 44.

There was still Roman business to be settled on behalf of the triumvirs, meanwhile, and so a law was passed by April 27 formally assigning Syria and Spain to the consuls for five years. The matter was still contentious and the gangs were out. Four people were killed and many wounded in the brawls, with Crassus himself personally drawing a senator's blood. On the same day, a separate law extended Caesar's time in Gaul by five years. Just how that five years would be counted was a matter of disagreement from then until the civil war of 49 broke out, and modern scholars are scarcely less divided. It would appear that the law, improbably, did not set an explicit end date. Our most solid indication of how the situation was read comes in Hirtius' continuation to these commentaries, where he says that in 51 both Caesar and the Gauls knew he would have only one more summer (of the year 50) in which to campaign, and both planned their strategies accordingly. The end of 50 and the beginning of 49 then saw the outbreak of civil war as Caesar returned to Italy. So the campaigns of this summer of 55 were in effect the first steps of the new proconsular term.

Without the delays of earlier years, Caesar rejoined the army earlier than usual in response to reports that two German nations, the Usipetes and the Tencteri, had crossed the Rhine and invaded Gaul. Caesar's story is blunt and painful. He defeated them without loss of Roman life while his men slaughtered some vast number of the enemy. Caesar is quite barefaced in asserting the intention and the achievement of slaughter, so much so that he happily exaggerates. Read his text carefully and he manages to imply without saying that the whole of the enemy force was slaughtered (with many killed, the rest threw themselves into the river and perished) and he gives a number for them of 430,000. The number certainly shocks: we just have to remember that it cannot possibly be the number of fatalities. The likelihood that Caesar had a count of the enemy that was anywhere near accurate is very slight. In battle many were killed, certainly; afterwards the rest fled, quite probably; many were seen plunging into the river to escape, very likely indeed; every last one of them drowned or was killed by hostile action on trying to leave the river—quite impossible. Forty years later, the Usipetes, Tencteri, and Sugambri crossed the Rhine again and defeated and killed a Roman general. A mighty force they must have been to lose 430,000 and recover in a generation.[1]

What we can take away from the episode is that Caesar had the chance to act ruthlessly and did so and wanted it known that he had acted with no limits and no leniency to destroy an enemy force. Just as with the previous year's enslavement of Aduatuci captives, we should pause to consider with horrified astonishment the logistics and manpower requirements of slaughter on such a scale, whatever the numbers.

"Germany," that place across the Rhine, that supreme otherwhere, was at this instant less threatening than before, with the invading

[1] In 2015, archaeologists at the Vrije Universiteit Amsterdam reported discovery of a probable site for this battle no longer needful, estimating 150,000 fatalities on a site at the joining of the Meuse and Waal rivers.

army destroyed. Caesar took a chance on that estimate of safety and led his men to the Rhine and beyond. They crossed the river in good order, spent eighteen days there without seeing an enemy, lay terrorist waste to several towns, and returned to Gaul. It's hard to evaluate a show of force for effect, but this was scarcely a great military achievement. Caesar's narrative, however, makes the crossing itself a mighty work by recounting the building of the bridge his army used, an achievement no aficionado of military prowess who reads this book ever fails to praise.

The main thing to recall about this bridge is that Caesar didn't need one—boats would have done just fine—, but there was ostentation to begin with in building the bridge (to impress the local population) and ostentation again in talking about it in great deal in his report of the year. The self-praise has had its desired effect.

If the story is accurate, it is impressive. In a 400-yard-wide channel, twenty-six substantial piers had to be roughed out and sunk into the riverbed over ten days' construction. Experts observe that that kind of pile-driving required equipment and management—and boats from which to work. The resulting bridge's roadbed would have been about 25 feet wide, so the piers, angled to support, were perhaps 40 yards apart. (Where did he cross? Somewhere on the 75-mile stretch of Rhine between Cologne and Koblenz.)

So the great mission to Germany was a bust. No enemies, no battles, no victories, no plunder. After demonstrating the strength of his presence, Caesar heard that the Sugambri had gathered a large force in woodland fastnesses and were prepared to do battle. So he turned around and marched back to Gaul looking for another adventure and put the best face he could on the crossing.

Slaughtered enemies and going boldly where no Roman had gone before were not enough for Caesar, however, and so he took one more cast at Pompey-rivaling glory this year, achieving another anticlimax. He made for Britain.

Just how much Caesar knew of Britain is hard to read, for we can barely surmise who and how reliable his sources might have been. We meet here for the first time a remarkable Gaul, Commius, leader of the Atrebates, a nation from the vicinity of Lille, easily into the

"Belgic" regions where Caesar was more skeptical of native aptitude for civilization. For this trip to Britain, Commius appears as trusted partner and guide, as indeed is plausible for one coming from a territory that now hosts one portal of the modern Channel Tunnel. Commius, with a cavalry detachment, accompanied Caesar and sought to negotiate with the Britons but found himself held as prisoner or hostage, released when Caesar concluded negotiations. (The next year he would accompany Caesar to Britain again and negotiate more successfully on his behalf. For the time being, the Atrebates were untaxed by Caesar, but we will see relations with them deteriorate in 53–52. Commius joined the great revolt of 52, remaining hostile into 51, when he eventually made peace on condition that he need not deal with Romans again. A gaudy later story has him fleeing the mainland, pursued in a small boat by Caesar himself, escaping to permanent refuge in Britain.)

The crossing to Britain, both this year and in 54, was challenging for Caesar for several reasons. The tides and currents of the open ocean were hard for Romans to imagine and manage when all their sea experience came from the tideless Mediterranean. Heavy-laden rowing ships were anything but nimble in the waters of the English Channel. On both trips, Caesar's arrival in Britain put him at some disadvantage, which he describes, both in terms of position and condition of his ships. He took two legions on this trip, the tenth and the seventh, quickly realized that he had no force with which to do anything, and made his way back to Gaul by late September.

Here again, he made more story than was strictly called for, the better to make an impression. Caesar's success in telling the story is reflected seventy or so years later in the version told by the writer Valerius Maximus (3.2.23), who turns the brave centurion of the tenth legion we meet here into a much more dramatic hero named Cassius Scaeva. By the fourth century, when the emperor Julian recounts the lives of his predecessors he makes Caesar the first to leap from a boat and make his way ashore. Garbled glory is still glory, and it was this book, not whatever happened on that shore, that created the glory.

At the end of the campaigning season, Caesar stayed on in Gaul for a while, leaving after the first of the year with orders to his commanders to assemble a grander fleet for the next summer.

The junta of Pompey, Crassus, and Caesar made it through this year at least with their hands firmly on the reins, but in the consular elections failed to keep the insurgent Ahenobarbus from victory. In a brawl in the Campus Martius the night before the election, Cato's torch-bearer was killed and Cato wounded in the arm, while Ahenobarbus himself fled home.

Caesar was voted a thanksgiving of twenty days, to the further delight of urban working men. Cassius Dio was skeptical:

> From Britain he had won nothing for himself or for the state except the glory of having conducted an expedition against its inhabitants; but on this he prided himself greatly and the Romans at home likewise magnified it to a remarkable degree. For seeing that the formerly unknown had become certain and the previously unheard-of accessible, they regarded the hope for the future inspired by these facts as already realized and exulted over their expected acquisitions as if they were already within their grasp; hence they voted to celebrate a thanksgiving for twenty days.

A year later, when his brother had joined Caesar in the hope of padding his fortune, Cicero complained that there wasn't a speck of money or treasure to be gotten in Britain, only slaves.

Cato, winning a praetorship for 54 in the same election as Ahenobarbus, proposed handing Caesar over to the Germans in expiation for this year's massacre but found no support for his outrage. This was a good time for Caesar to think about grander British schemes for the next year and to imagine his successes. Things would prove more complicated than he hoped.

IN THE CONSULSHIP OF POMPEY AND CRASSUS

1. The following winter, the year Gnaeus Pompey and Marcus Crassus were consuls, the German Usipetes and the Tencteri as well crossed the Rhine in a mass of people, not far from where the Rhine flows into the sea. They crossed because they were harassed and warred on for years by the Suebi and kept from farming.

The Suebi are much the greatest and most warlike of Germans. They are said to have a hundred cantons, each sending out a thousand armed men a year to fight. The others stay at home to feed themselves and the rest, then the next year they take up arms, while the first stay home. Thus neither farming nor the theory and practice of war languish. There are no private, individual farms among them, nor may they stay farming more than a year in one place. They live mostly on milk and livestock, not so much on grain, and they are big on hunting. With all this—diet, daily exercise, liberty (since from boyhood they are used to no duty or discipline and do absolutely nothing they don't like), they grow strong and produce men of immense bodily size. They have habituated themselves in the coldest regions to having no clothing except animal skins, small enough to leave most of the body bare. They bathe in rivers.

2. Merchants are allowed access there as buyers for what's seized in war, more than out of any desire to import anything.

Even draft animals, which the Gauls love and buy at great price, the Germans do not import, but they use native ones, small and scrawny, trained by daily use to be hard-working. In cavalry battles they often leap from horse and fight afoot, and train their horses to stay where they are so they can go back to them swiftly at need. They think nothing more shameful or feeble than using saddles. However few they are, they dare face any number of saddled horsemen. They do not let wine be imported to them, for they think it softens men for hard work and makes them womanly.

3. They count it worthy of high praise for a people to have land lying unused all around their borders, as a sign that many nations have been unable to withstand their power. So on one side of the Suebi some five or six hundred miles of land reportedly lie abandoned.[2] On their other side are the Ubii, whose nation was large and flourishing by German standards. They are a little gentler than the others, though of the same race, because they border the Rhine and many merchants come selling to them and because proximity accustoms them to Gallic ways. Though the Suebi through many wars found themselves unable to drive from their borders the Ubii, because the nation was large and powerful, they made them tributaries nonetheless and rendered them far weaker and less proud.

4. The Usipetes and Tencteri we named were in the same situation, enduring Suebi violence many years, finally driven from their land, wandering three years through much of Germany, ending at the Rhine, where the Menapii live.[3] These had fields, farmhouses, and settlements on both banks of the river.

[2] Exaggeration or error. C. may have actually written "one hundred."
[3] Around Emmerich, just at the German/Dutch border, almost the farthest point downstream where the Rhine could be readily crossed without modern technology.

Frightened by the arrival of such a multitude,[4] they abandoned the farmhouses they had across the river, setting garrisons this side of the Rhine to stop the Germans crossing. Trying everything, unable either to fight (having too few ships) or to pass Menapian guards secretly, the Germans feigned return to their homes and lands. After three days' travel they turned back again, making the journey in one night on horseback, overwhelming the Menapians unwary and unawares. They had gone back across the Rhine to their settlements without fear, reassured by scouts that the Germans had left. Killing them and seizing their boats before Menapians this side of the Rhine could learn of it, the Usipetes and Tencteri crossed the river, seized all the farmhouses, and lived the rest of the winter on Menapian supplies.

5. Learning of this, Caesar feared Gallic irresolution, for they are whimsical in making plans and often eager for revolutions, and so decided not to trust them. Gauls indeed by custom force travelers to stop, willing or not, and ask them what they have heard or learned about anything. Crowds in towns surround merchants to make them say where they have come from and what they have learned there. Excited by what they hear, they often form plans on important matters, then have to regret them on the spot, since they are slaves to unreliable rumors and many travelers make up stories to please them.

6. Knowing that custom, Caesar set out for the army earlier than usual, to avoid worse war. On arrival, he found his suspicions were fact. Embassies from some nations had gone to ask the Germans to leave the Rhine: everything they had asked for would be arranged. Led on by this, the Germans were roaming more widely, coming to the territory of the Eburones and Condrusi, clients of the Treveri. Summoning the Gallic chiefs,

---

[4] After action, C. says (4.15) there were 430,000 of them.

Caesar decided not to let on what he knew, but calmed and encouraged them, then raised a cavalry troop and determined to fight the Germans.

7. Gathering grain, he set out with select cavalry for where he had heard the Germans were. A few days away from them, their ambassadors arrived, making this speech: The Germans would not attack the Roman people first nor would they refrain from fighting if attacked, because this was custom with them from their ancestors: fighting, not negotiating with any attacker. This they added: they acknowledged they had come unwillingly, driven from their homes. If the Romans wanted their good will, they could be useful friends. Either Rome should assign them land or let them hold what they had won by fighting. They yielded only to the Suebi, whom not even the immortal gods could match. Otherwise there was no one anywhere they could not defeat.

8. Caesar answered appropriately, but ending thus: There could be no friendship with them if they stayed in Gaul, nor was it true they had seized others' land because they could not protect their own. There was no unoccupied land in Gaul to give to such a crowd without doing harm, but they could settle, if they wished, among the Ubii, whose representatives were with him, complaining to him of Suebian aggression and seeking help. He would order the Ubii to do this.

9. The ambassadors said they would report this to their people, discuss, and come back to Caesar in three days—asking meanwhile that he not move camp any closer. Caesar said even this could not be granted. He knew they had sent most of their cavalry some days before across the Meuse among the Ambivariti, to plunder and forage. He thought they were delaying to wait for these cavalry.[5]

[5] I omit here as inauthentic a paragraph of generic description of the Meuse and Rhine.

11. When Caesar was no more than about ten miles from the enemy, the ambassadors returned as agreed. Meeting him on the road, they asked urgently that he go no farther. Failing in this, they asked him to send to his cavalry who had gone on ahead and to forbid them from fighting, then allow them to send ambassadors to the Ubii. If their chiefs and senate gave assurance on oath, they would then obey conditions set by Caesar. Could he give three days for this? Caesar figured this all amounted to three days' delay for their cavalry to return, but said he would go no more than three or four miles that day, to water his troops; as many of them as could should meet there again the next day so he could judge their demands. Meanwhile he sent messengers to the prefects who had gone ahead with the whole cavalry: they were not to attack the enemy and if they were attacked to endure until he came closer with the army.

12. When first the enemy spotted our cavalry—5,000 of ours, while they had barely 800 horse (because their men crossing the Meuse to forage had not returned)—, our men were unconcerned, because the ambassadors had just left Caesar, requesting a day of truce. But they attacked and quickly threw our men into confusion. As we rallied, their tactic was to dismount and go about gutting horses and unhorsing many of our men, putting the rest to flight, hounding them in terror so they did not stop until they came in sight of our infantry. Seventy-four of our cavalry were killed in that fight, notably the brave Aquitainian Piso, born of a very distinguished family. His grandfather had held the throne in their country and was called friend by our senate. When his brother was surrounded by enemy, Piso snatched him from danger, then was himself thrown down when his horse was wounded, fighting back as bravely as he could. Surrounded and wounded repeatedly, he

fell. When his brother, who had left the field, saw this from afar, he spurred his horse and threw himself against the enemy and was also killed.

13. After this battle, Caesar thought he should not receive ambassadors or undertake negotiations with people who pled for peace, then waged war by treachery and ambush. He judged it crazy to wait for enemy forces to be increased and the cavalry to return. Knowing the weak Gallic character, he guessed how much prestige the enemy would gain from that one battle and decided to give them no time for consultation. Settling his plans and sharing with the legates and quaestor his intention to let no day pass without battle, it luckily happened next morning that a crowd of Germans, employing the same treachery and dishonesty, came to him in camp with all their leaders and elders. They both excused themselves, supposedly, for attacking the day before contrary to what they had promised and indeed themselves asked, and at the same time they were looking to win a truce by their dishonesty. Caesar was delighted to have them present themselves to him and ordered them detained. He led all his troops from camp and ordered the cavalry to follow the infantry, judging them spooked by the recent fight.

14. Quickly covering seven miles in triple line,[6] they reached the enemy camp before the Germans realized what was happening. In sudden terror at everything, with no time for consulting or taking arms, the Germans were confused whether to lead men against their enemy, defend camp, or seek safety in flight. They showed their fear, shouting and rushing about as our soldiers, enraged by the previous day's treachery, invaded their camp. The ones there who could reach weapons

[6] In battle formation, thus ready to pounce.

resisted our forces for a while and fought from among carts and baggage. The remaining crowd of children and women (they had left home and crossed the Rhine with all their people) began to flee every which way. Caesar sent cavalry to chase them down.

15. When the Germans heard hubbub behind and saw their people being killed, they discarded their weapons, abandoned their standards, and fled the camp. Reaching the junction of Meuse and Rhine, despairing of escape with so many killed, the rest threw themselves into the river and perished there, overcome by fear, exhaustion, and the force of the river. Every man of ours returned safe to camp, with only a few wounded, after a terrifying war with an enemy 430,000 in number. Caesar allowed those he had detained in camp to leave. Fearing punishment and torture from the Gauls whose land they had plagued, they said they wanted to stay with Caesar. He granted them this liberty.

16. After the German war, Caesar for many reasons decided he should cross the Rhine, especially because he saw how easily Germans were persuaded to come over to Gaul. He wanted them to fear for their own property, realizing that the Roman people's army could and would cross the Rhine. Moreover, the Usipetes and Tencteri cavalry that I mentioned crossing the Meuse for plunder and forage and so missing the battle had crossed the Rhine (after their people fled) to the Sugambri, joining with them. When Caesar sent messengers to demand that those who had fought in Gaul surrender, they replied: The Roman people's empire stopped at the Rhine. If he thought it wrong for Germans to cross to Gaul against his will, why should he claim any rule or power across the Rhine?

Meanwhile the Ubii, the only ones across the Rhine to send ambassadors to Caesar, sought friendship and gave hostages, urgently asking him to bring help, because they were hard pressed by the Suebi. If affairs of state kept him from doing so, would he at least send his army across the Rhine to help and offer hope for the future? The Roman army won such a reputation and name even among the remotest German nations in defeating Ariovistus and in this last battle that they knew they could be kept safe by the reputation and friendship of the Roman people. They promised a large fleet of boats for transporting the army.

17. Caesar decided to cross the Rhine for the reasons mentioned, but thought it neither safe nor appropriate to Roman dignity—or his—to use boats. Even if the breadth, speed, and depth of the river made bridge-building extremely difficult, he thought they had to try that or else not send the army across. He designed the bridge thus: pairs of beams a foot and a half thick, sharpened a little at the bottom and measured to the depth of the river, he tied together two feet apart. These he lowered into the river with cranes and fixed in place, pounding with mallets, not like stakes erect and perpendicular, but protruding and leaning forward following the flow of the river. He set other pairs joined the same way some forty feet from the others at the bottom, turned against the force and onrush of the river. These pairs as well were held apart at the top by beams two feet thick (the width of the joints), with braces inserted on each side. With those held apart and bound in opposite directions, the whole work was so strong and made in such a way that the more the force of water drove it, it was bound even more tightly. These stood firm, covered by material overlaid lengthways and with poles and woven mats. Piles were also driven at the downstream side at an angle, set down as buttresses and joined with the whole structure to take the force of the river, and others a little above the bridge so that if barbarians sent tree trunks or boats

to knock the bridge down, their force would be lessened by these defenses and not harm the bridge.

18. Ten days after lumber began to be assembled, the job was done and the army brought over. Caesar left a strong guard at each end of the bridge and made for Sugambri country. Meanwhile, representatives from many nations came seeking peace and friendship. He replied generously, directing them to bring him hostages. But the Sugambri, once the bridge-building began, prepared to flee, encouraged by Tencteri and Usipetes who were with them. They had left their country, taken all their possessions, and hidden in waste and woods.

19. Caesar stayed a few days in their territory, burning the villages and farmhouses and hacking down their grain, then took himself to the Ubii and promised them help if they were pressed by the Suebi. He found from them that the Suebi, learning about the bridge-making from scouts, held council in their way, sending messengers in all directions, telling people to abandon their towns and leave their children, wives, and property in the woods; then all who could bear arms should gather in one place in the middle of the land the Suebi controlled. Here they decided to await Roman arrival and fight it out. When Caesar learned this, having done everything that he had brought the army across for—terrifying the Germans, punishing the Sugambri, freeing the Ubii from attack—and having spent eighteen days in all across the Rhine, he decided he had accomplished what honor and expediency demanded and so returned to Gaul, demolishing the bridge.

20. With little of summer left and though the winters here come early, Caesar still made to set out for Britain, because he knew help came from there to our enemies in just about all the Gallic wars. If there wasn't time to fight, he still thought it would be very useful for him just to visit the island, see the

people there, and learn the places, ports, and approaches—all mostly unknown to the Gauls. No one went there impulsively except merchants, and only places along the shore and regions facing Gaul are known even to them. Calling in merchants from everywhere, he could not discover how large the island was, which nations lived there or how large they were, how they waged war, what their customs were, or which ports could handle a larger number of boats.

21. Before taking a chance, he thought it good to inform himself by sending Volusenus with a warship. He ordered him to investigate everything and return at once. He set out himself with his whole force for the Morini,[7] because the crossing there to Britain was shortest. He ordered boats from all the neighboring areas and the fleet he had built the last summer for war with the Veneti to gather there. Meanwhile, with news of his plan getting out and reported to Britain by merchants, representatives of numerous nations on the island came to him, promising to give hostages and accept the rule of the Roman people. Hearing this, with generous promises and encouragement to persist in their view, he sent them home and with them sent Commius, whom he had made king over the Atrebates when he defeated them, whose courage and wisdom he had tested and thought reliable, and who had a high reputation in this region. He commanded him to visit as many nations as possible and encourage them to keep faith with the Roman people, telling them Caesar would arrive soon. Volusenus explored the whole area as best he could without daring to leave ship and trust himself to barbarians, returning to Caesar on the fifth day and reporting what he had seen.

[7] Around Boulogne, some 400 km from his Rhine bridge, so perhaps ten days' to two weeks' march: we are now well on in July.

22. While Caesar delayed there to prepare ships, representatives from most of the Morini came to him, apologizing for their former behavior, saying they had waged war on the Roman people as barbarians unaware of our ways and that they would promise to do what he commanded. Caesar thought this timely, since he wanted to leave no enemy behind his back but had no capacity—because of the season—for making war and no desire to let such minor matters come ahead of Britain, so he commanded from them a large group of hostages. When these were brought, he accepted their loyalty. With about eighty cargo boats gathered and assembled, which he thought were enough for carrying two legions, he assigned the other warships to his quaestor, legates, and prefects. There were eighteen cargo ships besides, which were held by the wind about seven miles away,[8] prevented from coming to the same port: these he assigned to cavalry. The rest of his army[9] he gave to the legates Titurius Sabinus and Aurunculeius Cotta to station among the Menapii and those districts of the Morini that had not sent him representatives. He ordered the legate Sulpicius Rufus to hold the port with guard he thought sufficient.

23. Settling these matters and seizing a good time for sailing after midnight, he ordered the cavalry to go on to the farther port and take ship there and follow him. As they did this, a little slowly, he reached Britain around mid-morning with his first ships and saw enemy forces stationed on all the cliffs.[10] The lay of the land, with the sea hemmed in by cliffs

[8] The coastline runs here north and south; prevailing southwesterly winds would have pushed them to the tiny river mouth of the Slack at Ambleteuse.

[9] He took two legions with him to Britain and left one to guard the port and thus five more for Sabinus and Cotta.

[10] The Britons had excellent information about Caesar's plans. Caesar clearly chooses to say "hills" rather than use the word he has available for "cliffs," but the setting is unmistakable: from a little below Folkestone to north of Dover, except for two very short stretches where those towns are, the famous cliffs come within a few

close by, let a spear hurled from the heights reach the shore. Judging this no suitable place for landing, he waited at anchor until the ninth hour for the other ships to gather. Summoning then his legates and military tribunes, he reported what he had learned from Volusenus and what he wanted to happen. Then he reminded them that military strategy and especially maritime tactics demanded, when movement was rapid and unreliable, that everything be managed instantly, just at a nod. Letting them go and seizing wind and tide at a favorable moment, he gave the order, weighed anchor, and advanced about six miles from there, halting the ships on a broad and level shore.

24. But the barbarians had grasped the Roman plan and sent ahead cavalry and charioteers (whom they regularly use in battle), then followed with their remaining forces, to keep our men from leaving ship. So the difficulty was immense because the ships—for their size—could only halt in deep water, but the soldiers, in strange territory, their hands full, burdened with large, heavy weapons, had to jump from the ships, find their feet in the waves, and fight the enemy all at once, while the others had hands free to hurl weapons fearlessly and spur on their experienced horses either from dry land or going a little ways into the water, knowing the ground well. Terrified and completely inexperienced at this kind of fighting, our men did not show the enthusiasm and zeal they bring to land fighting.

25. Caesar saw this and ordered the long ships—strange to look at for barbarians and easy to handle—to pull back and row to station opposite the enemy's open flank, from there to beat

---

yards of the water and stand 50–100 meters high. Lympne to the south and Deal to the north are generally canvassed as likely locations for the eventual landing. The crossing there, the closest from the continent to Britain, is about 20 miles.

back and drive off the enemy with slings, arrows, and cata-pults. This was immensely useful to our side. The shape of the ships, their movement by oars, and the unfamiliar kind of catapult made the barbarians halt in fear and draw back a little. As our men hesitated, especially because of deep water, the eagle-bearer of the tenth legion, praying the gods that it would go well for the legion, said "Jump, comrades, unless you want to hand over the eagle to the enemy. I will surely have done my duty to the republic and our general!" When he had said this in a great voice, he hurled himself from the ship and began to carry the eagle toward the enemy. Then our men encouraged each another not to allow a disgraceful loss to occur and all leapt from the ship. When the first men in neighboring ships saw this, they followed and approached the enemy.

26. Both sides fought hard. Our men, unable to keep ranks or stand fast or follow their standards, assembling by whatever standards each one found from another boat, were greatly con-fused. The enemy on the shore, knowing all the shallows, saw individuals leaving ship. They spurred horse and made for us while we were entangled, many of them surrounding a few of ours, some hurling weapons against our force from the open flank. When Caesar realized this, he ordered skiffs from the long ships and also scout boats to be filled with soldiers and sent to help those he saw struggling. As our men made dry land and their comrades followed, they attacked the enemy and put them to flight, but were unable to go farther because the cavalry had not been able to hold course and reach the island. In this one thing his old luck failed Caesar.

27. As soon as the fleeing enemy regrouped after being over-come in battle, they sent ambassadors for peace to Caesar, promising to give hostages and do as he ordered. With these legates came Commius of the Atrebates, whom I said Caesar

had sent ahead to Britain. As he left ship, bringing them Caesar's orders as his representative, they had seized him and thrown him in chains. With battle done, they sent him back; pleading for peace, they put blame on the mob and asked their poor judgment be excused. Caesar complained that after spontaneously sending ambassadors to the continent seeking peace from him they had given battle for no reason, but said he would forgive their poor judgment and demanded hostages. They gave him some immediately and said they would summon others from a distance and hand them over in a few days. Meanwhile they ordered their people to go back home, while the chiefs came from all over and began to entrust themselves and their nations to Caesar.

28. Peace thus settled, three days after arriving in Britain the eighteen ships mentioned above as carrying cavalry had set out from the upper port in a light wind. As they approached Britain and were seen from camp, such a storm sprang up suddenly that none could hold course, but some were blown back where they came from, others were driven in great danger down to the lower part of the island, toward the setting sun. These dropped anchor but were awash with water and had to put out to sea on a hard night and make for the continent.

29. The moon happened to be full that night, which habitually makes the highest tides on the ocean, but our men did not know that. So the ships Caesar had brought ashore were filled with waves at the same time the storm pounded the ones lashed at anchor. Our men had no way of managing or helping them. Several ships were wrecked, while the rest, losing lines, anchors, and tackle, were made useless for sailing; hence a great upset—it had to happen—for the whole army.[11] There

---

[11] In military parlance, the situation is FUBAR.

were no other ships by which they could be taken back, they
had nothing they needed to repair the ships, and because they
were all set to winter in Gaul, grain had not been provided for
the winter here.

30. Knowing this, the British chiefs who had come to Caesar after the battle talked among themselves, seeing the Romans short of cavalry, ships, and grain and knowing how few
soldiers were there by how small were the camps, smaller still
because Caesar had crossed the legions without their usual
baggage.[12] They decided it best to rebel and keep our men from
grain and supplies, dragging the business out until winter.
When these were defeated or prevented from returning, they
were sure no one afterwards would cross to Britain to make
war. So gradually they slipped out of camp and began to bring
their men quietly from the farms.

31. But Caesar, without knowing their plans, still suspected
what was coming from what happened to his ships and from
the interruption in sending hostages, so he prepared resources
for all events. He brought grain from field to camp daily and
used the lumber and metal from the most seriously damaged
ships to repair others and ordered what was useful for that
purpose brought from the continent. Since the soldiers put
themselves to work enthusiastically, though he had lost twelve
ships in all, he made the rest ready to sail well enough.

32. Meanwhile, the seventh legion was sent for grain as
usual, suspecting no attack then. When some of the locals
were still in the fields and others were coming to camp, men
stationed outside the camp gates reported to Caesar that more

---

[12] An oddly precise note surviving in a writer almost 300 years later: Athenaeus
6.273b: "Julius Caesar, the first person to make a crossing to the British Isles with
1,000 ships, took a total of only three slaves with him, according to Cotta, who was
serving as his second-in-command at the time."

dust than usual could be seen in the direction where the legion had gone. Caesar suspected, rightly, some new barbarian plot. He ordered the cohorts on watch to set out with him in that direction, commanded two of the others to stand watch and the rest to arm themselves and follow quickly. A little way from camp, he saw his men hard pressed by the enemy, scarcely able to stand, the legion crowded together with weapons hurled against them from all sides. Since grain had been reaped in the other regions, the enemy suspected that our men would come here and so hid themselves in the woods by night. Then when our men laid down weapons and scattered to gather grain, they suddenly attacked, killing a few and throwing the rest into confusion, surrounding them with cavalry and chariots.

33. This is how they fight with chariots. First they ride around all sides and hurl spears, throwing the infantry ranks into confusion with fear of horses and the noise of the wheels. When they work their way among cavalry troops, they jump down and fight afoot. The charioteers pull a little way from the battle and arrange the chariots so that if their fighters are hard pressed by a mass of enemy, they would have retreat ready for them. Thus they enjoy the mobility of cavalry and the stability of infantry in battle and by experience and daily practice become able to control galloping horses even on a steep decline, steering and turning quickly, and even running out the pole to stand on the yoke, and then swiftly regain the chariot.

34. Caesar brought timely help to our side's disorder. When he arrived, the enemy halted and ours recovered from their fear. Then, reckoning the time wrong for attacking the enemy and joining battle, he held his ground and soon led the legions to camp. While this went on, keeping our men busy, the others in the fields slipped away. Storms followed for several consecutive days, holding our troops in camp and keeping the enemy

from fighting. Meanwhile the barbarians sent messengers in all directions reporting how few our soldiers were and how much booty could be gotten. Perpetual liberty was theirs if they could drive the Romans from camp. In short order a great many fighters on foot and horse were brought together and came to our camp.

35. Caesar, though he saw the same thing would happen as did days before—if the enemy were driven back they would escape danger swiftly—still, with about thirty horse that Commius of the Atrebates—mentioned before—had brought with him, set the legions in order before the camp. When battle began, the enemy couldn't long resist the onrush of our soldiers and turned tail. Following them as far as speed and strength allowed, our men killed some of them, burning farmhouses far and wide, and returned to camp.

36. Enemy ambassadors for peace came to Caesar the same day. Caesar doubled the number of hostages he had commanded before and ordered them taken to the continent, for with the equinox near he did not think he should risk winter sailing with battered ships. Seizing on favorable weather, he slipped anchor a little after midnight and all the ships came safe to the continent. But two cargo ships were unable to reach the same ports as the others and were carried a little farther down.

37. While some 300 soldiers came ashore from those ships and made for camp, the Morini (whom Caesar had left in peace when he went to Britain), inspired by hope of booty, first surrounded them with no great number of men and ordered them to lay down arms if they did not want to be killed. When the Romans circled for defense, quickly at the shouting about 6,000 more appeared. Hearing this, Caesar sent all his cavalry from camp to help them. Meanwhile our soldiers resisted the enemy attack and fought bravely for more than four hours,

losing a few wounded and killing some of them. After our cavalry came into view, the enemy threw away their weapons and turned tail. A large number of them were killed.

38. Next day Caesar sent the legate Labienus with the legions he had brought back from Britain against the Morini who had rebelled. Because the marshes were dry, they did not have the places to hide they had used the year before. Almost all surrendered to Labienus. But the legates Sabinus and Cotta, who had led legions to Menapian territory, had wasted their fields, cut down their grain, and burned their farmhouses, then returned to Caesar after the Menapii had hidden themselves in the deepest woods. Caesar made winter quarters for all the legions among the Belgae. Two British nations sent hostages there: the others failed to do so. For all this, on Caesar's report the senate voted a supplication of twenty days.

FIFTH COMMENTARY

54 BCE

Caesar began the year with gritted teeth as his persistent adversary Domitius Ahenobarbus took office as one of the consuls for the year. The other was Appius Claudius Pulcher, the eldest brother of the vile Clodius, but himself a solid citizen: de facto leader of the distinguished family of Claudii, widely respected as an augur. (In 63, he had reported as augur his prediction of a civil war, which all took as fulfilled by the outbreak and suppression of Catiline's revolt.) He had just married his daughter to Pompey's son, an alliance suggesting his continuing support for the junta, which he had first demonstrated two years before when he was in the cloud of powerful senators who went to Lucca to ratify the generalissimos' bargain. In 53, he would go out to Cilicia in southern Asia Minor as proconsul and do a miserable job that his successor, Cicero, had to clean up.

Back from further Gaul at the beginning of the year, Caesar made his one extended trip to his other sphere of responsibility, Illyricum, to inspect and shore up defenses against the Pirustae, a people from the region of modern Montenegro/Albania who were raiding into Roman territory farther north along the Adriatic. This took Caesar only a few weeks.

As he made his way back through the Po valley, to linger a while monitoring the news from Rome before going on toward Gaul and Britain, he stayed at Verona with the father of the poet Catullus. Their dinner party had more than a touch of awkwardness about it, for the younger Catullus had very recently written some stinging verses about Caesar, both about his habit of plunder and about his financially and sexually scurrilous sidekick Mamurra.[1] We don't know how the dinner went, and Catullus may have died not many months later.

During the winter, Caesar also found time to study Cicero's *On the Orator*. It was both a work about rhetoric but also a veiled manifesto about a Roman political system in which the qualities of what old Cato had called the "good man skilled at speaking" mattered more in leaders than proficiency at conquest and plunder. Caesar took the work so seriously that he used his time in these months to write his own learned and polished reply *De analogia* (*On Analogy*). The work espoused a view of language more austere, rational, and disciplined than was usually to be found in old crowd-pleasers like Cicero. Caesar himself was much less frequently than Cicero on stage as a speaker, but was nonetheless highly successful and both widely and deeply well-read besides. Suetonius tells us that the work was written while Caesar was on the way from hearing cases in northern Italy back to his army. We should agree with Suetonius that the discipline and focus required to do this were impressive, if the story is true.

The friendly-enough literary competition would continue in the coming months when, by the end of the year, Cicero wrote an epic poem on Caesar's expedition to Britain before continuing to an account of his own exile and return. Caesar praised the first book of that memoir highly. This renewed friendship also took the form of, and was nurtured by, the appointment of Quintus Cicero, the orator's younger brother, to serve as a legate with Caesar in Gaul for what would turn out to be three years. He was unabashedly there to enrich himself. We welcome that news because it also means we are better informed about affairs in camp by the surviving correspondence between the two brothers.

---

[1] Peter Green had fun translating Catullus 29 lampooning Mamurra (and Caesar): "O military Supremo, was this then your aim, / While you were in that final island of the west, / To let this shagged-out prick, your crony, chomp his way / Through twenty million, maybe thirty?" In another poem, Catullus 11, this vignette of travel to the ends of the earth shows awareness of C.'s adventures in 55: "or toil across high-towering Alpine passes / to visit the monuments of mighty Caesar, / the Gaulish Rhine, those rude back-of-beyonders / the woad-dyed Britons."

Mamurra and Oppius appear now alongside Balbus as Caesar's staff contacts with the world of politics and money back at Rome. (They undoubtedly got very rich themselves in the course of their service.) Balbus, for example, was in Rome the winter of 55–54, went out to join Caesar in Gaul in the spring and went on to Britain with him, then returned to Rome that winter and stayed there until May of 53. Correspondence was one thing, but the dispatch of a trusted agent was another, and it is reasonable that Balbus would have seen Pompey whenever he was at Rome and functioned as the most confidential line of communication between the two generalissimos. In his turn, Pompey sent his own man, Vibullius Rufus, to Gaul on similar errands at least once or twice. The "chief of staff" of this whole enterprise, staying close to Caesar and managing all his affairs, was in this period Pompeius Trogus, a Roman citizen of Gallic origin with a good knowledge of the region and some connections. Aulus Hirtius, who would eventually write the eighth of these commentaries, was apparently his successor. Caesar's attention to affairs at Rome never flagged and so we know of several letters he wrote to Cicero while actually in Britain this summer. (Pliny the elder reports that Caesar could write, with relays of secretaries, as many as seven letters at one time.)

The real march north for Caesar this year came at the end of May. The trip was longer than usual, for he had to go all the way north, first to the land of the Treveri (around modern Trier), with four legions, to bully into submission the locals, divided for leadership between the Roman-friendly Cingetorix and the resistant Indutiomarus, then on to the coast to supervise fleet preparations. He was also concerned to round up the heads of a number of Gallic nations to take along as virtual hostages, to make sure that their people did not take the opportunity to revolt. Dumnorix the Haeduan, as fearlessly unimpressed with Caesar as he had been in 58, tried to induce the other Gauls to refuse to go along (he told them they would be taken to Britain and killed there), then tried to escape back home himself. Caesar illustrates Dumnorix's admirable zeal for liberty, then reports he had him hounded down and killed. Dumnorix went down calling on his men to save him and proclaiming himself a free man from a free people.

After about three weeks' delay waiting for favorable winds, Caesar returned to Britain with five legions in August and September. This visit left more time for exploration and skirmishes with the locals, but in fact was as fruitless as the first. He says that the local chief Cassivellaunus promised to pay him tribute, but we may reasonably guess that with no Roman presence again north of the channel for most of a hundred years, payment fell quickly into arrears. There was some trade with a people called the Trinobantes on the Essex shore north of the Thames estuary, but not much substantial other contact.

The delays in the British trip and its duration meant that the question of winter quarters was pressing when Caesar returned. There was a food shortage in Gaul generally, so he was forced to distribute his forces to several locations some distance from each other in northern Gaul. He himself waited at Amiens until all were settled, by then realizing he would have to stay in Gaul himself this year rather than face challenging winter travel.

Caesar tells frankly the memorable story of the disaster that ensued. The Eburones under Ambiorix attacked and massacred one and a half legions in the winter quarters closest to them. Caesar makes it clear that it was the legate Sabinus whose irresolution and borderline cowardice lost the day. Making that clear also made it clear that Caesar himself, spreading his forces out in small groups far apart, bore no responsibility. The Nervii not far away took heart and besieged Quintus Cicero in his camp (using siegework tactics they had learned by imitating what Caesar did to them earlier in the war) until the general came rushing in pell-mell to the rescue with two under-strength legions: Caesar was quite the hero. Finally, Indutiomarus and the Treveri sought to entrap Labienus similarly, but Indutiomarus' rival Cingetorix rallied to the Romans, and so Labienus was able to use local cavalry in his defense and succeeded in defeating and killing Indutiomarus and his forces. By now it was late in the year and Caesar's resolution to stay in Gaul to repair the position in which he found himself was firm. He ordered conscription of three more legions from northern Italy, one of which was nominally designated for Pompey. By the time they could join Caesar in early 53, he had ten legions in the field but his forces were clearly shaken and unsure just how pacified Gaul would remain.

Failed invasions, fatal insurgencies, and recalcitrant consuls did not entirely ruin the year for Caesar. Remembering Pompey's great theater, Caesar had his own project for Rome, building a new basilica in the traditional forum, as well as his whole new forum, the "forum of Julius," a lavish extension of Rome's central market and assembly space reaching north from the old gathering place between the Capitoline and Palatine hills. Early in 54, Caesar had made Cicero a large loan, had of course looked out for Quintus at his right hand, and had welcomed other patronage requests to place promising young men with the army, and so he now came back to ask Cicero to work with Oppius on plans for the Forum Iulii and for a huge new construction in the Campus Martius, not far from Pompey's theater, to use as a voting assembly place for Roman citizens. The cost of the land (perhaps for just the forum) came to 60 million sesterces, no inconsiderable sum compared to the 40 million a year that would later be imposed on all of Gaul as an annual tax.

There was bad news from Rome for Caesar on his return from Britain. His daughter Julia, married to Pompey in 59, died this summer. Her funeral was huge and noisy, with a crowd carrying her body off to bury in the Campus Martius. Well and good for Caesar's standing in Rome, but the relationship with Pompey was inevitably attenuated by the loss.

But for both the generalissimos, the year ended badly. No elections could be held, between the riotous mobs and the political maneuvers of the senators. It was not until the summer of 53 that consuls and praetors were finally elected for a year already half done—and this was the winter that Caesar had to stay in Gaul, trapped between the uncertainties of his situation there and the instability at Rome.

IN THE CONSULSHIP OF
DOMITIUS AHENOBARBUS AND
APPIUS CLAUDIUS PULCHER

1. When Domitius and Claudius were consuls, Caesar left winter quarters for Italy, as he did every year, telling the legates he left in charge of the legions to build and repair as many ships as they could that winter, specifying their shape and kind. To load and beach them quickly he made them a little lower than is usual on our sea, especially because he knew frequent changes of the tide made waves lower there. For transporting cargo and animal herds, he made them a little broader than we use on other seas. He ordered them all made nimble, for which it helps to be lower. He ordered things needed for arming ships brought from Spain.

Concluding his trials in nearer Gaul, he left for Illyricum, hearing that the part of the province near the Pirustae was devastated by raids.[2] When he arrived, he summoned soldiers from the cities and bid them gather in a particular place. Hearing this, the Pirustae sent ambassadors to tell him that none of what had happened arose from official policy and showed themselves ready to make full amends for damages. Hearing

---

[2] His second visit (the last was two years earlier) to his other province. The border raids were probably around modern Lake Ohrid on the Albania/Macedonia border. The Pirustae had made peace with Rome in 167 BCE but now were plaguing other nations subject to Rome.

their speech, Caesar demanded hostages and ordered them delivered on a specific day; unless they did so, he would wage war against their nation. When they were brought as ordered on the day, he assigned arbiters between the nations to assess the quarrel and establish penalties.

2. When these things were done and trials completed there, he returned to nearer Gaul and then headed for the army. When he got there, going around all the winter quarters, he found that the soldiers, with extraordinary energy, short on everything, had equipped about 600 ships of the kind we described and 28 warships, and not much was left for their being ready to launch in a few days. Praising the soldiers and those who had led the work, he showed what he wanted done and ordered all to gather at the port of Itius,[3] where he knew the crossing to Britain was easiest, twenty-five or thirty miles' distance from the continent. He left enough soldiers for that task and with four legions (but no baggage train) and 800 cavalry he left for the country of the Treveri. That nation did not come to councils or obey his orders and was said to be encouraging the Germans across the Rhine.

3. This nation, by far the strongest of Gaul in cavalry, has huge forces of infantry as well and extends to the Rhine. Two men struggled for leadership there, Indutiomarus and Cingetorix. The latter came to Caesar as soon as the legions' arrival was known, to assure him that he and his people would remain loyal and never cease to be friends of the Roman people, and to report what was going on among the Treveri. But Indutiomarus began to gather cavalry and infantry and make ready for war. Those unable to bear arms because of age, he hid in the

---

[3] Location uncertain, still in the region between Boulogne and Calais; he arrives in early June.

Ardennes forest[4]—which stretches huge through Treveri country from the Rhine to the boundary with the Remi.

But then some leaders of that nation, drawn by friendship
for Cingetorix and fear of the coming of our army, came to
Caesar to deal with him for themselves, since they could not
make provisions for their nation. Indutiomarus, afraid all
would abandon him, sent legates to Caesar to say that he did
not want to leave his own people and come to Caesar. Better
to keep his nation loyal and to keep the masses from rashly
getting into trouble if all the nobility should leave. With the
whole nation in his hands, he would come to Caesar in camp
if allowed, trusting his own and his nation's future to Caesar's honor.

4. Caesar, though he understood why he said this and what
was keeping Indutiomarus from his plan, still didn't want to
waste the summer among the Treveri when everything was
ready for the British war, so he ordered Indutiomarus to come
with 200 hostages. When he brought them—including his son
and all his relatives,[5] summoned by name—Caesar reassured
Indutiomarus and encouraged him to remain loyal. Then he
still summoned all the leaders of the Treveri, reconciling them
one at a time with Cingetorix. Cingetorix had earned this, but
it was also of great importance that the authority of a man so
outstandingly faithful to Caesar should be built up among his
own people. Indutiomarus took this badly. Already hostile toward us, he flared up much worse with resentment.

[4] Caesar never describes the Treveri as having fixed settlements of any kind,
hence the forest hideouts.

[5] By the end of this year, Indutiomarus will be leading a major insurrection
against Caesar, which suggests that C. may have let the hostages go on return from
Britain, imprudently. A year from now, reported at 6.2, when Indutiomarus is dead,
it is his "relatives" (exact same expression as here) who take over leadership of the
Treveri.

5. Settling affairs thus, Caesar came to the port of Itius with the legions. There he found that 60 ships, built among the Meldi, couldn't hold course, blown back by storms, and had returned where they came from.[6] The rest were ready to sail, equipped with everything. 4,000 cavalry from all Gaul gathered there, as well as leaders from all nations, a few of whom, proven in loyalty, he left in Gaul. He decided to take the rest along as hostages, fearing Gallic uprising in his absence.

6. There with the rest was Dumnorix the Haeduan, of whom we've spoken before. Caesar really wanted him along, recognizing a strong figure, eager for revolution and rule, widely respected in Gaul. And in the Haedui council Dumnorix had said Caesar was giving him their throne—which the Haedui took badly, without daring to send ambassadors to Caesar to reject or deplore the decision. Caesar learned this from his allies. Dumnorix asked every which way to be left in Gaul, partly out of inexperience and fear of the sea, partly because he said his religious obligations stood in the way. After he saw that he was stubbornly refused and gave up hope, he started canvassing the Gallic leaders, calling each aside and urging them to stay on the mainland. He was frightening them, saying it was no accident Gaul was being stripped of its leadership. Caesar's plan was to take them to Britain and murder them there because he was afraid to kill them where Gaul could see. He pledged faith to them asking they swear to do together what they knew would help Gaul. These words were reported to Caesar by many people.

7. Knowing this, Caesar, because he greatly esteemed the Haedui, decided he had to control and constrain Dumnorix however he could. As he saw Dumnorix's delusions increas-

---

[6] From Meaux, on the Marne northeast of Paris; they returned to Caesar's depot at the mouth of the Seine, where they had entered the ocean.

ing, he needed to make sure no harm came to Caesar or the republic. So while spending about twenty-five days there, because northerly winds, blowing there year-round, prevented sailing, he worked to keep Dumnorix to his commitments while finding out all his plans.

Finally he got decent weather and ordered infantry and cavalry to board ship. While everyone was distracted, Dumnorix and his Haedui cavalry began leaving camp for home without Caesar's knowledge. Hearing this, Caesar interrupted his departure and put everything aside to send most of the cavalry to pursue Dumnorix and ordered him returned. If he resisted and disobeyed, he was to be killed. He couldn't expect Dumnorix to act sensibly after Caesar departed, when he was flouting his authority face to face. When he was summoned, Dumnorix began to resist and fight back and call on the loyalty of his men, regularly proclaiming himself a free man from a free nation. As ordered, they surrounded the man and killed him. All the Haedui cavalry returned to Caesar.

8. After this, Labienus was left on the mainland with three legions and two thousand cavalry to watch the ports, gather grain, keep track of what happened in Gaul, and plan as the circumstances of the moment suggested. Caesar sailed at sunset with five legions and as many cavalry as he left behind on the mainland. Carried on a light southwest wind, he lost headway around midnight when the wind dropped. Drifting farther with the current, at dawn he saw Britain on his left.[7] Then following the change of tide, he pressed with oars to reach that part of the island he had learned the previous summer was

---

[7] This gang that couldn't float straight wanted to go mainly due north, but wind and current took them north and east and so they looked back on the port side with alarm at the receding land. They made their way back to landing around Sandwich, a bit north of where they had likely grounded the year before.

best for landing. The bravery of the troops then was admirable, as they rowed tirelessly and kept the heavy transports up with the longboats. They all reached Britain about mid-day, with no enemy there in sight. Caesar later learned from captives that a great force had gathered there, but was frightened by the mass of ships. With last year's ships and the private ships made for profit, more than 800 were seen at one time.[8] They left the shore and hid themselves on higher ground.

9. Caesar landed his force and chose a good place for his camp, then learned from captives where the enemy forces had halted. He left ten cohorts and three hundred cavalry on shore to guard the ships, unworried because he left them at anchor on an open, sandy shore, with Q. Atrius put in charge of the ship garrison. By night he went forward about ten miles and spotted the enemy force.[9] They came by horse and chariot to the river from high ground to intercept our forces and began the fight. Driven back by cavalry, they hid in the woods, choosing a place extremely well fortified by nature and man, apparently prepared beforehand in some local war. Every approach was blocked by piles of felled trees. A few came out of the woods to fight and kept our men from getting beyond the barricades. Soldiers of the seventh legion, making a tortoise and driving a ramp up to the barricades, took the place and drove them from the woods with only a few of our

[8] In his grammatical work *De analogia*, written in this year, Caesar prescribed that unfamiliar words should be avoided as a mariner avoids rocks: "tamquam scopulum, sic fugias inauditum atque insolens verbum." The word *annotinis* ("last year's") appears in surviving ancient Latin literature here and in two scientific writers of a century later. The mention of ships-for-profit seems to suggest that various officers and camp followers had equipped themselves with boats that would be useful for freighting plunder or people captured into slavery back to the continent.

[9] If this distance is reliable, it would bring him to the vicinity of Canterbury, at appreciable risk of being surrounded and cut off, unless he had considerable confidence in his intelligence of the enemy's whereabouts.

own wounded. Caesar forbade chasing them further in flight, both because he did not know the ground and because they had used up most of the day and wanted time left for fortifying camp.

10. Next morning he sent cavalry and infantry out in three detachments to pursue the refugees. When they had gone a distance and the stragglers were already in sight, horsemen came from Quintus Atrius to Caesar to report that on the preceding evening a great storm had risen and battered almost all the ships and beached them, for their anchors and ropes did not hold and the sailors and helmsmen could not resist the force of the storm. From that battering of the ships much damage had been done.

11. Learning this, Caesar recalls legions and cavalry, bidding them halt on the way while he returned to the ships. He saw things were plainly just as he had learned from messengers and messages, with about forty ships lost, the rest able to be repaired but at great effort. He orders carpenters assigned from the legions and others summoned from the continent. He writes Labienus to prepare as many ships as possible for the legions with him. He judged it best to bring the ships all on shore and consolidate a single fortified camp, even though it took considerable work and effort. They spend about ten days on this, not even stopping the soldiers' work at night. With the ships beached and the camp strongly fortified, he leaves the same troops on ship garrison as before: he goes back where he had returned from. When he arrived, many British forces had gathered there from all over, by common agreement yielding supreme command and war leadership to Cassivellanus. In former times, continuous wars came between him and other nations, but when we arrived all the Britons were alarmed and put him in charge of war and command.

12. Inland Britain is inhabited by people traditionally said to have been born there, the coast by people who came from Belgium (they are called by names of the nations they came from) for booty and warfare, and after waging war they remained and began to till the land. There are infinitely many people and farmhouses everywhere very like Gallic ones, and a great number of cattle. They use bronze and gold coin or iron bars measured to a certain weight in place of coin. Tin is found in the inland regions, iron by the sea, but in small amounts. Bronze they import. There is timber of every kind you find in Gaul, except beech and fir. They think it not right to eat rabbit, chicken, or goose, but raise them for the delight of it. Their climate is milder than Gaul, the cold weather less severe.

13. The island is a triangle, one side facing Gaul. One corner on this side, by Kent, where almost all ships from Gaul come ashore, looks to the rising sun, while the lower corner looks south. This is about 500 miles long. Another side faces Spain and the setting sun, where lies Ireland, thought to be about half the size of Britain, but the crossing is about the same as from Gaul to Britain. Halfway is the island called Mona,[10] and many other islands are thought to lie there, where some claim that night lasts thirty full days in winter. We could not find out anything about this by our inquiries except that by careful water measures we saw the nights were shorter than on the continent. The length of that side, as the story goes, is seven hundred miles. The third side faces north, with no land facing, but the corner on that side mostly faces Germany. This side is about eight hundred miles long. The whole island around extends 2,000 miles.[11]

---

[10] Anglesey? Isle of Man?

[11] Measuring every foot of coastline gives a much larger modern number, but as a rough measure of the triangle of Great Britain from Kent to Cornwall to John o'

14. The most civilized people of them all are the ones who live in Kent, an entirely maritime area, not much unlike Gaul in customs. Inland they mostly do not plant grain, but live on milk and meat and dress in skins. All the Britons stain themselves with woad,[12] which produces the color blue, and so they are more horrifying to see in battle, with long hair and all their bodies shaved except for head and upper lip. By tens and twelves they have wives in common, especially brothers with brothers and fathers with sons. Children born of them are counted as children of the man to whom the mother was first brought as a virgin.

15. Enemy cavalry and charioteers battled our cavalry fiercely on the road, but ours were still victors all around, forcing them into the woods and hills, cutting them down in a furious chase, losing a few of our own. A while later, when our men were fortifying camp and heedless, theirs suddenly burst from the woods attacking those who were stationed outside camp and fought strongly. Caesar sent two cohorts to help, the first ranks of two legions, and when these stood fast with little space between them, our men were still frightened by the new style of fighting, so the Britons fought bravely through our lines and retreated safely. That day Quintus Laberius Durus, military tribune, was killed. The enemy were driven back when more cohorts were sent forward.

16. In all this sort of fighting, where they battled in plain sight before the camp, we realized that our men, weighed down by weapons and unable to leave their standards and pursue retreating enemy, were less ready for a foe like this. Cavalry

---

Groats and around, the approximation is credible. Tacitus' father-in-law Agricola would become the first Roman to circumnavigate the island more than a century later.

[12] A plant of the cabbage family.

fought at very great risk because the enemy deliberately withdrew, then when they had drawn our men a little away from the legions, they leapt down from their chariots and fought the uneven contest on foot. Their cavalry style of fighting brought equal danger in retreat and in pursuit. The Britons fought, moreover, nowhere in close order but in small numbers all spread out, and had troops posted so some could take up for others, with fresh unwearied troops relieving the exhausted.

17. Next day the enemy stayed on hills far from camp, with here and there a few of them showing themselves, harassing our cavalry, skirmishing more tentatively than the day before. But at noon, when Caesar sent three legions and all the cavalry foraging with the legate Gaius Trebonius, suddenly they flew against the foragers on all sides, not even avoiding the standards where the legions were. Our men attacked them fiercely, driving them back and not abandoning the chase until the cavalry, confident of support as they saw the legions following, drove the enemy headlong, killed a large number and gave them no chance to regroup or stop or dismount their chariots. In this rout, the auxiliaries they had gathered from everywhere departed, and after that the enemy never fought with us with their full strength.

18. Learning their plans, Caesar led the army to the river Thames in Cassivellaunus' territory, a river able to be crossed—with difficulty—in only one place.[13] Arriving there, he saw huge enemy forces aligned on the opposite bank, protected there by sharp stakes fixed before them, with stakes of the same kind hidden underwater in the river. Finding this out from captives and refugees, Caesar sent cavalry ahead and ordered the legions to follow at once. The soldiers moved with

---

[13] Perhaps around Brentford, a little upriver from London.

such speed and momentum, just their heads out of the water, that the enemy could not resist the combined attack of legions and cavalry, and so left the bank and gave themselves to flight.

19. Cassivellaunus, as we have seen, gave up all hope of battle, released most of his troops and kept four thousand charioteers to watch our progress. He went off the road and hid in tangled woods. Where he knew we would pass he ordered people and livestock out of the fields into the woods and, when our cavalry poured out freely into farmland to plunder and pillage, he sent out his chariots by every road and path from the woods to fight our cavalry, at our great peril, and made them fear to roam farther. Caesar was left forbidding men to go far from the legions' line of march and was able to harm the enemy only by ravaging farmland and setting fires, as much as legionary soldiers could do on the march.

20. Meanwhile the Trinovantes were nearly the strongest people thereabouts,[14] whose young Mandubracius trusted Caesar and came to him in Gaul when his father, holding power among them, had been killed by Cassivellaunus and he himself avoided death by flight. They sent ambassadors now to Caesar promising to surrender to him and obey his orders and asking him to protect Mandubracius against harm from Cassivellaunus and send him home to rule and hold command. Caesar ordered them to supply forty hostages and grain for his army and sent them Mandubracius. They obeyed at once, sending the number of hostages and grain.

21. With the Trinovantes protected and sheltered against military attack, the Cenimagni, Segontiaci, Ancalites, Bibroci, and Cassi sent ambassadors and surrendered to Caesar. From them he learned about Cassivellaunus' town not far away, forti-

[14] From north and east of London, mainly modern Essex.

fied by forest and swamp, where a considerable number of men and livestock had gathered. The Britons call it a town when they fortify thick woods with walls and ditches to gather there routinely against enemy attack. Caesar went there with the legions. He found the place wonderfully protected by nature and engineering, but still he set out to attack from two sides. The enemy hesitated a little, unable to bear the onrush of our soldiers, then fled out another side of town. A great many livestock were found there and many fugitives were captured and killed.

22. While this went on there, Cassivellaunus sent messengers to Kent, where four kings ruled, Cingetorix, Carvilius, Taximagulus, and Segovax. He ordered them, gathering all their forces, to approach and attack our naval station by surprise. When they came near camp, our men broke out, killed many of them, captured their noble general Lugotorix, and brought our men home safe. Cassivellaunus had news of this battle. Troubled by suffering such losses, by the ravaging of his land, and especially by the loss of allies, he sent ambassadors to Caesar by way of Commius of the Atrebates to discuss surrender. Caesar, deciding to winter on the continent in case of sudden Gallic uprisings, with not much summer left (he knew the time could easily be dragged out), demanded hostages and set the annual tribute Britain would pay the Roman people.[15] He particularly ordered Cassivellaunus to do no harm to Mandubracius or the Trinovantes.

23. Accepting hostages, he led troops back to the coast and found the ships rebuilt. Launching them, because he had many captives and some ships had been lost in storm, he decided to return the army in two trips. And so for all the ships

[15] Cassivellaunus gave in quickly. Did he gamble that Caesar was unlikely to return and the promised tribute could go unpaid?

and sailings this year and the last, not one ship carrying troops
was lost. But of those sent back empty from the continent, the
ones from which the soldiers of the earlier crossing had dis-
embarked and the sixty Labienus had built later, few made
their place and almost all were driven back. When Caesar had
waited for them a while,[16] not wanting to be kept from sailing
by the season, as the equinox neared, he had to crowd the
soldiers in tighter and, when a great calm set in, they set off at
second watch and at dawn reached land, bringing all the ships
in safe.

24. When the ships were ashore and the Gauls' council at
Samarobriva[17] was done, because harvests had fallen short
through drought that year in Gaul, he had to arrange forces in
winter quarters differently from years before and assign the
legions among more nations.[18] He gave legate Gaius Fabius
one to take to the Morini, Quintus Cicero another for the Nervii, Lucius Roscius a third for the Esuvii, and a fourth he ordered to winter among the Remi in Treveri territory with Titus
Labienus. Three he stationed among the Belgae, putting quaestor Marcus Crassus and legates Lucius Munatius Plancus and
Gaius Trebonius in charge.[19]

One legion, lately drafted beyond the Po, he sent with five
cohorts to the Eburones, most of whom are between the Meuse

[16] A letter of Cicero's suggests they had stayed in Britain almost two months. Two
to three weeks intervened between first sailing and the end of Caesar's impatience.

[17] Amiens.

[18] He was *compelled* to a division of forces that went very badly for him. That's his
excuse. Further excuse is in the remark below that they were all stationed within a
hundred miles (truer if he had said 200) of each other, and the one outlier was among
(apparently) quiet and peaceful folk.

[19] The most senior legate, Labienus, was given the hosts who had seemed most
restive and dangerous since Indutiomarus' sedition (5.3 above). Marcus Crassus now
replaces his brother Publius, who had been with Caesar but had left to join his father,
the triumvir, in the east. Munatius Plancus was in his early thirties, with a long career
of shifting allegiances ahead of him.

and Rhine rivers and ruled by Ambiorix and Catuvolcus. He ordered legates Quintus Titurius Sabinus and Lucius Aurunculeius Cotta to lead them. Arranging the legions thus he thought he could easily deal with the grain shortage. The camps of all these legions—except the one he'd given Lucius Roscius to take to the most quiet and peaceful region—were within less than a hundred miles of each other. He decided to linger in Gaul himself until he knew the legions were settled and the camps fortified.

25. Born to high station among the Carnutes was Tasgetius, whose ancestors had ruled that nation. For his power and his kindness to him—he had depended on his distinctive energy in all his battles—Caesar restored him to the rank of his ancestors. Reigning now a third year, he was killed by his enemies, many of the ringleaders coming from his own city. The affair was reported to Caesar. He worried the city might revolt on encouragement of the many involved and ordered Lucius Plancus and his legion swiftly from Belgium to go to the Carnutes, to winter there, seizing and sending him those involved in Tasgetius' murder. By then he had report from all the legates and the quaestor to whom he had assigned legions that they had reached and fortified their winter quarters.

26. Some fifteen days after they were in quarters a sudden uprising and revolt began, led by Ambiorix and Catuvolcus. Though they had presented themselves to Sabinus and Cotta at their border and brought grain for the camps, nevertheless on urging from messengers sent by the Treveran Indutiomarus they stirred up their people, suddenly overrunning our woodgatherers, and came with great force to attack the camp. Our men snatched up arms and mounted the rampart. They prevailed in a cavalry battle by sending out the Spanish horsemen on one side. The enemy lost hope and drew back from attacking.

Then as customary for them they all shouted that someone of our side should come to parley: they had things to say of mutual interest that they hoped could lessen the disagreements.

27. Gaius Arpinius, equestrian and a friend of Sabinus, was sent to parley with them, and with him one Quintus Junius from Spain, who had for a while been Caesar's messenger to Ambiorix. Ambiorix spoke to them so: He acknowledged how much he owed to Caesar's generosity toward him, freeing him from paying what he had been paying his neighbors, the Aduatuci, and freeing as well his son and nephew, whom, when they'd been sent among hostages, the Aduatuci had kept in servitude and chains. What he had done in attacking the camp was not by his will or judgment, but he had been forced by the people. They had no less authority over him than he over them—such was the nature of his regime. For to the people the justification for war was that they could not resist the fast-rising conspiracy of the Gauls. In all humility, he could easily prove he was not so inexperienced that he thought he could overcome the Roman people with his forces.

But Gaul was of one mind: this day was set for attacking all Caesar's winter camps, so no legion could come to the aid of another. Gauls could not easily refuse Gauls, especially concerning a plan for regaining their common freedom. He went along out of loyalty but was now reckoning what he owed for the kindness of Caesar. He warned, indeed prayed, Sabinus as his guest-friend to look out for the safety of himself and his troops. A huge band of German mercenaries had crossed the Rhine and would be here in two days. They should think whether, before the neighbors could notice, to lead troops from camp and take them to Cicero or Labienus, the one a bit less than fifty miles away from them, the other rather farther. He promised and confirmed by oath he would give them safe conduct through his land. In doing so, he was looking out for his own nation—to free it of quartering obligations—and paying back Caesar for all his kindness. With this speech, Ambiorix left them.

28. Arpinius and Junius reported what they heard to the legates, who were alarmed by the sudden news and thought they should not ignore the report, even from an enemy. They were especially concerned and incredulous that the lowly and weakling Eburones should dare by themselves to make war on the Roman people. They took the matter to a council; a great quarrel erupted among them. Aurunculeius Cotta and numerous tribunes and first rank centurions thought nothing should be done in a hurry. They should not leave winter quarters unless Caesar ordered them. They claimed they could withstand any Gallic forces—or even Germans—in fortified camp. Their evidence was that they had strongly withstood the first attack of the enemy, wounding many besides. They were not short of grain. Help would arrive from nearby camps and from Caesar. And besides, what was more foolish and embarrassing than to take advice on great matters from the enemy?

29. Sabinus rejoined loudly that it would be too late when larger enemy forces joined up with additional Germans or when neighboring winter camps endured some disaster. Time for discussion was short. He thought Caesar had left for Italy—the Carnutes would not otherwise have planned Tasgetius' killing, and the Eburones, if Caesar were nearby, would not have approached our camps so contemptuously. His eye was not on the enemy but on the facts: the Rhine was nearby, the Germans were outraged at the death of Ariovistus[20] and our earlier victories, and Gaul was on fire over subjection to

---

[20] Ariovistus' death has gone unmentioned till now; cf. 1.53.

the Roman people's rule and the many humiliations that extinguished their former military renown. Finally, who could convince himself Ambiorix would stoop to such designs without good reason? His own view was safe either way. If there was no challenge, no danger in joining the nearest legion; if all Gaul was in league with the Germans, only in speed was there safety. What could come from the advice of Cotta and the others? If not immediate risk, at least fear of starving under a long siege.

30. The argument went both ways, with Cotta and the first officers pushing back strongly. "You win," said Sabinus, "if that's how you want it," loud enough for most soldiers to hear: "I'm not the type to be terrified by you with danger of death. These men will understand, and if something serious happens, they'll hold you accountable. If you let them, in three days they would join the nearby camps to face the common fortunes of war there, not be left cast out and abandoned far from the others, to die by sword or starvation."

31. Everyone leapt to their feet, laying hands on both and pleading that disagreement and stubbornness not lead to the worst danger. Easy enough, to stay or go, if everyone thought and voted as one; but they saw no safety in disagreement. The argument lasted till midnight. Finally Cotta was persuaded and gave in; Sabinus' opinion prevailed. It was declared they would march at first light. The rest of the night was wakeful, every soldier looking to his kit: what would he take with him, what winter equipment would he be forced to abandon? They thought of everything dangerous about staying, how exhaustion and night watches would increase risk. So at first light they left camp in a long line, heavily laden, like men believing Ambiorix's argument was not that of an enemy but of their greatest friend.

32. The enemy, in the noisy and wakeful night, sensed they were leaving and set ambush in the woods on both sides of their way. Well-hidden, a couple of miles off, they awaited the Roman coming. When most of our line had descended into a steep valley, they showed themselves suddenly on both sides of the defile, crowding the rear and blocking the vanguard from ascending. They began battle in a setting entirely bad for our men.

33. Then at last Sabinus, as if he had foreseen none of this, took fright and ran around arranging his cohorts, timidly, as though everything he needed was lacking—which happens often enough to those who need to stop and plan in the midst of action. Cotta, who had thought this could happen en route and so had advised against marching, was everywhere he was needed and did his duty as general and soldier in battle, calling out and encouraging the troops. Since the line of march was long and the two could not be everywhere and see what was needed in each place, they ordered it passed along that baggage should be abandoned and that forces should gather in a circle. In a crisis of this sort, that advice is not bad, but it still turned out badly. It took away our soldiers' hope and made the enemy keener to fight, for we appeared to act only out of great fear and despair. It also happened—as it had to—that soldiers left their standards and hurried to find and take whatever they valued most from their baggage. There was shouting and weeping everywhere.[21]

34. The barbarians were not without a plan. Their leaders sent orders up the line for no one to give way. The booty was theirs and whatever the Romans left would be kept for them. They should think everything depended on victory. Our men,

---

[21] Big Roman soldiers don't cry; stern editors blush and think about deleting this sentence.

bereft of leadership and luck, relied on their courage above all and whenever any cohort attacked, many enemy fell. Ambiorix sees this and orders it passed along that they should throw spears from a distance and not go closer, yielding ground wherever the Romans attacked, but pursue them when they returned to their standards.

35. This command they obeyed exactly. When a cohort left the circle and attacked, the enemy drew back quickly. That cohort was necessarily exposed and took spears thrown on the open side. When they began to go back where they had come from, they were surrounded by those who had retreated and by the ones near them. If they held their ground, they had no chance to show their courage and in the crowd they could not dodge spears thrown by so many. With so many disadvantages and many wounds, they still stood fast most of the day, fighting from dawn to the eighth hour, doing nothing to be ashamed of. Then Titus Balventius, first spear just last year, a man strong and greatly respected, took a javelin wound in each leg. Quintus Lucanius, of the same rank, fighting heroically, was killed helping his son, who had been surrounded. The legate Lucius Cotta, cheering on every cohort and rank, was wounded in the face by a slingshot.

36. Troubled by all this, Sabinus, seeing Ambiorix at a distance encouraging his troops, sent his interpreter Gnaeus Pompeius[22] to him to ask for mercy for him and his men. Ambiorix responded to the plea: If Sabinus wanted to talk to him, fine. He hoped he could win safety for the soldiers from the people. Sabinus himself would not be harmed, and for that, Ambiorix pledged his own faith. Sabinus consulted with the

[22] Likely the father of the historian Pompeius Trogus on Caesar's staff. Originally himself a Celtic Gaul, he would have obtained citizenship fighting for the great Pompey (hence the name).

wounded Cotta whether they should leave battle and confer with Ambiorix, hoping to win safety for themselves and their soldiers. Cotta said he would not approach an armed enemy and went on fighting.

37. Sabinus ordered the military tribunes and first rank centurions around him to follow, and when he neared Ambiorix, he was commanded to cast aside his weapons. He did as he was commanded and ordered his men to do likewise. Then while they talked terms together and Ambiorix designedly began a longer speech, he was gradually surrounded and then killed. They proclaimed victory and raised the war-whoop in their fashion, scattering our men with an attack. Lucius Cotta was killed fighting there along with most of the soldiers. The rest made it back to the camps they had left. One, Lucius Petrosidius, a standard-bearer, pursued by a great many enemy, hurled his eagle over the rampart and was slain fighting heroically before the gate. They barely held off the attack till nightfall, but after dark, despairing of rescue, they all killed themselves to the man. A few slipped away from battle and through sketchy woodland paths made it to legate Titus Labienus' camp and reported what had occurred.

38. Elated by victory, Ambiorix and his cavalry departed immediately for the Aduatuci, his kingdom's neighbors. They paused neither night nor day, ordering infantry to follow. Reporting events and rousing the Aduatuci, next day they reached the Nervii and urged them not to miss the chance of freeing themselves forever and avenging themselves on the Romans for the injuries they had suffered.[23] Two legates had been killed and a large part of the army destroyed. It would not be hard to

---

[23] We are about ten days from the end of October 54 BCE. Here the Nervii, said to have been wiped out at 2.28, rise again. In 7.75 they will have 5,000 fighters to contribute to the siege of Alesia.

surprise and kill the legion wintering with Cicero. Ambiorix promised his support. His speech easily won over the Nervii.

39. So they sent messengers at once to the Ceutrones, Grudii, Levaci, Pleumoxii, and Geidumni, all under their sway, gathered all the forces they could, and rushed unexpected to Cicero's camp: news of Sabinus' death had not reached him.[24] Here too inevitably some soldiers who had gone out in the forest for firewood and lumber were cut off by the sudden arrival of cavalry. They were surrounded. Then with a large force, the Eburones, Nervii, Aduatuci, and all their allies and followers began to attack the legion. Our men rushed to arms, mounting the rampart. They barely held the day, for the enemy counted entirely on speedy attack—winning this, they were sure of lasting victory.

40. A message was sent from Cicero to Caesar at once and the couriers were promised great rewards, but all roads were watched and they were captured. From lumber collected for fortification, 120 towers went up at night. Everything needed was accomplished with incredible speed. The enemy attacked camp next day with a much larger force, filling in the ditch. Our men fought back the same as the day before, and again on the following days. No hour of night saw effort lessen: there was no rest for the weary or the wounded. Whatever the next day's attack required was gotten together at night. Many sharp stakes were fire-cured, many wall spears were made.[25] Towers were boarded over, with protecting tops and covers made of woven wicker. Cicero himself, though in poor health, left him-

[24] Cicero was south of Brussels, near the Sambre, not far south of Waterloo. Caesar was at Amiens, some 125 miles away.

[25] "Wall spears" were five to six feet long, usually planted atop a rampart close together to create a pointed barricade. The fire-cured stakes were shorter, planted out farther.

self no time for rest, even at night, until a crowd of protesting soldiers made him spare himself.

41. Then the leaders and princes of the Nervii who could approach Cicero with some claim of friendship said they wished to speak with him. Permission granted, they argued the same as Ambiorix had done to Sabinus. All Gaul was in arms, the Germans had crossed the Rhine, the winter quarters of Caesar and the others were assailed. They reported Sabinus' death as well and invoked the example of Ambiorix. The Romans were wrong to hope for help from people fearing for their own affairs. Their intentions for Cicero and the Roman people were to deny them nothing but winter quarters—they did not want the practice to become a habit. They were free to leave camp and go where they wished without fear. Cicero gave them one answer: The Roman people were not in the habit of accepting terms proposed by armed enemies. If they would disarm, they would have his support sending representatives to Caesar. He had hopes, considering Caesar's fairness, that they would get what they wanted.

42. Disappointed in their hope, the Nervii surround camp with a rampart ten feet high and a ditch fifteen feet deep. They had learned this from us in prior years' encounters and were taught by captives from our army, but without suitable iron tools they were forced to hack the turf with swords and bring up the dirt in hands and cloaks. One could tell how large the force was, for in less than three hours they completed a fortification two or three miles around, then in the next days began to build towers as high as the rampart and prepared hooks and tortoises the way the same captives had showed them.

43. On the seventh day of siege, when great winds sprang up, they started launching fiery projectiles of molten clay from slings and heated spears against the huts covered in the Gallic

manner with thatch.[26] They quickly caught fire and in the strong wind spread flame throughout the camp. The enemy shouted as if victory were over and done, moved forward towers and tortoises, and began to climb the rampart with ladders. Our soldiers were so brave and alert that, with fire and flying spears on all sides, seeing all their baggage and possessions aflame, not only did no one think of leaving the rampart to slip away, but almost no one even looked back and they went on fighting fiercely and powerfully. This was by far the worst day for our men, but ended with a great many enemy wounded and killed. They had crowded up under the rampart with those behind giving those in front no room for retreat. When the flames died down a bit and in one place a tower was brought up to touch the rampart, the centurions of the third cohort pulled back from where they stood and moved back all their men, then with words and gestures invited the enemy to enter if they wished. None of them dared to advance. Then stones flew on all sides, they were driven back, and the tower set ablaze.

44. There were heroic men, centurions, in that legion, ready for promotion to the highest ranks, Titus Pullo and Lucius Vorenus. They were always competing for who was ahead, every year fiercely vying for position. Pullo, when the fighting was fierce at the wall, said, "Why hesitate, Vorenus? What chance to prove your courage are you waiting for? This day will settle our contest." Saying this, he went beyond the wall and rushed where the enemy seemed crowded thickest. Vorenus didn't stay within the rampart either, but followed, conscious of what everyone thought. At close range, Pullo threw his spear at the enemy throng and transfixed one running toward him.

[26] Both flying weapons may have been not only heated but set aflame with pitch or the like.

The man fell lifeless, protected by the shields of enemy who all hurled weapons at Pullo and left him no chance to retreat.

Pullo's shield was pierced, the point lodging in his belt. This pushed aside his scabbard and slowed his right hand reaching to draw his sword. The enemy surrounded him in his awkwardness. His rival Vorenus came to help him struggle. The whole crowd turned from Pullo right toward him, thinking Pullo run through by a spear. Vorenus went hand-to-hand with his sword, killed one and drove others back a little. Pushing on too eagerly, he fell and landed in a hollow. Now Pullo brought help to his surrounded rival, and both made it back inside the ramparts, with numerous kills and high acclaim. So fortune turned for each in their rivalry and competition. Each rival brought help and safety to the other, nor could you tell which outdid the other in courage.

45. As each day's siege fighting grew more serious, more dangerous—especially because many soldiers were wounded, leaving the matter to few defenders—so reports and messengers went oftener to Caesar. Some messengers were caught and tortured to death in sight of our soldiers. There was one Nervian named Verticus with us, of honorable birth, who had fled to Cicero when the siege began and shown him loyalty. He convinced a slave, promising him freedom and great rewards, to take a message to Caesar. He took it wrapped around a javelin and came, unsuspected, a Gaul among Gauls, all the way to Caesar. From him they learned of the danger to Cicero and the legion.

46. Caesar received the report late afternoon and immediately sent a messenger to the Bellovaci for quaestor Marcus Crassus, whose quarters were twenty-odd miles away. He ordered the legion to start at night and come quickly. Crassus left immediately with the messenger. He sent another to legate

Gaius Fabius, to bring a legion to Atrebates territory, where he knew he would have to go himself. He wrote Labienus to come with a legion to the Nervii, if it could be done without endangering the republic. He did not think he should wait for the rest of the army, which was a bit farther away. He brought about 400 cavalry from camps nearby.

47. Learning mid-morning from runners of Crassus' approach, he covered about eighteen miles that day. He put Crassus in command at Samarobriva and assigned him a legion, because he left there the army's baggage, native hostages, public documents, and all the grain collected there for surviving the winter. Fabius, as ordered, hardly hesitating, met him on the way with his legion. Labienus, hearing of Sabinus' death and slaughtered cohorts, with all the Treveri forces approaching, feared if he made a similar flight from camp he would not be able to sustain an enemy attack, especially from those heartened by recent victory. He wrote back to Caesar how dangerous it would be to bring his legion from quarters, wrote what had happened among the Eburones, and reported that all the horse and foot of the Treveri had set down a couple of miles from his camp.

48. Caesar approved his advice, even if it meant giving up on three legions and settling for two and still putting his one hope for common safety on speed. He came by long marches to the Nervii. There he learned from captives what was happening with Cicero and how dangerous things were. Then he convinced a Gallic cavalryman with a large bribe to take a message to Cicero. He sent it written in Greek characters,[27] so our

---

[27] Dio 40.9.3 says it was not only in Greek but in Caesar's private code, which we know of from Suet. Jul. 56.6 (a simple letter substitution or pixxiv wyfwxmxyxmsr, if you prefer); Polyaenus 8.23.6 gives a Greek text supposedly of the short note that doesn't in fact match what Caesar says here. The Gauls knew at least the Greek alphabet (see 6.14), so the code was still necessary.

plans would not be understood by the enemy if intercepted. If he could not reach Cicero, Caesar advised him to tie the message to a throwing spear's strap and throw it into the fort. In it he said he would arrive very soon with legions and encouraged him to maintain his old courage. The Gaul, fearing danger, threw the spear as ordered. By chance it stuck in a tower unnoticed by our men for two days and was seen on the third by a soldier, taken down, and brought to Cicero. He read it then recited it to the assembled troops, filling all with great happiness. Then the smoke of fires was seen from afar, erasing all doubt of the coming of our legions.

49. The Gauls, alerted by scouts, abandon siege and make for Caesar in full force: about 60,000 armed men.[28] Cicero took the chance to ask Vertico, mentioned above, for a Gaul to take a message to Caesar. He tells him to go cautiously and carefully. He writes in it that the enemy has left him and turned its whole force to Caesar. The letter was brought to Caesar around midnight. He alerts his men and encourages them to fight. Next day at dawn, he moves camp and goes three or so miles, spotting enemy forces across a valley and a stream. It was very dangerous to fight such a force on disadvantageous ground. Then, knowing Cicero was free of siege, he thought he could relax his speed, stopping to fortify camp in the most favorable position he could. Small as it was for a force of seven thousand with no baggage, still he shrinks it as much as possible with narrow lanes, thinking to make himself contemptible in the eye of the enemy. He sends meanwhile scouts in all directions to see where to cross the valley most easily.

50. Both sides held their positions that day, with a few cavalry skirmishes by the river. The Gauls were awaiting large

---

[28] He holds off 60,000 enemy with 7,000 of his own?

forces not yet arrived. Caesar was looking to see if he could pretend fear to lure the enemy to his position, across the valley, to fight in front of his camp. If he could not do this, he would scout the fords to cross valley and stream less dangerously. At dawn enemy cavalry approached camp and joined battle with ours. Caesar deliberately ordered our cavalry to withdraw and return to camp and for the camp to be fortified by a higher rampart on all sides and the gates barred, and to do this with much rushing about and appearance of fear.

51. Encouraged by all this, the enemy cross over their forces and form on uneven ground as our men come out from the rampart. They close and hurl spears into our fort from all sides. Sending around heralds they order this proclamation: Anyone, Gaul or Roman, who went over to them before the third hour could do so without danger; after that, no opportunity. They so disrespected us that when we blocked the gates with single rows of turf, seemingly unbreakable, some began to tear down the rampart bare-handed, while others were filling the ditch. Then Caesar burst out from every gate. Swift-rushing cavalry put the enemy to flight, so none could stand to fight at all. He killed a great many and stripped all of their weapons.

52. He hesitated to go farther, seeing woods and swamps between and no chance left to harm the enemy even slightly. On the same day, he reached Cicero with all his forces safe. The enemy's towers, shelters, and fortifications surprised him. When the legion formed up in ranks he saw not even one-tenth of them unwounded. From this he judged how dangerous it had been and how bravely done. He praised Cicero and the legion deservedly. He praised individually by name the centurions and tribunes whose great courage he learned from Cicero's account. He heard from prisoners the true fate of

Sabinus and Cotta. Next day he made a speech, recounting what had happened, consoling and heartening the soldiers. He said they should endure the disaster brought by the legate's fault and folly, because by the kindness of immortal gods and by their own courage, the loss was atoned for, leaving neither lasting joy for the enemy nor lasting pain for them.

53. News of Caesar's victory flew unbelievably fast through the Remi to Labienus. The camp of Cicero was more than fifty miles away and Caesar reached it after the ninth hour, but by midnight a roar went up at the camp gates, signifying the victory and congratulations from the Remi to Labienus. When this news reached the Treveri, Indutiomarus, who had decided to attack Labienus' camp the next day, fled by night and took his forces back to Treveri country. Caesar sent Fabius and his legion back to quarters, choosing to winter himself with three legions in three camps around Samarobriva. He decided to stay with the army all winter, because the uprisings in Gaul had been so considerable.

The harm done by Sabinus' death led almost every Gallic nation to think about war, sending messengers and legates back and forth to ascertain what might be done, how war might begin, and holding night gatherings in remote places. No part of the winter passed for Caesar without concern for some news of schemes and unrest among the Gauls. He was informed by Lucius Roscius, whom he had put in charge of the thirteenth legion, of a great gathering of forces among the Gallic nations called Armorican, massing to attack him no more than seven miles from his quarters—but departing on hearing news of Caesar's victory, a departure that looked like flight.

54. Caesar summoned leaders from every nation. Frightening some by revealing what he knew was going on and encouraging others, he kept most of Gaul to its obligations. But the

Senones, one of the strongest and most respected Gallic nations, decided to kill Cavarinus, whom Caesar had made king among them.[29] (His brother Moritasgus ruled when Caesar came to Gaul, his ancestors before that.) When Cavarinus realized this and fled, they chased him to their borders, driving him from home and kingdom, then sent representatives to Caesar to justify themselves. He ordered their whole senate to come to him, but they did not heed him. Having a few leaders ready to begin hostilities so impressed these barbarians and made such a change of intentions among all that there was almost no nation free of our suspicion except the Haedui and the Remi, whom Caesar had always specially honored—the Haedui for their ancient and constant loyalty to Rome, the Remi for their recent service in the Gallic war. I do not know if this is surprising, especially because—among many other reasons—a people thought to be more courageous than all others in war were extremely unhappy to have lost so much of their reputation by taking Roman orders.[30]

55. The Treveri and Indutiomarus let no time pass all this winter without sending ambassadors across the Rhine, recruiting allies, offering money, and saying that with most of our army slaughtered a much smaller part remained. But no German nation could be persuaded to cross the Rhine, saying that having experienced both the war of Ariovistus and the crossing of the Tencteri, they would not tempt fortune again. Failing this hope, Indutiomarus still gathered and trained forces, acquired horses from neighbors, and recruited exiles and criminals from throughout Gaul with promise of great rewards. He

[29] We will meet the ringleader of this insurgency, Acco, among the Senones in 6.4.

[30] Other reasons included death and taxes – Roman slaughter and invasion, tribute imposed, general devastation of the countryside. Instead he mentions only wounded pride. Note the first person singular verb here.

had thus gained such a reputation in Gaul that embassies hastened to him, publicly and privately seeking his influence and friendship.

56. Seeing their spontaneous approach—Senones and Carnutes driven by guilty conscience, Nervii and Aduatuci preparing war against the Romans—and knowing he would have no shortage of volunteer forces if he wanted to emerge from his country, he summoned an armed council. In Gallic custom, this is the start of war, where by a general law all armed youth assemble. The last to arrive is tortured horribly and killed in public view. In the assembly he declared Cingetorix, the other party's leader and his own son-in-law (whom we have before[31] seen staying loyally with Caesar), to be a public enemy and confiscated his property. This done, in the assembly he reports that on invitation of the Senones, Carnutes, and many other Gallic nations, he would march that way through Remi territory and lay waste to the land after first attacking Labienus' camp. He orders what he wants done.

57. Labienus, keeping to a camp well fortified by nature and effort, was not afraid for himself and his legion; he was thinking how not to miss any chance for success. When he hears of Indutiomarus' speech in council from Cingetorix and his family, he sends messengers to neighboring nations and summons cavalry from all sides, giving them a date to assemble. Meanwhile, Indutiomarus roamed near his camp almost daily with all his cavalry, partly to learn the layout of the camp, partly to parley or to intimidate. Most of his cavalry threw spears across the rampart. Labienus kept his men inside the fort and did what he could to make himself seem fearful.

[31] 5.3.

58. Every day Indutiomarus approached the camp more defiantly, so one night Labienus brought the cavalry he had summoned from nearby nations inside and kept all his forces inside the guarded camp so there was no way this could be reported or disclosed to the Treveri. Following daily habit, Indutiomarus approached camp and spent most of the day there, his cavalry throwing spears and challenging ours to fight with highly insulting language.

No answer from our men until they are seen dispersing and scattering at evening. Suddenly Labienus sends out all his cavalry through two gates. He strictly commands and orders that when they drive the terrified enemy to flee (he accurately foresaw what would happen) they should all make for Indutiomarus alone and wound no one else until they see him killed. He didn't want him to escape by gaining time while we hung back with the others. He offers the killers great rewards and sends infantry to support the cavalry. Fortune approves his plan; when all pursue him, Indutiomarus is trapped and killed at the ford of the river. His head is brought back to camp. The returning cavalry chase and kill whoever they can. At this news, all the Eburones and Nervii forces that had gathered go away and Caesar had a somewhat more peaceful Gaul afterwards.

SIXTH COMMENTARY

53 BCE

If we are right to believe that Caesar wrote each commentary in the winter months following the conclusion of that year's campaigns, we then conclude that he wrote the fifth and sixth commentaries together late in 53 and released them to Roman readers together. There are mild stylistic patterns that make this argument plausible, but certainty remains elusive. If Suetonius is right, it was a shaggy and unkempt Caesar who greeted the year 53. After the disastrous loss of Sabinus and his men, Caesar left his hair and beard to grow until he had taken vengeance. By summer 53, he will presumably have had his shave and a haircut, two bits of grooming, restored.

Quite apart from the events of the year at home and with the army, the commentary on the year 53 is remarkable for its extensive ethnographic description of Gauls and Germans and their ways of life. The Gallic section is all true, mostly, except for some stretchers (as Huck Finn would say) and one quite large gap. He describes the warrior culture and goes at some length into stories about the druids, but the usual ancient descriptions of Gaul include as well a class of bards, the singers of songs and tellers of tales. Caesar is writing to illuminate and impress, not to give here or anywhere a comprehensive factual record. (One scholar suggests that his knowledge is overdetermined by his familiarity with the Haedui.) The patronizing ethnographic tone has the effect of firmly distancing the Gauls from the Romans, not merely as "other" but as fundamentally different in kind, as living in a very different world from the Romans. When he comes to the Germans, he begins unreliably and veers off into sheer fantasy by the time he is done.

The year began with a delicate dance as Caesar recruited new soldiers to fill the gaps from the disastrous losses late in the previous year. Pompey himself was still in the vicinity of Rome, seeking to overshadow ordinary politics—"for the republic's sake" as Caesar puts it in his introduction to this year. That phrase is a bit of a stretcher, for Pompey held an office and title (proconsul of Spain) that at least required him to remain outside the city *pomerium* and should have sent him about his business to his province. (He let his legates in the field look after things.) His pious pretext was that he was needed to supervise the grain supply at Rome.

The narrative of this commentary is the slackest and least interesting of Caesar's seven. He mounts a successful raid on the Nervii, punishment for last year's treachery, and yields a great haul of captured men and cattle, which he then hands over generously to his soldiers. Moving west, based now out of Paris rather than Amiens, he attacks the Senones, then returns northeast to harass again the Eburones and Treveri. Labienus seems always to be in his element in these northeastern frontier territories and had good success with the Treveri. Impatient with the constant need to fight, Caesar makes a particular point of hounding the Eburones to the Rhine and beyond. Though their leader Ambiorix escapes, the Eburones themselves cease to play any part in Gallic affairs afterwards. It is safe to assume the slaughter was substantial.

At campaign's end this year, he summons a council of Gaul to Reims and there makes a show-trial execution of Acco, the Senones' rebel leader. Happy, perhaps a little smug, to have made his point so dramatically, Caesar could return to Italy for the first time in two years, confident he was leaving Gaul at peace.

While Caesar was on these campaigns, the collapse of normal politics continued at Rome. Undistinguished consuls, Domitius Corvinus and Messalla Rufus, were finally elected in July of the year. The streets were contested by the gangs of Clodius and of Annius Milo, who had come to the fore as tribune of the people in 57, earning the distinction in the years after of being the oligarch's thug of choice, leading gangs of slaves and hirelings in the street fighting that grew worse each year. Later in 53, he was a candidate for consul, but once again elections could not be held. His street-fighting main rival Clodius was a candidate for praetor in the same debacle.

With Caesar in further Gaul for two full years and Crassus on his expedition to Parthia, Pompey had the upper hand in Rome if anyone did, but the atmosphere inside the senate was no less poisonous than on the streets. The younger Cato, never to emerge as a power in his own right, was yet a force for obstruction and aggravation of quarrels during the electoral deadlocks of these years.

And then in June, the earth moved under Pompey's feet. Crassus died in Parthia.

Crassus doubtless thought himself the new Alexander, but when faced with Parthian archers, his imagination failed him. He expected the Parthians to run out of arrows, but they did not. He was heavily defeated on the battle field at Carrhae (modern Harran, on the Turkish/Syrian border 1,500 miles east of Rome). His son Publius, who had fought well as a legate of Caesar's in Gaul, died in the battle himself.

After the battle, the two forces remained in edgy contact. Taking horse to go forward for a negotiation with the Parthians, Crassus was caught up in a clumsy scuffle that escalated into a brawl and left him dead and his forces leaderless. Cassius Dio says the Parthians poured molten gold into the corpse's mouth to symbolize his rapacity.

Where in 56 the Lucca meeting, reinforced by the marriage of Caesar's daughter to Pompey, had created a ruling trio with at least some checks and balances to keep them aligned, now constraints were slackened and Pompey and Caesar could eye each other at a distance with freshened ambitions. The poet Lucan a century later would say that the problem was that Caesar could not stand to have anyone rank ahead of him in Roman politics and Pompey could not stand to have anyone his equal. That's as good an explanation as any for what would now unfold, probably already inevitable in 53.

The year ended then with the generalissimos staking out their ambitions, the public offices empty, and the gangs of Milo and Clodius battling each other in the streets of Rome.

IN THE CONSULSHIP OF
DOMITIUS CORVINUS AND
MESSALLA RUFUS

1. Caesar had many reasons to expect a broader Gallic uprising and so ordered conscription conducted by legates Marcus Silanus, Gaius Antistius Reginus, and Titus Sextius.[1] Simultaneously he asks the proconsul Pompey, since he was still in command near the city for the republic's sake, to order the men he had, as consul, sworn in from Cisalpine Gaul to come to the standards and set out for Caesar. It was important for the future of Gallic opinion for Italy to appear to have such resources that, after any loss in war, strength would be made up and even enhanced in short order. Pompey granted this for the republic's sake and for friendship, so the draft was quickly completed with three legions—thus double the number of cohorts lost with Sabinus—enrolled and brought together. By his speed and the size of his forces, he taught the Gauls what the Roman people's wealth and discipline could do.

2. With Indutiomarus dead, as we reported, command is passed to his relatives by the Treveri. They go on wooing the Germans and promising money. Unable to prevail nearby, they solicit nations farther away. Persuading a few, they confirm the

---

[1] The troops were to be raised in Caesar's part of northern Italy, Cisalpine Gaul, to replace the losses of the preceding fall.

deal by swearing mutual oaths and offering them money in return for hostages. They connect with Ambiorix by treaty and alliance.

Caesar found this all out, seeing war prepared everywhere: the Nervii, Aduatuci, and Menapii and all the Germans this side of the Rhine were in arms, the Senones did not come when commanded and were sharing their plans with the Carnutes and other neighbors, and the Germans received from the Treveri frequent embassies wooing them. He thought he would soon have to consider war.

3. The winter not yet over, he collected the four nearest legions and marched to the Nervii. Before they could assemble or flee, he captured a great many cattle and men and assigned his soldiers the booty.[2] Ravaging their fields, he forced them to surrender and give hostages. With that quickly over, he returned the legions to quarters. Announcing as usual a Gallic council for early spring, when all had arrived except the Senones, Carnutes, and Treveri, he took it as a sign of the beginning of war and revolt and moved the council to Lutetia among the Parisii—seeming to put everything else aside.[3] But the Parisii lived near the Senones and had within living memory campaigned with them, but were thought now to be aloof from their plotting. Announcing the council's move from the tribunal, he left the same day for the Senones and reached them with long marches.

4. Acco, the leading plotter, having heard he was approaching, summons people to gather in the towns. Before they can accomplish this, the Roman arrival is reported. They have to

[2] When he is generous with captured spoils, he can mention it. When he keeps them for himself, not.

[3] The settlements of Gallic/Roman Lutetia were on and near the Île de la Cité of modern Paris.

abandon their plan and send legates to Caesar to plead. They approach him using as intermediaries the Haedui, a nation long loyal. On their urging, Caesar willingly forgives the Senones and accepts their excuse, thinking summer a time for war, not inquisition. Demanding a hundred hostages, he leaves them guarded by the Haedui. The Carnutes send representatives there, using the Remi, whose dependents they were, to plead for them: they receive the same answers. Caesar ends the council and orders up cavalry from the nations.

5. With this area of Gaul at peace, he applies himself heart and mind all to war with the Treveri and Ambiorix. He orders Cavarinus and the Senones cavalry to accompany him, to prevent revolt due to Cavarinus' hot temper or the hatred he had earned there. With all this settled, he took it for granted that Ambiorix would not face open battle, so he reviewed other plans. The Menapii were neighbors of the Eburones, protected by an unbroken line of swamps and woods: the only nation in Gaul never to send peace ambassadors to Caesar. He knew they were guest-friends with Ambiorix and that they had, through the Treveri, become friends with the Germans. He decided to remove these supporters before provoking Ambiorix to war, so he wouldn't in desperation either hide among the Menapii or join up with people across the Rhine. Adopting this plan, he sends all the army's baggage to Labienus among the Treveri, and two legions besides. He goes himself with five legions traveling light to the Menapii. They gather no forces and rely on nature for protection, fleeing into the woods and swamps and taking their possessions along.

6. Caesar divides his forces with legate Gaius Fabius and quaestor Marcus Crassus and they build bridges quickly and go in three groups, burning farmhouses and villages, seizing numerous cattle and men. Their hand forced, the Menapii

send him ambassadors to sue for peace. He accepts hostages and tells them they will be his enemies if they welcome either Ambiorix or his representatives to their land. With this settled, he leaves Commius of the Atrebates and some cavalry among the Menapii as guards. He himself sets out for the Treveri.

7. While Caesar is doing all this, the Treveri were gathering a huge infantry and cavalry force to approach Labienus, who was wintering in their territory with one legion. Only two days' march away, they learn the two legions sent by Caesar had arrived. Making camp nearly fifteen miles away, they decide to wait for German reinforcements.

Labienus hears the enemy plan and hopes their impulsiveness will give him the chance to fight. Leaving five cohorts to guard the baggage, he marches against the enemy with twenty-five cohorts and many cavalry, making camp with less than a mile between them. Between Labienus and the enemy was a river, steeply banked and hard to cross. He did not mean to cross nor did he expect the enemy to—their hope for reinforcements was increasing daily. He says straight out in council that since Germans are reported approaching he will not risk his own and his army's fortunes and so will move camp at dawn the next day. This is swiftly reported to the enemy—some of the many Gallic cavalry naturally favored their countrymen. Labienus summons his tribunes and centurions that night, tells them his plan, and orders them to move camp with more noise and hubbub than was Roman custom, the better to make the enemy suspect fear. Thus he makes departure look like flight. This report too is taken by scouts to the enemy before dawn—the camps were that close.

8. Scarcely had the rear guard left the fortifications when the Gauls were urging each other not to let the plunder they expected get away. With the Romans frightened, waiting for

German reinforcements would take too long. Their pride should not let them fail to attack such a small band, fleeing and weighed down, with their great forces. They did not shy from crossing the river and joining battle on uneven ground. Labienus expected as much, going forward steadily as if marching, to lure them across the river. Then he sent the baggage a little ahead and set it on a hill. "Soldiers, you have the chance you wanted: you have the enemy weighed down and on uneven ground. Show your officers here the courage you've often shown your general—imagine he is here watching you."

Then he orders standards to turn about and battle lines to be formed. Leaving a few cavalry squads to guard baggage, he sets the rest of them on the flanks. Quickly our men raise a shout and hurl spears against the enemy. When the enemy unexpectedly saw men they thought were fleeing turn standards and march against them, they could not withstand the assault and were thrown into flight at first encounter, making for nearby woods. Labienus pursued with cavalry, killing many, capturing more, accepting their surrender a few days later. The Germans coming to help saw the Treveri in flight and took themselves home. Indutiomarus' relatives, fomentors of revolt, went with them and abandoned their nation. Rule and command were handed to Cingetorix, whom we have shown was faithful from the beginning.

9. After arriving among the Treveri from the Menapii, Caesar decided to cross the Rhine for two reasons: first, because troops from there had been sent to the Treveri to fight him; second, so Ambiorix would not have a refuge there. So he began building a bridge a little above where he had crossed before. Knowing now how to proceed, the soldiers enthusiastically accomplish the work in a few days. Leaving a strong guard among the Treveri at the bridge, in case of any sudden

uprising, he brings his remaining forces and cavalry across. The Ubii, who had given hostages and surrendered before, send ambassadors to justify themselves to him, explaining they had sent no forces to the Treveri from their nation and betrayed no allegiance. They beg and beseech his forgiveness: a general hatred of Germans should not make the innocent pay penalties instead of the guilty. They promise more hostages if he wants them. Hearing them out, Caesar learns it was the Suebi who had sent troops; he accepts the apology of the Ubii and asks directions for approaching the Suebi.

10. A few days later he learns from the Ubii that the Suebi were gathering all their forces in one place and ordering nations under their authority to send infantry and cavalry. Knowing this, he looks to his grain supply and chooses a good place for camp. He tells the Ubii to take all their cattle and belongings from the countryside into towns, hoping a barbarous and ignorant people could be led by shortage of rations into fighting in unequal conditions. He orders numerous scouts out among the Suebi to learn what they are doing. They do as ordered and report in a few days later. All the Suebi with all their and their allies' gathered forces, after they heard reliable news of the Roman army, withdrew to the farthest end of their territory. A vast forest there called Bacenis reaches far into their country and is like a natural barrier protecting Cherusci and Suebi from each other's attacks and incursions. The Suebi had decided to await Roman arrival at the edge of this wood.

11. As we get to this point,[4] it seems appropriate to set out how Gaul and Germany live and how these nations differ from one another. In Gaul, in all the nations and cantons, even al-

---

[4] As he sets out to smite the German Suebi, his reader of yearly installments would not remember what he had said about them and their German neighbors at 4.1–4.

most in every home, there are factions, whose leaders are the
men they judge to have the greatest authority. All affairs and
plans come down to their choice and judgment. And so from
of old it appears to have been established that no commoner
should lack support against the powerful. No aristocrat allows
his people to be oppressed or cheated. If he does otherwise,
he has no authority among his own people. This state of affairs obtains in all Gaul, for all the nations are divided into the
two groups.

12. When Caesar came to Gaul, the Haedui led one faction,
the Sequani another.[5] Less strong, because the greatest influence had long belonged to the Haedui, who had many followers, the Sequani connected themselves with the Germans and
Ariovistus, winning them over with lavish expenditures and
promises. After several successful battles, where all the Haedui
nobles were killed, the Sequani moved so far ahead in power
that they brought most Haedui clients over to their side, took
the sons of princes as hostages, and made them swear openly
they would never conspire against the Sequani. They forcibly
occupied some neighboring territory and took leadership of all
Gaul. Out of necessity Diviciacus came to Rome to beg help
from the senate but went home without success. At Caesar's
coming things changed. Hostages were returned to the
Haedui, old clients came back and new were gotten for them
through Caesar, because those who joined their friends found
a better life and fairer regime. As they advanced again in influence and honor, the Sequani lost the leadership. The Remi
replaced them. Because they were thought to stand equally
high with Caesar, those who for old enmities would not join

[5] In 1.31 Caesar reported that the Haedui said the other faction was led by the
Arverni, followed by the Sequani, who together had invoked German support. In that
passage he told the story about Diviciacus repeated here with different emphasis.

the Haedui promised to be clients of the Remi, who looked after them carefully and so acquired sudden new influence. As things stood, the Haedui were by far the first nation, while the Remi held second rank of honor.

13. In all Gaul, two sorts of men stand out in rank and esteem. (For commoners are treated almost like slaves, venturing nothing on their own, being asked no advice. Many, oppressed by debt or huge levies or vengeful potentates, swear themselves into service to nobles who have all the rights over them that masters have with slaves.) One of these two sorts are the druids, the other the knights.

The former busy themselves with affairs of the gods, look after public and private sacrifices, and interpret religious laws. Many young men swarm to them for instruction, for they are highly honored. The druids rule on almost all public and private disputes and if there is a case of a crime committed, a murder done, or a suit about inheritance or property, they decide it and set rewards and penalties. If any individual or group does not stand for their ruling, they are banned from sacrifice—the most serious penalty they have. Those who are banned are counted as wicked and criminal and others all shun them, avoiding their approach and conversation to prevent any defilement. They have no legal standing and share in no office.

One man presides over all the druids, holding highest rank among them. On his death, either some distinguished survivor succeeds or, if there are several equal, they compete for the leadership by vote of the druids, but sometimes by force of arms. At a fixed season, they sit together at a sacred place in land of the Carnutes,[6] thought to be the center of all Gaul.

---

[6] Medieval and modern Chartres, ever a site of pilgrimage.

Here everyone with disputes from everywhere assembles and heeds their decrees and judgments. It's thought their craft was discovered in Britain and migrated to Gaul, and often even now men who want to learn it more precisely travel there for training.

14. Druids consistently abstain from warfare and do not pay tribute like the rest. Aroused by such rewards, many gather to them for training spontaneously, others are sent by relatives and family. There they are said to memorize a huge number of verses. Some remain in training twenty years. They think it wrong to write these things down, while in most other matters, both public and private records, they use Greek writing. They seem to do this for two reasons: because they did not want the teaching spread among the masses and did not want learners to trust in writing and pay less attention to memory. It is often the case for many that reliance on writing reduces attention to learning and memory. Above all they try to teach that souls do not die but pass from one person to another after death.[7] They think this specially inspires courage and disregard for fear of death. They debate and transmit to the young much more about the stars and their movements, the extent of the world and its lands, the origins of things, and the strength and power of the immortal gods.

15. The other class is the knights. When necessary and some war arises (which used to happen yearly before Caesar's coming, nations attacking other nations or repelling attacks), they all take part in war. The most fortunate in family and wealth have the most clients and slaves[8] about them. This is the only kind of power and influence they recognize.

---

[7] This version of metempsychosis may have come from Greek colonists and travelers.

[8] C. borrows here *ambactus*, a Celtic word for "slave"; exceedingly rare in Latin, he

16. The whole nation of Gauls is much devoted to rituals, so those who suffer serious illness or face battle and danger either sacrifice human victims or promise to do so and use the druids as ministers of these sacrifices. Unless human life is rendered for human life, they think the power of immortal gods cannot be appeased. They conduct sacrifices of this kind publicly. Some have immense artificial figures whose frames made of wicker they fill with living people. Set ablaze, the people die swallowed in flames. They think punishing those who are caught in theft or robbery or some other crime is pleasing to the immortal gods, but when the supply of criminals runs out, they lower themselves to punish even the innocent.

17. The god Mercury they worship most;[9] of him there are many images, him they claim as inventor of all the arts, him the guide of roads and journeys, and he they think has great influence over business and commerce. After him, Apollo and Mars and Jupiter and Minerva.[10] They think of them about what other nations do: Apollo banishes disease, Minerva teaches rudiments of working and making, Jupiter holds sway in the skies, Mars controls wars. To him, when they decide to wage war, they usually promise to offer what they seize in battle. When they prevail, they sacrifice captured animals and gather the rest of their plunder in one place. In many cities heaping mounds of these things can be seen, nor does anyone much dare to scorn religious practice and hide captured prop-

uses it here in a way that assumes it will be understood. Compare 3.22, "loyal men they call *soldurii*," marking that Gallic word as unfamiliar.

[9] Toutatis was his Gallic name, rather grander than wing-footed Roman Mercury.

[10] The first three were Belenus, Esus, and Taranis when they were at home, embodying the power of sun, war, and thunder, but Belenus ranked after the other two. Which Gallic god is meant by "Minerva" is not clear.

erty for themselves or steal from the mounds.[11] For that crime the worst punishment, with torture, has been established.

18. Gauls all claim to descend from father Dis,[12] saying this is revealed by druids. So they measure time by the number not of days but nights. Birthdays and first days of months and years are observed with night and the following day. In other customs of life they most differ from others in this, that they do not allow their sons to approach them in public until they are grown enough to take on military service. They think it shameful for a son of boy's age to be seen in public by his father.

19. Whatever money husbands get as bride-gift from their wives, they add to the bride-gift a similar amount appraised from their own property. A single accounting is kept of all this money and profits are saved. The surviving spouse receives both parts with the accumulated profits. Men have power of life and death over wives, as over children. When a well-born paterfamilias dies, his relatives assemble and, if there is suspicion about the death, they interrogate wives as they would slaves. If they find something, they torture them with fire and rack, then kill them. Funerals, by Gallic standards, are magnificent and lavish. They add to the flames everything the living held dear, even animals. In recent memory, beloved slaves and clients were burned together after the regular funeral was over.

20. Nations thought better governed have it sanctioned by law that anyone hearing rumor or report about the state from neighbors should take it to a magistrate and not share with

[11] The hiding and stealing are wrong because they take for private use what should be offered and left to the gods.

[12] In their language, Cerunnos. Taking origin from a god of the underworld means coming up out of the ground and thus claiming an unshakable title to that stretch of earth.

anyone else, because impulsive and inexperienced men are often known to be frightened by false rumors, to be driven to rash conduct and decisions on highly important matters. Magistrates conceal what they think and share with the public what they judge useful. It is not allowed to speak of the state except in assembly.

21. German ways are very different. They have no druids to manage divine affairs nor are they keen on sacrifices. They count only gods they can see, gods whose riches plainly help them, Sun and Vulcan and Moon. They have not even a rumor of the rest of the gods. Life is all in hunting and military exercise.[13] From childhood they train for labor and hardship. They have great praise among them for those who remain longest without sexual experience. Some think this makes for height, muscle, and strength. Indeed to have had knowledge of a woman before age twenty they think very shameful, and there is no hiding it, inasmuch as they bathe together indiscriminately in rivers and use skins or small covers of reindeer hide, leaving most of the body naked.[14]

22. They are not keen on farming.[15] Most of their food consists of milk, cheese, and meat. No one has a fixed amount of land or his own boundaries. Each year magistrates and leaders assign each family and assembled community as much land as they think best (and where) and require relocation the next year. They offer many reasons for this: to avoid men giving up war for agriculture out of habit; to avoid people trying to extend

[13] Compare Tacitus *Germania* 15 a century and a half later: "They don't do much hunting and prefer to spend their time at leisure, given to eating and sleeping." Tacitus *Germ.* 20 does agree with Caesar about their deferral of sexual initiation.

[14] Commentators enjoy this passage, particularly the questions it raises of bathing suit design and visual techniques for detecting sexual experience.

[15] This passage resembles what he says of the German Suebi in 4.1, but there he had them farming enthusiastically.

landholdings far and wide with the powerful driving the weak from their land; to keep people from building with more care than just to avoid cold and heat; to prevent the rise of greed for money, which begets factions and quarrels;[16] to keep the commoners tranquil when they see their wealth equal to that of the most powerful.

23. The greatest boast of their nations is to have desert and wasteland around them as far as possible. This they think proof of courage: neighbors driven from lands and withdrawing, no one daring to settle nearby. They think they will be safer with fear of sudden invasion removed. When a nation either defends itself in war or wages it, magistrates are selected to be in charge of the war with power of life and death. There is no common magistrate in peacetime, but leaders of regions and cantons give judgments and placate quarrels among their people. Brigandage beyond the boundary of a nation is not disreputable, indeed they commend it as training the young and suppressing laziness. And when one of the first men says in council that he will lead and that willing followers should declare themselves, men who like the cause and the man rise to promise support and are praised by the assembly. Those unwilling to follow are thought deserters and traitors and are no longer trusted in anything. Harming a guest they think wrong. Visitors of whatever purpose they keep from harm and regard as inviolable; the homes of all are open to them and food is shared.

24. And there was a time when Gauls outdid Germans in courage, waging war against them and sending colonies across the Rhine because they had too many people and too little land. The most fertile places in Germany are around the Hercynian

---

[16] Tacitus (*Germ.* 5) thinks the Germans all but immune to the use and lure of money, except a few peoples along the Rhine.

wood, which I see was known by rumor to Eratosthenes and some Greeks (who called it Orcynian).[17] The Volcae Tectosages claimed this land and settled there, continuing there till now with a high reputation for justice and warrior glory. They live with the same poverty, neediness, and endurance as Germans, using the same food and clothing. Proximity to our provinces and familiarity with seaborne imports bring the Gauls many things to use and keep, so they gradually grew accustomed to defeat, losing many battles and not even claiming to be the Germans' equals in courage now.

25. This Hercynian wood (mentioned above) extends nine days' journey across for someone traveling light. It cannot be otherwise delimited and they do not know how to measure distance. It arises in the land of the Helvetians, Nemetes, and Rauraci and stretches straight along the Danube to the land of Dacians and Anartes. Here it bends leftwards away from river lands and touches on the boundaries of many nations in its vastness. No one from this part of Germany claims to have reached the wood's farthest point, even traveling sixty days, or heard where it begins. We know many kinds of beasts are native there that are not seen elsewhere. Here are the ones most unlike others and worth recording in memory:

26. There is an ox shaped like a deer, with one horn emerging between his ears from mid-forehead, taller and straighter than horns we know; at the top, it spreads wide like a hand's palm or a tree's branches. Male and female are alike, with horns the same size and shape.[18]

---

[17] Aristotle had heard of the place as one where rivers ran north. For C., the tract begins with the modern Black Forest and extends east beyond his ken.

[18] This is likely the reindeer, which ranged much farther south in antiquity than today.

27. There are ones called elk, in shape and mottled pelt like a goat, but a little larger, bereft of horns, and their legs have no joints or ligaments. They do not lie down to rest and if they chance to be struck and fall they cannot rise or lift themselves up. Trees are their beds: they lean against them and recline slightly to take their rest. When hunters learn from their hoof-prints where they usually go to rest, they tear up all the trees there by the roots or hack into them enough to leave them standing in appearance only. When the elk lean on them out of habit, they bear down on them with their weight and collapse along with them.

28. A third species are called *uri*.[19] They are a little smaller than elephants with the appearance and color and shape of bulls. They are very strong and very fast and unsparing of any man or beast they see. These they carefully snare in pits and kill them. By this work young men harden themselves and practice this kind of hunting. The ones who kill the most, showing the horns publicly as evidence, win great praise. Not even when caught very small can they learn to be with men and become tame. The size and shape and appearance of their horns differ greatly from those of our cattle; these are assiduously sought out, tipped with silver, and used as cups in the most lavish feasts.

29. When Caesar learned from Ubian scouts that the Suebi had retreated to the forest, he feared grain shortage because, as we said, Germans are not keen on farming. He decided to go no farther. Not to relieve the barbarians entirely from fearing his return and to slow their reinforcements, he drew back his troops and had the end of the bridge touching the Ubian

[19] Apparently a wild ox, but the word appears here first and is rare after.

shore cut back some 200 feet and built a four-story tower at its end. He left a guard of twelve cohorts to watch the bridge and strengthened the place with heavy fortifications. He put young Gaius Volcatius Tullus in charge of the guard and the place. When grain began to ripen, he left to fight Ambiorix, by way of the Ardennes forest, largest in Gaul, reaching from the Rhine and the Treveri to the Nervii, some five hundred miles broad. He sends Lucius Minucius Basilus and all the cavalry ahead, for what might be accomplished by speedy travel and timeliness. He warns them to prohibit making fires in camp to avoid any sign at a distance of their coming. He says he will follow quickly.

30. Basilus does as ordered. Completing the journey quickly with no one expecting him, he surprises many in the fields unawares. With information from them he makes for Ambiorix himself, to where he was said to be with only a few cavalry. Fortune is powerful in war as in all things. It was a great accident that Basilus fell on Ambiorix unawares and unready, arriving in sight of all ahead of any rumor or messenger. It was also great luck for Ambiorix to escape death when all his military equipment was seized, his carts and horses captured. It happened because his farmhouse was surrounded with forest—as Gallic homes usually are (they look for nearby woods and rivers to ward off the heat) and in a tight spot his comrades and attendants held off our cavalry attack a little while. They fought while some of his men got him on horse and so the woods concealed his flight. Fortune brought him into danger and helped him escape it.

31. It is unclear whether Ambiorix had deliberately not gathered his forces, thinking he would not have to fight, or was caught short by time and the sudden arrival of our cavalry, while thinking the rest of our army was following after. But

certainly he sent messengers through the country ordering all to fend for themselves. Some fled into the Ardennes, some into neighboring wetlands. Closer to the ocean they hid themselves on islands the tide predictably forms. Many left their lands and chanced lives and property among strangers. Catuvolcus, king of half of the Eburones, who had plotted with Ambiorix, now weary with age and unable to bear the effort of war or flight, swore every curse at Ambiorix for initiating the scheme and ended his life by eating yew berries, which abound in Gaul and Germany.

32. The Segni and Condrusi, counted among the German population but living between Eburones and Treveri, sent legates to Caesar to ask he not count them as enemies or judge all Germans this side of the Rhine to be of one purpose. They had no thought of war, sending no forces to Ambiorix. Caesar investigated by questioning prisoners and ordered they give back to him any Eburones who had fled to them. If they did that, he said he would not cross their borders. Dividing his forces three ways, he collected the baggage of all legions at Aduatuca—that's the name of a fort nearly in the midst of the Eburones, where Sabinus and Cotta had settled for winter.[20] He liked the spot for various reasons, now especially because the fortifications of last year were still standing—thus reducing work for the soldiers. He left the fourteenth legion, one of the three recently conscripted in Italy, to guard the baggage. He put Quintus Tullius Cicero in charge of legion and camp and gave him two hundred cavalry.

33. Dividing the army, he ordered Titus Labienus and three legions to go toward the ocean near the Menapii. Gaius Trebonius with an equal number of legions he sent to lay waste to

[20] Likely modern Tongeren, Belgium.

land near the Aduatuci. He decided to go with the three remaining to the Sambre river, where it flows into the Meuse,[21]
and to the farthest Ardennes, where he heard Ambiorix had
gone with a few cavalry. On leaving, he promises to return in
a week, when he knew grain was due the legion left for guard
duty. He told Labienus and Trebonius to return by the same
day if they could do it without harm to the republic. They
would take counsel together again, discuss enemy plans, and
so begin war again.

34. As we said, there was no fixed force, no town, no garrison defending itself with arms, but a multitude scattered
everywhere. Wherever a hidden valley or wooded spot or boggy
wetland offered someone hope of protection or safety, he
camped. These places were known locally and the matter required great care, not so much to protect the whole army (no
danger could befall when the others were all scattered and
frightened), but to save individual soldiers. Eagerness for booty
took some too far away and the woods with hidden and unsure
paths kept groups from entering. If Caesar wanted the business finished and this nation of criminal men killed, he needed
to send out more troops and distribute them. If he wanted to
keep companies by their standards, as the set plan and custom
of the Roman army demanded, the setting protected the barbarians, who did not lack bravery in laying secret ambushes
and surrounding scattered individuals. In difficulties like
these, whatever could be foreseen was foreseen. Better to leave
some damage undone, even if everyone was on fire for re-
venge, than suffer injury and lose soldiers. Caesar sent mes-

---

[21] A good example of C.'s inaccuracies; the Sambre does not flow into the Meuse
and probably never did. Writing a few months later back in winter quarters, Caesar
could err.

sengers to neighboring peoples, inviting them with hope of
booty to plunder the Eburones. Better to risk a Gaul's life in
the woods than a legionary soldier's; better that the nation's
history and name should be eradicated by an overwhelming
force for such a crime. A great number gathered quickly from
all sides.

35. While this was going on all over Eburones territory, the
seventh day approached, which Caesar had set for returning
to the baggage and the legion. Here one sees how much fortune counts in war and what accidents it brings. The enemy,
scattered and frightened, as we showed, was no force to offer
the slightest cause for fear. Rumor reached the Germans across
the Rhine that the Eburones were being plundered and everyone was invited to share. The Sugambri, closest to the Rhine,
welcoming the Tencteri and Usipetes in flight as we said—
raise two thousand cavalry and cross the Rhine in ships and
boats twenty-five miles downriver from the bridge Caesar built
and the guard he left. They reach the Eburones' borders, collect
many who had scattered in flight, and seize a great many cattle—for which barbarians are very greedy. Encouraged by booty
they go farther: swamps and forests do not slow down men
born for war and banditry. They ask prisoners where Caesar is.
They find he has gone on farther and his whole army has left.
Then one of the prisoners says: "Why do you chase wretched
and meager spoils when you could be richly fortunate? In three
hours you can reach Aduatuca. There the Roman army collected all their possessions. There is so little guard they cannot
even man the wall and no one ventures out of the fort." Offered
this hope, the Germans leave hidden the booty they had gotten
and make for Aduatuca following the guide from whom they
had learned this.

36. Cicero,[22] who all these days had most carefully kept soldiers in camp at Caesar's behest, allowing not even a servant to leave the fort, on the seventh day, hearing Caesar had gone farther away and no rumor of his return, was unsure Caesar would observe the promised number of days. He was influenced at the same time by some saying his patience meant they were effectively besieged. He had no reason to fear misfortune within three miles of camp with nine whole legions and a huge cavalry on campaign and with the enemy scattered and almost destroyed, so he sent five cohorts foraging in nearby fields, with only one hill between them and camp. A fair number of legionaries were invalids in camp; some 300 of them had recovered enough during these days and were sent out under one standard. A great many servants and a large herd of beasts of burden remaining in camp were allowed to go along with them.

37. Just then by chance German cavalry ride in and without breaking stride try to break into camp through the back gate. Concealed by woods on that side they were not seen before reaching camp. Peddlers camping by the rampart did not have time to retreat. Our men are surprised and confused by the event. The cohort on duty barely withstand the first attack. The enemy pour around the sides looking for entry. Our men hold the gates with difficulty. Other approaches are protected by the lay of land and the fortifications. The whole camp is in fear, everybody asking each other the cause of the uproar. They cannot see where to take the standards or where to form up. Some say the camp was already taken, others that the general and

[22] In a surviving fragment of a letter to the elder Cicero back at Rome, C. says that it was reckless of Quintus to stay shut in, rather blaming him for what happened. But in book 5, he had praised Quintus, and so here he goes light on him and the rebuke for him soon at 6.42 is very gentle: C. still needed the support of the elder Cicero back at Rome.

army were destroyed and the barbarians come as victors. Many imagine new superstitions about the place and think about the disaster of Cotta and Sabinus, who fell in the same fort. All are so panicked that the barbarians are convinced, as they had heard from a prisoner, that there was no guard inside. They try to break in and they encourage each other not to let such a prize slip from their hands.

38. Publius Sextius Baculus, a first centurion under Caesar whom we mentioned in earlier battles,[23] had been left behind sick with the garrison and now five days without food. Losing hope for his own and everyone's safety, he leaves his tent unarmed. He sees the enemy threatening and everything in crisis. He snatches arms from bystanders and takes a stand at the gate. The centurions of the cohort on duty follow him. For a little while they keep up the fight. Sextius faints with serious new wounds; dragged back by hand, he was barely rescued. In this respite, the others recover confidence enough to dare stand on the walls and put up a show of resistance.

39. Foraging done, meanwhile, our soldiers hear shouting. Cavalry rush forward; they realize how dangerous things are. But here is no fortification to welcome them in their fear. New conscripts without military experience[24] turn to the military tribune and the centurions, awaiting instruction. No one is so brave as not to be frightened by this news. Seeing standards at a distance, the barbarians leave off attacking, thinking at first it's the return of the legions that captives said had gone farther; but then, sneering at the small numbers, they attacked from all sides.

40. The servants run to higher ground nearby. Quickly dislodged, they rush among the standards and companies—

---

[23] 2.25, 3.5.
[24] These had been in Caesar's army about five months.

frightening fearful soldiers the more. Some think they can break out quickly if they form a wedge, with camp so close. Even if some were surrounded and fell, surely the rest can be saved. Others think they can make a stand on high ground and all suffer the same fate. The veteran soldiers, the ones coming out together behind a standard, did not like this. Encouraging each other under command of Gaius Trebonius, the Roman knight who was in charge of them, they break through the enemy's middle ranks and make it all into camp, safe to a man. The servants and cavalry, following them in the same rush, are saved by their courage. But those who took a stand on high ground, having no military experience, could neither stay with the plan they had chosen (to protect themselves on higher ground) nor imitate the speed and force they had seen save the others. Trying for camp, they came down to difficult ground. Some centurions promoted for courage from lower ranks in other legions to higher ranks in this, wanting not to lose the glory they had already won, fell fighting heroically. Their courage drove back the enemy. Some soldiers, safe beyond all hope, come untouched to camp, but some are surrounded by barbarians and perish.

41. The Germans gave up hope of storming camp, seeing our men now inside the fortifications. They retreated across the Rhine with the booty they had hidden in the woods. Even after the enemy left, there was such terror that when Gaius Volusenus, who had been sent out with cavalry, arrived at camp that night, he could not make them believe Caesar was nearby with his army intact. Fear had so seized minds that they said half-crazed that the cavalry had returned in flight after all the rest were destroyed. The Germans would never have attacked if the army were safe. Caesar's coming removed this fear.

42. Returning and knowing how war goes, Caesar complained only that cohorts had been sent out from their garrison posts, for nothing should have been left to the least chance. He saw fortune's power displayed in the sudden arrival of the enemy, much more again in turning the barbarians away at almost the rampart itself and the camp gates. The most astonishing thing was that the Germans, who had crossed the Rhine to plunder the land of Ambiorix, had detoured to the Roman camp and done Ambiorix a most desirable service.

43. Caesar sets out again to harass the enemy, collecting a large force from neighboring states and sending them in all directions. Every town and farmhouse in sight was aflame. Livestock were being slaughtered, booty gathered from everywhere. Grain was not only consumed by so many beasts and men, but was pounded flat by the season and the rains. If anyone hid for now, when the army left they would perish from want of everything. With cavalry out in all directions, it often came to the point that captives would look about for the fleeing Ambiorix, saying he was almost still in sight. Hoping to pursue him and making vast efforts, thinking they would win the highest praise from Caesar, they almost outdid nature, seeming always just a little away from the greatest good fortune. And yet Ambiorix took himself off through hiding places and thickets, making for other regions and places under cover of night, with no protection more than four horsemen, the only people to whom he would trust his life.

44. The countryside was devastated; Caesar took his army, with loss of two cohorts, to Durocortorum[25] among the Remi, summoning there a council for Gaul. He conducted an inves-

[25] Reims.

tigation of the conspiracy of the Senones and Carnutes and imposed our ancestors' punishment[26] on Acco, under severe sentence for leading that conspiracy. Some fled, fearing trial. Forbidding them fire and water, he set two legions facing the Treveri, two among the Lingones, and the six remaining among the Senones at Sens for winter quarters. Providing grain for the army, he left for Italy, as he had intended, to hear cases.

[26] Shackling, stripping, whipping, and beheading with an axe.

SEVENTH COMMENTARY

52 BCE

The unconscionable, flamboyant, ambitious, outrageous Publius Clodius was killed in a stupid fight on the Appian Way on January 18. He was making a visit to the old Roman town of Aricia south of Rome on the Appian Way a couple of miles past the site of the modern papal summer home at Castel Gandolfo, in territory that had been Latin before there was a Rome. He had thirty armed slaves with him, as who would not if you were the most reviled man in Rome in a lawless time? About halfway back to Rome, as chance had it, he met his great rival Milo heading in the other direction to Lanuvium (a bit farther down the Appian Way), therefore also with a retinue, some of whom were professional gladiators. (He was also accompanied by his wife, a daughter of the dictator Sulla.) Like Jets and Sharks, the two groups passed each other, exchanging words and gestures of defiance and contempt. As they had almost passed each other, a fight broke out and Clodius was wounded by a javelin throw from the other side. His gang was routed from the scene and his fate was entirely in Milo's hands.

Milo decided his enemy was better off dead and so Clodius was killed in cold blood. Milo tried to slip away with his gang and dumped the body in the road for a passing senator to find, but there was no question who had done the deed. Clodius' funeral the next day then turned into the sort of incident that civil wars can spring from. His widow first had his body exposed to public view in the Forum on the *rostra*, the place where orators addressed citizens and mobs. Egged on from there by the widow and sympathetic tribunes, the funeral mob carried his body into the adjacent *curia*, the home of the senate, and set it up to be burned at the center of that hall. The fire flew up out of control and burned the entire venerable senate house to the ground. By nightfall that day, Rome had neither consuls (none had been elected during 53) nor a home for its senate.

On the day of the murder, Caesar arrived back in Ravenna to recruit additional forces and do his gubernatorial business. The Gauls were themselves well enough informed about events at Rome to draw the conclusion that the city's crisis would distract Caesar and likely keep him in Italy as long as possible. Some of them decided this was their opportunity for mounting revolt. The author of the revolt was an Arvernian noble named Vercingetorix, whom Caesar had once declared to be a friend. In the later winter months, there was restlessness, planning, and skirmishes designed to interfere with the Romans' food supply. Labienus as senior legate needed to stay close to quarters until Caesar could arrive.

The year was a long one because Caesar as *pontifex maximus* had ordered an intercalary month inserted between February and March to bring dates and seasons in line. Waiting on the season in Ravenna, Caesar launched negotiations with Pompey to sustain their relationship in view of the crisis and the death of Crassus. What if, he suggested, they struck a new marriage bargain? Caesar would divorce Calpurnia and marry a daughter of Pompey while Pompey would marry Octavia, the sister of the boy (age 10 by now) who would become the future Augustus. In this sequence of conversations, Pompey still offered to guarantee that Caesar could stand for election to the consulship of 48 during the year 49 without having to give up his army and return to Rome and the prospect of criminal prosecution. Cicero, visiting Ravenna at this moment, was instructed to make sure that his client Caelius, a conservative tribune, did not quash the proposal. In these circumstances, Caesar was relieved and ready to think about heading to Gaul. We are not sure when he actually set out, but a reference here in the seventh commentary to Pompey having affairs in hand has us looking close to the first of March, thus at the end of the intercalary month.

For at that point, Pompey had succeeded in having himself elected consul without colleague, on a motion from Bibulus, Caesar's ex-co-consul of 59. Rumors had suggested that he and Caesar might try to be elected together, but with affairs in Gaul deteriorating, Pompey was spared the crisis of having to reject that partnership. Consul without colleague was almost but not quite the same as dictator. Pompey held sole executive power, but as consul he still had to meet with and care for the actions of the senate, which a dictator could avoid. He had the support of conservative die-hards like Cato and Ahenobarbus, and Ahenobarbus agreed to prosecute Milo for Clodius' murder—with Cicero famously acting for the defense.

Pompey ended by rejecting the marriage proposals Caesar had been floating and instead married a daughter of Metellus Scipio, whom Pompey then arranged (in August) to have elected as second consul for the year. Metellus was well rewarded for his daughter and his complaisance.

The near collapse of government and urban peace at Rome formed the backdrop to the year's beginning in Gaul. When Caesar arrived, he found the most concerted resistance he had yet faced, now centered not in the northern reaches of Belgic Gaul, where he had been based the last several years, but in the heart of the landmass itself, with Vercingetorix the ringleader representing the powerful Arverni people whose name survives on their land, the modern Auvergne. We have heard much by now of the Haedui, their neighbors to the north, and in this year Caesar will have to think of how to pacify and control those two powerful peoples side by side in the center of the territory that was the focus of his Gallic ambitions.

On arrival in Gaul, Caesar fended off an attack on Narbo, well west of the Rhone in what was already the Roman province. This was probably meant as a feint and a distraction, to pull Caesar's attention away from central Gaul. He had recruited by then 22 cohorts, a bit more than two full legions to add to his strength. On arrival, he found the Cévennes mountains still covered in snow and Vercingetorix to the north raising troops and support. A sharp move to the north over the mountains succeeded in drawing Vercingetorix back to defend his home territory and a short series of important victories—not dramatized in the commentary on this year—put Caesar in a good position.

There follow three great battles in a year that could easily have seen Caesar defeated and dead. Avaricum, Gergovia, and Alesia extend in a zigzag from west to east, along the boundary between Roman power and Gallic resistance. Caesar won the first, lost the second, and performed a miracle at the third. His own narrative is the best account of what happened, even if it takes some close reading to see just how badly handled Gergovia was and how carefully Caesar presents the truth in a way least damaging to himself. The year saw great and uneven bloodshed: 40,000 massacred at Avaricum, Caesar losing most of a thousand at Gergovia (including 46 centurions), and then the culminating siege of Alesia with Caesar pinned between two circular walls: the one with which he penned the occupants of the city inside and the one he used to defend himself against other Gauls attacking him from further outside. Discipline and manpower and doubtless wealth played strong parts in making that victory possible.

No reader of Caesar ever fails to see vividly the person and personality of Vercingetorix, the great hero of the Gauls—as Caesar tells it. If Ali needed Frazier, then Caesar needed Vercingetorix (once he had survived victorious himself!) to show how great a general he had been. There are just traces and hints that the situation on the Gallic side was more complicated and collegial than Caesar lets on. For example, Vercingetorix seems never to have been in actual command of any of his battles and was never at risk of being killed or captured in them. It was only when the whole revolt collapsed that he was forced to surrender to Caesar, who kept him imprisoned for six tumultuous years of civil war until Caesar could return to Rome for a grand and long-deferred triumph. Vercingetorix ended his life as a prize exhibit in the triumphal parade and was then summarily executed when he had no further contribution to make to Caesar's glory.

The Arverni had been the most culpable but also the most powerful of the rebels. The Haedui, who had played Caesar deftly in all the earlier years of the war, usually on his side, were also in revolt this year. But when the year and the war was done, Caesar was careful not to punish those peoples harshly. He needed them for Rome's future in Gaul and he did for them what the allies did not do after World War I for Germany. He made them live and thrive and find it easier to accept subjection than to continue in thoughts of rebellion. We see very little of how Caesar managed this, but it may be the most important single thing he did in Gaul.

Back at Rome as the year progressed, Caesar could not have been entirely at ease about Pompey's positions. The collapse of his marriage arrangement was one sign, the disposition of the consulship another, and then there was vacillation and signs of betrayal on the question of how Caesar might return to the consulship. As long as he was away from the city, his enemies and rivals could hold back their full support, to keep him alert and attentive.

Caesar reacted by welcoming into his retinue refugees from the purges of this year at Rome. Milo was condemned to exile in April and left the city, but a series of Clodius' hangers-on were also condemned at the hands of Cato and Ahenobarbus and they fled the city for Gaul and Caesar's welcome. Caesar also made sure to intervene in the elections for the tribunate back at Rome, to be sure that in 51, 50, and 49 there would always be at least one loyal follower with the power to veto anti-Caesarean acts. This precaution was shown to be necessary when the consular elections saw Cato defeated (good news for Caesar), but the successful candidate Marcellus was outspokenly hostile and would do all he could to thwart Caesar's plans.

But Caesar succeeded. The defeat of Vercingetorix won him a thanksgiving of twenty days and the chance to stay on in Gaul a while longer. From now until the great crisis of 50/49, Caesar stayed north of the Alps, wintering this year at least at Haeduan Bibracte. He would come back to Italy when there was a Rubicon to think of crossing, late in 50.

IN THE CONSULSHIP
OF POMPEY

1. Gaul was quiet. Caesar proceeded to Italy, as planned, to hear cases. There he learns of Clodius' murder and hears of the senate's decree that the youth of Italy should take the oath;[1] he decides to hold a draft across the whole province. This news passes swiftly to Transalpine Gaul. Gauls add to it and make up stories as opportunity suggests, that Caesar is detained by unrest at Rome and cannot rejoin the army while such disturbances last. Seizing this opportunity, people already unhappy to be subject to the Roman people's rule begin openly, daringly to make plans for war. Gallic leaders summon meetings in woods and wild places, complaining about the death of Acco and observing that the same could happen to them. They bemoan the common lot of Gaul. With every promise and bribe they challenge men to begin war and liberate Gaul, risking their necks.

They say the first consideration, before their secret plotting becomes known, is to keep Caesar from the army. Easy to do, because legions would not dare leave winter quarters without the general nor would the general travel without guards to the legions. In all, better to be killed in battle than fail to regain the warrior's glory and the liberty handed down by their ancestors.

---

[1] Clodius was killed Jan. 18, 52 BCE and the decree passed affecting the youth (age 17–46) a day or so later.

2. With all this in the air, the Carnutes say they will shrink from no danger for the common good and promise to be the first to initiate hostilities. Since for now they cannot (to avoid word getting out) take the precaution of hostages, they ask all to swear and sanction before their military standards (that is how their most solemn ceremonies are conducted) that the Carnutes will not be abandoned by the others once war begins. All praise the Carnutes, with everyone present swearing the oath, and they leave the assembly with an agreed date for action.

3. When the day arrives, the Carnutes, led by Cotuatus and Conconnetodumnus, desperate characters, swarm on signal to Cenabum,[2] slaughtering and plundering the Roman citizens gathered there to do business, including Gaius Fufius Cita, a respectable Roman knight charged by Caesar with acquiring grain. The news reaches all Gallic cities swiftly, for whenever something important or remarkable happens, they shout it through fields and regions, others taking it up in turn and sending along to nearest neighbors—as then happened. What occurred at sunrise in Cenabum was heard of among the Arverni by the end of the first watch,[3] some hundred and fifty miles away.

4. And there likewise was Vercingetorix, Celtillus' son, an Arvernian, a youth of immense influence, whose father had dominated Gaul and been killed by his own people for seeking to be king. Vercingetorix gathers his dependents and fires them up. When his plans are known, the city is in arms. He is opposed by his uncle Gobannitio and other princes opposed to tempting fate. He is driven from the town of Gergovia but persists, enlisting needy and ruined men in the countryside. Gathering this band, he wins over everyone from his nation

[2] Orléans.
[3] About twelve hours later.

he chances to meet. He encourages them to take arms for their common liberty. With a huge force now, he drives from the city the opponents by whom he was banished just before. He is acclaimed king by his people. He sends embassies in all directions, adjuring loyalty.

He quickly reels in the Senones, Parisii, Pictones, Cadurci, Turoni, Aulerci, Lemovices, Andes, and all the rest along the ocean coast. All agree to yield command to him. Offered power, he orders all these to give hostages, orders that a specific number of soldiers be brought at once, and states how many weapons each city should prepare at home and by when. He is particularly attentive to cavalry. With his attention to detail he combines great severity of command, coercing the reluctant with heavy punishment. Any serious offence he punishes with death by fire and torture; for lesser matters, he cuts off ears or gouges out eyes, sending victims home as an example for others, terrifying others by the extent of their penalty.

5. These punishments quickly raise an army. He sends the Cadurcan Lucterius, a hugely daring man, to the Ruteni with some troops while he himself makes for the Bituriges. On his arrival, the Bituriges send legates to the Haedui, to whom they were pledged, asking help the better to resist enemy forces. The Haedui, advised by the legates Caesar had left with his army, send cavalry and infantry forces to support the Bituriges. When they reach the Loire, separating Bituriges from Haedui, they linger a few days, not daring to cross the river, and go home, telling our legates they returned fearing treachery from the Bituriges, whose plan they had learned. If they had crossed the river, the Bituriges from one side and Arverni from the other would surround them. Whether they did this for the reason they gave the legates or out of treachery, we cannot say

for certain, for nothing is clear. On their retreat, the Bituriges immediately join the Arverni.

6. Hearing this report in Italy, Caesar left for Transalpine Gaul, knowing city affairs had reached a more settled state through the courage of Pompey. When he arrived, he had difficulty knowing how to reach the army.[4] If he summoned the legions to the province, he knew they would have to fight on the way without him. If he made for the army, he saw he could not trust his own safety just then even to the peoples who were quiet.

7. Meanwhile, Lucterius the Cadurcan who had been sent to the Ruteni wins them for the Arverni. Going on among the Nitiobriges and Gabali, he receives hostages from both, gathers a large army, and seeks to break into the province toward Narbonne. At this report, Caesar put marching to Narbonne ahead of all other plans. Arriving, he encourages the fearful, sets garrisons among the Ruteni (in the province), the Volcae Arecomici, the Tolosates, and around Narbonne, in the areas closest to the enemy. He orders some of his forces from the province and the recruits he had brought from Italy to assemble among the Helvii, who border the Arverni.

8. With things settled (Lucterius was stopped and pushed back because he thought it dangerous to pass between the garrisons), Caesar makes for the Helvii. Even though the Cévennes, separating Arverni from Helvii, blocked the way with deep snow during the year's hardest times, still he cleared six feet of snow and opened the roads by the soldiers' untiring effort, arriving in Arverni country. Taken by surprise, they thought themselves protected by the wall of the Cévennes, with

---

[4] Pompey's election took place just before the first of March. Caesar's difficulty was that his troops were in winter quarters north of Vercingetorix and his forces.

the roads open at that season not even to a lone traveler. Caesar orders cavalry to roam as widely as possible to terrify the enemy. Rumor and messengers bring the news immediately to Vercingetorix. All the Arverni surround him in terror, pleading that he look to their property and not let it be plundered by the enemy, especially when he could see the whole war was now upon them. Touched by their pleas, he moves camp from the Bituriges back among the Arverni.

9. Caesar waits there two days, having anticipated what Vercingetorix would do, then leaves the army to bring in the recruits and cavalry. He puts young Brutus in command, telling him to have cavalry range as widely as possible in all directions. He would try to be away from camp no more than three days.[5] With these arrangements, he surprises his own men by arriving at Vienne by very long marches. Picking up fresh cavalry there (sent on there some days before) and resting neither night nor day on the way, he goes through Haedui country to the Lingones, where two legions are wintering. If the Haedui have any designs on his own safety, he will outrun them. On arrival he sends to the other legions to bring them all together in one place before news of his coming could reach the Arverni. Vercingetorix, learning this, takes his army back among the Bituriges and from there begins the attack on Gergovia, a town of the Boii, whom Caesar had defeated and settled there under the Haedui after the Helvetian war.

10. This created a serious problem for Caesar's planning. If he kept the legions in one place for the rest of winter, he could protect the Haedui's dependents, lest all Gaul should revolt for

---

[5] He lies to Brutus (the future assassin) to keep him on station. His route takes him north perhaps as far as Dijon, some 200 miles. He has gotten past the barrier Vercingetorix thought would keep him from his troops and can gather the eight legions in that area.

thinking he could not protect his friends. If he broke quarters early, he would be short of grain because of transport difficulties. It seemed best to endure whatever challenges rather than lose support of his allies by suffering such an insult. So he encourages the Haedui to keep up supplies and sends messengers to tell the Boii of his approach, encouraging them to remain loyal and face enemy attack dauntlessly. Leaving two legions and all the army's baggage at Agedincum, he marches to the Boii.[6]

11. Arriving next day at Vellaunodunum, a Senones town, he decided to attack and in two days walled it around—to leave no enemy behind him and to have readier grain supply. The third day, legates emerge from town to discuss surrender. He orders them to collect their weapons, surrender cattle, and give six hundred hostages. He leaves legate Gaius Trebonius[7] to accomplish this. He leaves for Cenabum of the Carnutes as soon as possible. The Carnutes had just heard of Vellaunodunum's siege, expecting it to be prolonged, and were preparing a garrison to send to protect Cenabum. Caesar arrives in two days, pitching camp before the town. Prevented by the late hour, he defers attack until the next day, ordering whatever supplies the troops need. Since a bridge over the Loire reached Cenabum, he fears they will flee town at night, so he orders two armed legions to keep watch.

Just before midnight, the Cenabans emerged quietly from town and began to cross the river. When Caesar heard this from scouts he sent the soldiers he had ready to burn the gates and seize the town. They captured all but a few enemy, because

---

[6] Agedincum is modern Sens, considerably farther from the scene of action than even Dijon. The conciseness of these two paragraphs conceals bold and far-ranging action on C.'s part. (Vellaunodunum, mentioned next, is somewhere south of Paris, probably between Orleans and Auxerre.)

[7] Trebonius will be another assassin.

the narrow bridge and paths kept most from fleeing. He destroys and burns the town, gives booty to the soldiers, takes the army across the Loire, and marches into Bituriges territory.

12. Vercingetorix, learning Caesar had arrived, breaks off his attack and marches against Caesar. Caesar had begun attacking Noviodunum,[8] a Bituriges town on his route. When ambassadors come out to ask him to pardon them and spare their lives, he orders them—the better to finish business as rapidly as what he had already accomplished—to collect weapons, surrender horses, and give hostages. While hostages are being produced and the rest taken care of, he sends some centurions and soldiers in to look for weapons and horses. Enemy cavalry are seen in the distance, coming ahead of Vercingetorix's forces. When the townspeople saw this and came to hope for assistance, they raised a shout, seized arms, closed the gates, and began to man the walls. The centurions in the town, when they understood from gestures the Gauls had a new plan, drew swords, seized the gates, and got all their men out safely.

13. Caesar orders horsemen led out of camp and joins battle with cavalry. As they struggle, he sends out about 400 German horse, which he had planned to keep with him from the beginning. The Gauls could not resist their attack. Put to flight, they escaped to their own lines, losing many on the way. After this rout, the townspeople were terrified again, so they seized the ones they thought had stirred up the people and took them to Caesar and surrendered them. After that, Caesar marched to Avaricum,[9] the largest and best fortified town among the Bituriges, in rich farming country. He was sure if he took that town he could bring the Bituriges under his sway.

---

[8] Neung-sur-Beuvron, a tiny place now, south of Orléans.
[9] Bourges.

14. After this string of losses at Vellaunodunum, Cenabum, and Noviodunum, Vercingetorix calls a council. He declares the war needs to be conducted very differently from before. They should focus entirely on one thing, keeping Romans from fodder and supplies. It will be easy, because they have abundant cavalry and are helped by the season of the year. Fodder cannot be harvested; the enemy will have to scatter to search in farmhouses; they can all be cut down daily by horsemen. Private property was less important than safety. Villages and farmhouses should be burned a distance from the road in every direction, wherever the Romans might go foraging. Gauls have plenty of supplies, supported by those in whose territory war is fought. The Romans would either be unable to endure shortages or would go farther from camp at great danger. It did not matter whether they were killed or just stripped of their baggage, because without it they could not make war. Towns should be burned if they were not protected from every danger by their position and fortifications, so they would not be left to countrymen avoiding service or to Romans as sources of supplies and plunder. If this seems harsh and burdensome, they should think how much worse for their children and wives to be taken into servitude and for themselves to be killed: which had to happen to the defeated.

15. Everyone agrees with this view. In one day more than twenty Bituriges cities are burned. Fires are seen everywhere. Though everyone feels the pain, they offer themselves this consolation, that because victory was all but certain, they would soon recover their losses. In council together they discuss whether to burn Avaricum or defend it. The Bituriges prostrated themselves to the Gauls, to keep from being forced to burn with their own hands the fairest city in all Gaul, the stronghold and ornament of their nation. They say they would

defend it by taking advantage of its position, with swamp and river on almost all sides and one very narrow approach. Their prayer is approved, with Vercingetorix at first opposed, then yielding to their pleas and pity for the people. Suitable defenders for the town are chosen.

16. Vercingetorix follows Caesar on shorter marches and chooses a campsite protected by marsh and wood, fifteen miles from Avaricum. From trusted scouts he learned hour by hour the doings at Avaricum and ordered what he wanted done. He was watching all our foraging and grain collecting, attacking our men individually when they went too far and inflicting serious losses—even though as far as could be arranged, our men went out at irregular times by different ways.

17. Pitching camp by the side of town that had a narrow approach, as we described, but no river or marsh, Caesar began to prepare a ramp, move up a protective shed, and raise two towers. (The site made a surrounding wall impossible.) He kept asking the Boii and Haedui for grain. The latter, not caring much, were not much help, while the former, because their nation was small and weak, without many resources, quickly consumed what they had. The army had the gravest difficulty with food supply, because the Boii were poor, the Haedui apathetic, and barns had been burned—so much that for several days soldiers had no grain and forestalled outright famine with cattle driven from remote villages. But not one word there was heard unworthy of the majesty of the Roman people and their own earlier victories.

Indeed, when Caesar addressed individual legions at work and said he would abandon the siege if the shortage were too acute, they all begged him not to. For years of service under his command they had never let themselves be disgraced and nowhere abandoned their task half-done. They would take it as a disgrace to abandon the siege they had begun. Better to endure every difficulty than not avenge the Roman citizens who had died through Gallic treachery at Cenabum. They gave the same messages to centurions and tribunes to be taken to Caesar.

18. When the towers neared the wall, Caesar learned from prisoners that Vercingetorix, consuming all his fodder, had moved camp nearer Avaricum. He had gone on with cavalry and the light infantry who usually fought with them to ambush our men where they thought they would forage next day. Knowing this, Caesar left quietly at midnight and arrived at the enemy camp in the morning. They soon heard from their scouts of Caesar's coming and hid their carts and baggage in thick woods, drawing up their troops on high, open ground. Told of this, Caesar immediately ordered the baggage gathered up and weapons made ready.

19. The hill sloped gently, surrounded on all sides by a tricky and tangled marsh no more than fifty feet broad. Breaking up the bridges, the Gauls stayed on the hill, confident of their position. Arranged by nations they held the marsh's fords and meadows, ready to overwhelm the Romans if they tried to penetrate the marsh and became stuck. Whoever saw how close they were would think them ready to fight on nearly even terms, but whoever saw how different their positions were would know it was just an empty show of courage. Caesar saw his men were angry that the enemy could bear to face them so close at hand. They demanded the signal for battle, so he told them what they would lose and how many brave men would die for such victory. Seeing them prepared to refuse no danger for his glory, he said he would deserve to be guilty of the utmost injustice if he did not cherish their lives more than his own safety. Consoling them, he leads them

back in camp that day, beginning to prepare what he needed
to besiege the town.

20. When Vercingetorix returned, he was accused of betrayal. He had moved camp nearer the Romans, he had left
with all the cavalry, he had left his considerable forces without
a commander, and when he left, the Romans swiftly and op-
portunely appeared. This could not all happen accidentally
without planning. He preferred to rule in Gaul at Caesar's pleasure rather than because of their support.

Thus accused, he responds: He had moved camp at their
urging, because fodder was running short. He had approached
the Romans because he was convinced the place would almost
defend itself. Cavalry support should not be sought in swampy
ground and would have been useful there where he took them.
He deliberately did not transfer command to anyone when he
left, to keep the mob from forcing battle. He saw they were all
weaklings, wanting to fight just because they could not hold
out longer. If the Romans had just happened to arrive, they
should thank their fortune and if they had instead been invited
in by some turncoat, they should thank *him*, because from the
higher ground they could see how few the Romans were and
despise the bravery of men who did not dare to fight and
shamefully retreated to camp.

He didn't need to win his command from Caesar by treachery, since he could have it by victory, victory now assured for
himself and all Gauls. But he would give them back his command, if they thought the honor for him outweighed the rescue for them. "To know I speak honestly, listen to Roman soldiers." He brings out slaves he had captured out foraging a few
days earlier and tortured with hunger and chains. They had
been told what to say when interrogated—that they were legionary soldiers; driven by hunger and need they had secretly
left camp to see what grain or livestock they could find in the

fields. The whole army was oppressed by similar shortages: no one had any strength left, no one could endure the work. The general had decided to withdraw in three days if they made no progress in besieging the town. "These are the gifts you have from me," said Vercingetorix, "whom you accuse of treason. By my efforts you see a great victorious army taken down by famine without a drop of your blood. I have taken care no nation will welcome them when they shamefully flee."

21. The whole crowd shouts out and clatters arms in the way they do for someone whose speech they approve. Vercingetorix is their supreme leader. No one doubts his loyalty. War could be waged with no greater prudence. They decide to send 10,000 men chosen from the whole army into the town and not trust the common welfare to the Bituriges alone, because they knew that the whole of victory lay in holding this town.

22. Gallic schemes of every sort challenged our soldiers' exemplary courage, for their nation is greatly clever, ever ready to imitate and do whatever they learn from others. So they snared hooks with nooses, then dragged them inside with engines. They tunneled under our ramp, the more knowledgeably because there are great ironworks among them and every kind of tunneling is known and practiced. They covered the whole wall with towers on all faces and wove hides over them. In sallies by night and day they set fire to the ramp or attacked soldiers busy working. They matched the height of our towers, as these were forced up higher every day by work on the ramp, by adding to their towers with timbers. They intercepted our tunnels, slowing their progress with sharp, bent stakes and boiling pitch and huge rocks, preventing them from reaching the walls.

24. So the siege bogged down, but the soldiers, slowed the while by cold and endless rain, worked incessantly to overcome obstacles and in twenty-five days raised a mound 330 feet wide

and eighty feet high. When it almost reached the enemy wall, Caesar, attentive as always, urged them not to let up working a moment. Just before the third watch[10] smoke was noticed rising from the mound, which the enemy had set on fire from a tunnel. Then a shout rose along the whole wall and they burst from two gates either side of the towers. Some threw torches and dry wood down from the wall onto the mound, pouring down pitch and other stuff that could feed fire. One hardly knew where to run first or where to render aid. By Caesar's arrangements, two legions were always on watch in front of the camp and the rest at work by shifts, so it was quickly arranged that some resisted the sally and others pulled back the towers and broke down the ramp,[11] while the whole mass rushed from camp to extinguish the fire.

25. They fought everywhere the rest of the night. The enemy's hope of victory constantly reawakened, especially when they saw the towers' covering burned away, exposing us and making it hard for us to approach to offer help. Fresh troops continually replaced the weary. They thought the whole salvation of Gaul hung in that moment. As we watched, something happened worth recalling and not to be passed over. A Gaul stood before the town gate, hurling into the fire from near the tower balls of pitch and tallow that were handed to him. Shot by a dart fired from his right, he fell lifeless. Another nearby stepped over his body and took up the same function and was killed the same way by a dart; a third succeeded him and a fourth likewise the third. The post was not abandoned by defenders before the fire in the ramp was put out, the enemy driven back on all sides, and the fighting ended.

---

[10] Around midnight.
[11] Most likely they hacked a trench in the ramp to make it easier to fight the fire.

26. Having tried everything and succeeded at nothing, next day the Gauls decided to flee the town at Vercingetorix's encouragement and command. Trying in the dead of night, they hoped to do this without great loss of men, particularly because Vercingetorix's camp was not far from town and the swamp running between slowed Roman pursuit. They were preparing to do this by night when their womenfolk suddenly rushed into the open, throwing themselves weeping at the feet of their husbands, begging in every way that they not hand them and their children to the enemy to be punished, for by nature they were too weak to take flight. When they saw the men standing by their plan (in extreme danger fear is impervious to pity) they began to shout out and betray the flight to the Romans. The Gauls greatly feared the roads would be seized by Roman cavalry and abandoned the plan.

27. Next day Caesar moved a tower forward and completed the works he had begun. A great rainstorm broke, making him think it helped his plans, for he saw guards somewhat casually arranged on the wall. He ordered his men to slack off and showed them what he wanted done. Hiding legions inside protective sheds, he encouraged them to grasp at last victory's fruit for all their efforts, offering the first to climb the wall a reward, then gave the soldiers the signal. They suddenly flew out on all sides and quickly gained control of the walls.

28. Startled and scared, the enemy were dislodged from walls and towers into squares and avenues, making their stand in tight clusters, thinking that if they were attacked on any side, they could form a line and fight it out. They realized no one was coming down to level ground but the wall was swarmed on all sides. Fearing that hope of escape would vanish, they downed arms and in a headlong rush made for the remotest parts of town. Some were killed there by infantry

when they crowded the narrow passage at the gates, while others got out the gates only to be killed by cavalry. No Roman bothered with plunder. Angered by the slaughter at Cenabum and the laborious siege, they spared neither the age-weary nor women nor children. Of the whole 40,000, scarcely 800, who fled town at first uproar, made it safe to Vercingetorix. He took the refugees in quietly, late at night, fearing insurgency born of pity as they flooded into the camp. So he posted trusted men and tribal leaders a distance down the road, there to divide up the refugees and have them taken to their own people in whatever part of camp had fallen to them originally.

29. Next day Vercingetorix summoned a council, consoling and encouraging all not to be downcast, not to be upset at the loss.[12] The Romans won not by courage in battle but by trick and by siege skill, at which they themselves were inexperienced. They were wrong to think everything in war might turn out favorably. He never liked defending Avaricum—they were his witnesses. The irresponsibility of the Bituriges and the hasty acquiescence of the others made them take this loss. They would quickly remedy it with greater victories. By his efforts, they would reunite the nations that had stood aside from other Gauls and make one plan for all Gaul, whose solidarity not even the whole world could resist. The task was all but accomplished. Meanwhile it was fair for him to ask them, for the common welfare, to start fortifying camp, to resist sudden enemy attacks more readily.

30. This speech did not displease the Gauls, especially because he was not downcast over taking such a loss. He did not hide and avoid the public eye. He was thought better at foresee-

---

[12] Four times in this paragraph and the next Caesar uses or puts in the mouth of V. the mild word *incommodum*, "a set-back, a reverse," to describe this ghastly slaughter.

ing and anticipating because at the outset he had wanted to burn Avaricum, then later to abandon it. Adversity diminishes authority for other generals, but his reputation instead increased by the day after the loss. They found hope in his assertion about bringing in other nations. For the first time, the Gauls began to fortify camps. They were so frightened that, although unaccustomed to hard work, they thought they should endure everything they were ordered to do.

31. Vercingetorix worked as enthusiastically as he had promised to recruit other nations, luring their leaders with gifts and promises. He picked men suited for this task, whose skillful speech or existing friendships could win others over. He clothes and arms the refugees from Avaricum. To strengthen his reduced forces, he orders up a fixed number of soldiers by nation (saying how many and by when they should be brought to camp) and orders all archers—there were many in Gaul—to be found and sent to him. With this he quickly replaced what had been lost at Avaricum. Meanwhile Teutomatus, Ollovico's son and king of the Nitiobriges, whose father had been acclaimed as a friend by our senate, came over with a great body of his own cavalry and mercenaries from Aquitania.

32. Caesar stayed at Avaricum a few days collecting a large grain supply and other provisions, resting the army after toil and privation. With winter almost over, the season was calling him to war and he had decided to march on the enemy, whether it was to draw him out from swamps and woods or to thwart him with siege. But leaders of the Haedui come to him as legates asking for help in crisis for their nation. The danger was immense. Though single magistrates had of old been created and held royal power for a year, now two held office, each claiming he had been appointed according to their laws. One

was Convictolitavis, a charismatic young man of good family, the other Cotus, born of ancient line and himself of immense influence and large family. His brother Valetiacus had held the same office the previous year. The whole nation was in arms, the senate split, the people split, each man with his own followers. If the quarrel lasted much longer, one faction would be fighting the other. It was Caesar's attention and influence that could prevent this.

33. Caesar knew it was bad to let go of the war and the enemy but he knew as well what disasters arise from dissension. To keep a great nation and close ally of the Roman people, one he had always supported and favored in everything, from descending to arms and violence and to keep the less reliable faction from seeking help from Vercingetorix, he decided to forestall them. Because by Haedui law holders of the highest magistracy could not leave their borders, he decided not to appear to disrespect their custom and law and to go himself among the Haedui, summoning the whole senate and the rivals to convene at Decetia.[13] When almost the whole nation had gathered there, he was told one brother had been declared elected by the other before a few invited witnesses, at a time and place different from what was proper, though the laws forbade two brothers of the same family not only from being made magistrates while both were alive but even from both serving in the senate. Caesar forced Cotus to surrender command and ordered Convictolitavis to take office, for he had been named by the priests, according to tribal custom, when the line of officeholders had broken.

34. Issuing this decision, he encouraged the Haedui to forget quarrels and strife, leave everything else aside, and devote

---

[13] Decize.

themselves to the war and to anticipating the rewards they would earn from him when Gaul was conquered. They should send him all their cavalry and ten thousand infantry quickly, which he would assign to watching the grain supplies. He divided the army in two: four legions he gave Labienus to lead among the Senones and Parisii, six he took himself among the Arverni to the town of Gergovia by the Elaver river.[14] He gave Labienus some cavalry, some he kept. Hearing this, Vercingetorix broke all that river's bridges and began to march along the opposite bank.

35. The two armies went their way each in sight of the other, pitching camp facing each other, the Gauls sending out scouts so the Romans could not build a bridge and bring troops across. Caesar's situation was difficult, not wanting the river to delay him all summer—the Elaver is not usually forded before autumn. To avoid that, he pitched camp in a wooded place opposite one of the bridges Vercingetorix had arranged to tear down. Next day he stayed back secretly with two legions, sending on ahead all the rest normally, with all the baggage. He spread out some cohorts so the number of legions would seem right. He ordered them go as far as possible and when he estimated by the time of day that they had made camp, using the timbers whose lower part had remained intact he began to remake the bridge. The work was quickly done. The legions crossed and chose a good place for camp. Then Caesar summoned the other legions back. Vercingetorix found out and went on ahead by long marches to keep from being forced into a fight.

[14] Gergovia was a fortified hilltop town a few miles south of Clermont-Ferrand and west of the Allier (Elaver) River. It lay about 100 miles south of Decize: C. was in rapid motion seeking to keep Gaul under control; V. was well informed. The broken bridges were meant to force C. to stay on the east side of the river as he made his way south.

36. In five stages from there Caesar reached Gergovia. In a cavalry skirmish that day he examined the city's position, on a high hill with all the approaches difficult. He despaired of storming the city and decided not to begin siege before preparing his grain supply. But Vercingetorix, camped near the stronghold, arranged the forces of individual nations around him at intervals and took all the high points on that ridge from which the town could be seen, giving a frightful appearance. He told the leaders of the nations with whom he had chosen to share his planning to gather with him daily at dawn, for whatever had to be arranged or reported. He let no day pass without cavalry and archers skirmishing, testing the spirit and courage of his men.

Opposite the town a hill at the foot of the ridge was fortified and steep all around. If our men could hold that, it looked as if they could keep the enemy from most of his water supply and from foraging freely. This place was held by a garrison, not a very strong one. In the dead of night, Caesar left camp, dislodged the garrison before help could come from town, and took the place, establishing two legions there. He built a double trench twelve feet wide from the main camp to the smaller one, so that even individuals could go back and forth safe from enemy ambush.

37. While this went on at Gergovia, the Haeduan Convicto-litavis—we saw him awarded the magistracy by Caesar—took a bribe from the Arverni. He conferred with young men led by Litaviccus and his brothers, youths of a great family. He shared the bribe with them and told them to remember they were free men born for rule. The Haedui were the only state preventing assured victory for Gaul, while the others were held back by their prestige. If they were brought over, there would be no way for Romans to stay in Gaul. He had benefitted somewhat

from Caesar's generosity, but only where he had a compelling
case: he owed more to their common liberty. Why should
Haedui need Caesar to rule on their own customs and law,
rather than have the Romans come to them? The young men
were quickly brought over by the magistrate's bribery and his
speech, promising they would even lead the plot, and so a plan
for accomplishing it was discussed. They were sure their nation would not be persuaded to undertake war rashly. They
agreed Litaviccus would command the ten thousand Caesar
had ordered sent to war and would supervise the march, while
his brothers would go on ahead to Caesar. They settled other
plans for how things should be done.

38. Litaviccus took over the army and when they were still
twenty-five miles from Gergovia he gathered them suddenly
and wept, saying, "Soldiers, where are we going? All our cavalry, all our nobles are dead. Our nation's leaders, Eporedorix
and Viridomarus, charged with treason by the Romans, have
been killed without trial. Hear it from the men who fled the
slaughter themselves. My brothers and all my relatives have
been murdered. My grief keeps me from describing what happened." They bring out men whom he had told what to say and
they tell the crowd what Litaviccus had declared: the Haedui
cavalry had all been killed, accused of consulting with the
Arverni; they themselves had hidden in the crowd of soldiers
and escaped from the midst of massacre.

The Haedui cry out and beg Litaviccus to do their thinking
for them. "As if it were a matter for thinking and not just the
urgent need to make for Gergovia and join up with the
Arverni. Can we doubt that after their wicked crime the Romans are hurrying to kill us? So if we have any spirit, let us
avenge the deaths of those who died shamefully: let's kill
these bandits!" He brings out some Roman citizens who were

there under his protection. He confiscates a large quantity of grain and supplies from them, tortures them cruelly, and kills them. He sends messengers through the whole Haedui nation, stirring them up with the same lie about the killing of the cavalry and the leaders, urging them to avenge their injuries just as he did.

39. Eporedorix the Haeduan was a youth born to high rank and had great influence there. Along with him, Viridomarus was of similar age and character but lower birth, recommended to Caesar by Diviciacus and advanced by him from modest beginnings to high rank. Summoned particularly by Caesar, they had arrived with the cavalry. These two quarreled over the leadership. In the struggle of magistrates, one fought with all his might for Convictolitavis, the other for Cotus. Eporedorix learns Litaviccus' plans and takes them to Caesar at midnight, begging him not to allow their nation to lose the friendship of the Roman people through the wicked schemes of young men. That's what would happen if so many thousands of men went over to the enemy. Their relatives could not neglect their wellbeing nor could the nation brush it off.

40. Caesar was greatly troubled by this news, for he had always specially favored the Haedui. Without hesitation he takes four light-armed legions and all his cavalry from camp, without time to shrink the camp perimeter, because everything depended on speed. Legate Gaius Fabius he leaves with two legions guarding camp. When he ordered Litaviccus' brothers arrested, he discovered they had just fled to the enemy. He urged the soldiers not to be discouraged in a crisis by the fatigue of a march. Advancing with great enthusiasm over twenty miles, they spot the Haedui line. He sends the cavalry to slow and interfere with their march, ordering that there be no killing. He directs Eporedorix and Viridomarus, whom their peo-

ple thought had been killed, to go ahead among the cavalry and call to their people. When they are recognized and Litaviccus' lie revealed, the Haedui hold out their hands in surrender, cast aside their weapons, and plead for their lives. Litaviccus and his followers—in Gallic custom abandoning patrons even in the worst misfortune is very wrong—flee for Gergovia.

41. Caesar sends messengers to the Haedui to say he had spared men he could have killed by right of war. With three hours' rest for the army, he departs for Gergovia. About half-way there, riders sent from Fabius tell him how dangerous things are: they report the camp attacked by huge forces, fresh troops constantly replacing tired ones, wearing ours down with incessant toil, for the size of our camp made the same men stay constantly on the rampart. Many were wounded by a mass of arrows and every kind of spear; our catapults were very helpful in surviving this. When the enemy withdrew, Fabius kept two gates open and blockaded the rest, adding protection to the rampart and preparing to face similar risks tomorrow. Hearing all this, Caesar reaches the camp before sunrise thanks to the great efforts of his men.

42. While this is going on at Gergovia, the Haedui take no time to think after hearing from Litaviccus' first messengers. Some are inspired by greed, the rest by a rage and impulsiveness deeply rooted in that people, taking mere rumor as certain fact. They plunder Roman citizens' property, killing some, dragging others into slavery. Convictolitavis abets the affair and drives the mob crazy: they would be too embarrassed to sober up after committing such crimes. They promise safety to lure the military tribune Marcus Aristius out of the town of Châlon on his way to his legion. They force others who are there for trading to do the same: harassing them constantly on the way, they strip them of their baggage, attacking them as

they fight back for a day and a night. After many are killed on both sides, they stir up a greater crowd to take arms.

43. Then news arrives: all their soldiers were in Caesar's power. They rush to Aristius, to assure him that nothing was done with official authority. They order an investigation into the stolen property, they confiscate property of Litaviccus and his brothers, and they send Caesar ambassadors to clear themselves. They do this to get their men back, but they are tainted by the crime and enamored of profiting from stolen property— many were involved in that—and frightened of punishment, so they begin making secret plans for war and stirring up other nations with embassies. Caesar knew this, but he addresses their representatives as calmly as possible: he would not judge the nation harshly for the ignorance and folly of the mob or lessen his generosity toward the Haedui. He anticipates a major uprising in Gaul. To keep from being surrounded by the united nations, he began to think how he could leave Gergovia and collect his whole army without making a departure in fear of revolt look like running away.

44. While he was thinking, he saw a chance for success. Entering the smaller camp to inspect it, he notices an enemy hill was abandoned where days before you could scarcely see it for the crowd. Astonished, he asks the refugees coming every day in great numbers for an explanation. They agree with what Caesar had found through scouts, that the back of that ridge was level but wooded and narrow where it approached the other side of town. The Gauls were very afraid of this place and had to think that with the Romans already on one hill, if they lost the other, they would be surrounded and shut off from escape and foraging. Vercingetorix ordered them all to fortify the position.

45. Realizing this, Caesar sends out cavalry squads after midnight and orders them to wander around noisily all over. At dawn he orders large amounts of baggage and mules out of camp and the mule-blankets removed. Muleteers should ride around the hills wearing helmets and looking and acting like cavalry. He adds a few horsemen ranging more widely for show. He tells them to head for a particular area by going the long way round. From Gergovia, looking down into the camp, they were seen far off. At such distance one could not tell for sure what was happening. He sends one legion toward the hill and after a little distance hides it in low ground and woods. The Gauls' suspicion increases and all their forces are shifted to fortify the hill. Caesar sees the enemy camp is empty. Covering their distinguishing markings and hiding the military standards, he takes straggling groups of soldiers from the larger camp to the smaller so as not to be seen from town. He shows the legates in charge of each legion what he wishes done. First, they should keep their soldiers from advancing too far out of enthusiasm for fighting or hope of plunder. He describes the disadvantages of the uneven ground. Speed is the only remedy: a time for surprise, not fighting. Saying this, he gives the signal and sends the Haedui at the same time on the right flank by another ascent.

46. The climb to the town wall was about a mile in a straight line with no turnings. Whatever added turns eased the climb but increased the distance.[15] At the middle of the long side, as the mountain's shape allowed, the Gauls had stretched a wall of large stones six feet high to slow our men's attack. Leaving

[15] C. has no way to measure altitude as we do, in feet above sea level. Depending on the starting point, the height of Gergovia is some 700–800 feet above the surrounding plain and the ascent for armed men certainly steep.

all the space below empty, they filled the upper part of the hill all the way to the town wall with camps crowded together. On a signal, the soldiers reach the fortification quickly, cross it, and seize three camps. They take them so quickly that Teutomatus, king of the Nitiobriges, surprised in a moment in his tent as he took midday rest, half-dressed and his horse wounded, scarcely snatches himself away from the hands of the plundering soldiers.

47. Having done what he intended,[16] Caesar ordered retreat sounded and immediately planted the tenth legion's standards—he was with them. Soldiers of other legions did not hear the trumpet sound—a large ravine separated them—but were restrained by tribunes and legates as Caesar had instructed. They were full of hope for swift victory and thought of the enemy's flight and successful battles before. They thought nothing was too difficult for courage to achieve, so they did not stop pursuit until they reached the town wall and gates. But then a shout rose throughout the city and those a distance from the sudden uproar were frightened—thinking the enemy within the gates—and rushed from town. Matrons threw clothes and silver from the wall, leaning down, breasts bared and hands outstretched, beseeching the Romans to spare them and not fail (as at Avaricum) to spare women and children. Some were lowered from the wall by hands and surrendered to our soldiers. Lucius Fabius, centurion in the eighth legion, who apparently said to his men that he was inspired by the plunder of Avaricum and would not let anyone scale the wall before him, took three of his squad to lift him up and he climbed the wall, then lifted each of them behind him.

[16] He puts a good face on a failure.

48. Meanwhile the ones going, as we said, to the other part of town to fortify it, first hearing the shouting and then upset by frequent rumors the town was held by the Romans, sent ahead cavalry and headed there in great haste. Each one arriving took a stand beneath the wall, enlarging the crowd of fighters. When a great mass had gathered, matrons who had just been reaching out to the Romans from the wall pleaded now with their own, showing their disheveled hair in Gallic fashion and bringing their children out to be seen. The contest was unequal in position and numbers for the Romans, while exhaustion from running and continuous fighting made it hard to resist fresh, sound troops.

49. Caesar saw that they were fighting on unfavorable ground and enemy forces were increasing. Fearing for his men he sent to Titus Sextius, left to guard the smaller camp, to bring cohorts quickly from camp and position them at the foot of the hill on the enemy's right. If he saw our men being driven back, he should make the enemy afraid to pursue them. Caesar went a little forward with the tenth legion from where he had stopped, awaiting the outcome of battle.

50. In hand-to-hand combat, the enemy trusted in their numbers and position, ours in their courage. Suddenly on our open flank appeared the Haedui, whom Caesar had sent from the right by another climb to create a distraction. By the similarity of their weapons to the enemy's, they frightened our men greatly. Even if it was noticed they had right shoulders bare, always an agreed sign, our soldiers still thought the enemy did it to deceive us. Then Lucius Fabius the centurion and the men who had climbed the wall with him were surrounded, killed, and thrown from the wall. Marcus Petronius, a centurion of the same legion, trying to hack open the gate, was overwhelmed by a mob. Despairing for himself and taking many wounds,

he said to the soldiers following him, "Since I cannot save myself and you, I will certainly look out for your lives, since I led you into danger in my desire for glory. When you get the chance, look out for yourselves." At once he rushed among the enemy, killing two and driving the rest a little back from the gate. When his men tried to help, he said, "It's useless to try to save my life, as blood and strength now fail me. So go while there's a chance and get to your legion." Fighting on, he soon fell, saving his men.

51. Our men were surrounded and driven back, losing forty-six centurions. The tenth legion, in reserve on more level ground, slowed the Gauls' relentless pursuit. Cohorts of the thirteenth took their place, coming from the smaller camp with legate Titus Sextius and taking higher ground. When the legions reached level ground, they turned their standards and stood against the enemy. Vercingetorix led his men from the foot of the hill back behind the fortifications. On that day almost seven hundred soldiers were lost.

52. Next day Caesar called an assembly to rebuke his impulsive and greedy soldiers for deciding for themselves where to go and what to do, not stopping when they had the signal and not letting tribunes and legates hold them back. He explained what uneven ground could do, which he had been thinking of at Avaricum, when he had thrown away assured victory when they caught the enemy leaderless and without their cavalry. He would not risk the slightest loss in battle on account of the uneven ground. Much as he admired their spirit—undeterred by the fortified encampment, the height of the hill, and the town walls—he still had to reproach their indiscipline and arrogance for thinking they knew better than the general about victory and how things would turn out. He expected restraint and self-discipline from soldiers no less than courage and spirit.

53. Giving this speech, he finally encouraged them not to be upset and not to credit enemy courage for what was merely the effect of uneven ground. Thinking as before of departure, he led the legions from camp and drew them up in a good position. When Vercingetorix did descend to level ground, Caesar mounted a brief and successful cavalry skirmish and then led the way back to camp. After doing the same the next day, he decided he had done enough to lessen Gallic arrogance and hearten his troops, and moved camp toward the Haedui. Even then the enemy did not pursue and on the third day he returned to the Elaver river, repaired the bridge, and crossed the army there.

54. Greeted by the Haedui Viridomarus and Eporedorix, he learned Litaviccus and all his cavalry had gone to stir up the Haedui. They would have to go ahead of him to reassure the nation. Even though he had seen Haeduan treachery on many occasions and judged their departure would in fact hasten the whole nation's secession, he still decided not to hold them back—not to be seen to do them an injustice or give reason to suspect him of fear. When they were going, he briefly outlined his services to the Haedui, how he had found them cast down, herded into towns, deprived of lands, all their forces taken away, obliged to pay tribute, giving hostages in the face of the worst insult. He had brought them to good times and prosperity, not merely restoring their former standing, but so that now they seemed at a historic height of prestige and influence. Making these representations, he let them go.

55. Noviodunum was a Haedui town well situated on the bank of the Loire.[17] Caesar had brought there all his Gallic hostages, his grain, his public money, and most of his and the

[17] Nevers.

army's baggage, as well as a great number of horses bought in Italy and Spain for this war. When Eporedorix and Viridomarus arrived, they learned the nation's situation. Litaviccus had been welcomed by Haedui at Bibracte. Convictolitavis the magistrate and many of the senate had gone to meet him. Legates had been openly sent to Vercingetorix to make peace and friendship. They both thought this opportunity was not to be missed.

Killing guards and the merchants gathered at Noviodunum, they divided up the money and horses and had the hostages led to the magistrate at Bibracte. The town—which they judged they could not hold—they burned so it would be of no use to Romans. They took off in boats what grain they could in a hurry, destroying the rest by river water or fire. They themselves began to collect forces from neighboring regions, to set garrisons and guards on the Loire banks, and to show cavalry around everywhere to inspire fear, hoping to keep the Romans from foraging or else drive them hungry back to our province. Their hope was much encouraged because the Loire had so swollen from snow it appeared impossible to cross.

56. Hearing this, Caesar decided to hurry, to fight before greater forces gathered there, whatever danger there was in building bridges. He did not change plan and turn his course to the province, as indeed some thought he should, not just for the disgrace and shame of doing so or for the hard roads and Cévennes mountains in the way, but mainly because he feared greatly for Labienus, separated from him with the legions he had sent with him. Surprising everyone, he reached the Loire in very long day and night marches. With his cavalry he found a ford there good enough to use in a crisis, where just arms and shoulders could reach free of the water to hold on to weapons. He set out cavalry to break the flow of the river and carried

the army across safe, startling the enemy when they first appeared. They found grain and a supply of livestock in the fields. Restocking the army thus he set out for the Senones.

57. While Caesar is doing this, Labienus leaves the reinforcements lately arrived from Italy at Agedincum to guard the baggage and sets out for Lutetia with four legions. It is the town of the Parisii, set on an island in the Seine. When the enemy learned he had arrived, huge forces from nearby nations gathered. Supreme command was given to Camulogenus of the Aulerci, weary with age but still raised to the honor for his unique knowledge of military affairs. When he noticed a large marsh flowing into the Seine and making all that land impassable, he stopped there and set to stop our troops from crossing.[18]

58. Labienus first tried to bring up sheds, fill the marsh with wicker frames and clay, and strengthen the road. Realizing how difficult this was, he left camp quietly at third watch, reaching Metiosedum[19] the way he had come. It is a Senones town on an island in the Seine, as we just said of Lutetia. Seizing some fifty boats, tying them together quickly and loading them with soldiers, he terrifies the townspeople with the novelty of it all, taking the town without opposition since many of them had been called away to war. Repairing the bridge the enemy had torn down days before, he crosses his army and makes downstream for Lutetia. Hearing this from Metiosedum refugees, the enemy orders Lutetia burned and its town bridges destroyed. They leave the marsh for the Seine bank and make camp opposite Lutetia facing Labienus.

---

[18] The Essonne river flows from the south into the Seine just above Paris and made a good line of defense to force Labienus to cross the Seine and approach the city on the right bank.

[19] Melun.

59. They had heard Caesar had left Gergovia, then that rumors of Haeduan revolt and successful insurrection in Gaul were afoot. Gauls were asserting Caesar was blocked from marching and crossing the Loire and so, forced by grain shortage, was heading to the province. The Bellovaci, previously unruly on their own, hearing of Haeduan revolt, began to gather forces and openly prepare war. With such reversals, Labienus knew he needed a very different plan from before and was thinking not of new conquest or of provoking the enemy in battle but of getting his army safe back to Agedincum. On one side of the river the Bellovaci, reputedly the bravest nation in Gaul, harassed him, while Camulogenus held the other with a fresh, disciplined army. And a considerable river cut the legions off from baggage and garrison. In such sudden crisis he saw that help would be found in courage and spirit.

60. Calling a council toward evening, he insists they carry out his commands promptly and carefully. The ships he had brought from Metiosedum he assigns to individual Roman knights. At the end of the first watch they should make downstream three and a half miles silently and await him there. Five cohorts judged least ready for fighting he leaves to guard camp. The other five of the same legion he orders to set out upriver just after midnight with great hubbub, taking all their baggage. He also seeks out small boats. These he sent the same way, propelled loudly by noisy oars. He himself sets out a little later in silence with three legions for the place where he had ordered the ships to land.

61. When he arrives, enemy scouts, arranged all along the river, caught unawares because a great storm had suddenly arisen, are overrun by our men. The infantry and cavalry cross quickly, supervised by the Roman knights in charge. About the

same time, near dawn, rumor in enemy camps says that there was unusual hubbub among the Romans, a large force was going upriver, and the sound of oars was heard in that direction, while farther down soldiers were crossing in boats. Hearing this and thinking our legions were crossing in three different places, they divided their forces also in three parts. Leaving a garrison opposite the camp and sending a small band toward Metiosedum, to go as far as the boats could go, they led their remaining force against Labienus.

62. First light and all our men are across and the enemy line comes in view. Labienus encourages the troops to remember their own former courage and successful battles and to imagine that Caesar, under whose leadership they had often overcome enemies, was there with them: then he gives the battle sign. At first contact on the right wing, where the seventh legion stood, the enemy are driven back, thrown into flight. On the left, which the twelfth legion held, the enemy first ranks fell, shot through with spears, but the rest fought back fiercely and none gave hint of flight.

The enemy leader Camulogenus was with his men, urging them on. With the issue of victory still unknown, the seventh legion's tribunes heard what was happening on the left and so revealed the legion's presence behind the enemy and attacked. Even then, no one gave way, but all were surrounded and killed—Camulogenus endured the same fate. Those left on guard opposite Labienus' camp, hearing battle joined, went to help their side and seized a hill, but could not withstand our victorious soldiers' attack. They mixed with other fugitives and any who were not hidden by woods and hills were killed by our cavalry. The business done, Labienus returns to Agedincum, where all the army's baggage had been left; from there with his whole army he came to Caesar.

63. War spreads as the Haeduan revolt becomes known. Embassies are sent in all directions. They strive to recruit allies with whatever influence, prestige, and money they can. Taking and executing the hostages Caesar had left with them, they frighten the reluctant. The Haedui asked Vercingetorix to come and share war planning with them. Succeeding, they urge that supreme command be given to them. That becomes controversial, so a council of all Gaul is called to Bibracte. Thronging from everywhere, they meet there. The matter is left to majority vote. To a man, all acclaim Vercingetorix their general. The Remi, Lingones, and Treveri were absent from this council, the former out of loyalty to Roman friendship, the Treveri because they were far away, facing German pressure—which is why they stood aside from the whole war and sent troops to neither side. The Haedui accept their loss of leadership with considerable unhappiness, complain of the reversal of fortune, and repine for Caesar's generosity to them. But after starting war, they dare not separate their planning from the others. Reluctantly the young men of great promise, Eporedorix and Viridomarus, defer to Vercingetorix.

64. Vercingetorix orders other nations to give hostages. Then he sets a date for doing so. All their cavalry—fifteen thousand in number—he orders to gather speedily. He says he will be content with the infantry he had before.[20] He will not tempt fortune or fight open battle but, with abundant cavalry, it will be perfectly easy to keep the Romans from forage and fodder. As long as Gauls would calmly destroy their own grain and burn their farmhouses, they will see that sacrifice of private property would give them permanent rule and freedom. Settling this, he orders ten thousand infantry from the Haedui

[20] Some 80,000.

and Segusiavi (the closest nation to our province) and to these he adds eight hundred cavalry. He puts Eporedorix's brother in charge of them and orders him to take war to the Allobroges. In another direction he sends the Gabali and the nearest Arvernian communities against the Helvii and similarly he sends the Ruteni and Cadurci to lay waste to the land of the Volcae Arecomici.[21] But he goes on encouraging the Allobroges with secret messages and representatives, hoping their minds were still unsettled after the earlier war. To their leaders he offers money, to the nation control of the whole province.

65. Against all these possibilities twenty-two cohorts were on guard, drafted from the province and posted on all sides by the legate Lucius Caesar.[22] The Helvii enthusiastically fight their neighbors and are defeated, driven back into their towns and forts. Their leader Gaius Valerius Donotaurus, son of Caburus, and many others are killed. The Allobroges set guards all along the Rhone to protect their territory alertly and strenuously. Caesar, knowing the enemy cavalry to be superior, with all roads blocked and no help possible from the province and Italy, sends across the Rhine to the nations he had pacified in earlier years, asking them for cavalry and light-armed infantry accustomed to fighting among cavalry. When they arrive, mounted on unsuitable horses, he takes horses from the tribunes and the other Roman knights and veteran reservists and gives them to Germans.

66. Meanwhile, enemy forces from the Arverni and cavalry summoned from all Gaul assemble. A huge body collected while Caesar marched toward the Sequani, skirting Lingones

---

[21] Where lay the Roman city of Narbonne.

[22] A cousin of Caesar, consul in 64, loyal through the civil war and the Ides of March, then proscribed by Antonius but survived. His son fought with Cato against Caesar, was pardoned by Caesar, then murdered by troops loyal to Caesar.

territory, the better to bring aid to our province. Vercingetorix settles in three camps nearly ten miles from the Romans and calls his cavalry commanders to council, declaring the time of victory was at hand. The Romans were leaving Gaul, fleeing to the province.[23] This was enough to gain immediate freedom, but little help for future peace and tranquility. They would gather larger forces and return: there would be no end to war. So the Gauls should attack them weighed down on the march. If they tried to rescue their baggage and were delayed, they would not complete the march. If—this he thinks more likely—they abandoned the baggage to assure their own safety, they would lose use of things they needed and would lose face. As for the enemy cavalry, none of them would dare go ahead of the line of march—no one should doubt that. To encourage them the more, he would bring his whole force before the camps and strike fear in the enemy. The cavalry shout as one that they would swear a most sacred oath that no one would be sheltered indoors nor allowed near children, relatives, or wives if he had not ridden twice through the enemy line.

67. The plan was approved and all forced to swear an oath. The next day the cavalry, divided in three, show two columns on our two flanks, while one ahead began to block the road. Told this, Caesar orders his cavalry as well to approach the enemy in three divisions. Fighting breaks out at once on all fronts. The march halts. The baggage is taken in among the legions. If our men struggled or were hard pressed on any side, Caesar ordered standards there and lines formed to fight. This slowed enemy pursuit and encouraged our men to hope for support. Finally Germans on the right take the high ground and drive the enemy away. They pursue them in flight to the

---

[23] V.'s claim is accurate. Caesar might call it strategic retreat.

river, where Vercingetorix stayed with the infantry, and kill several. Seeing this, the rest fear they will be surrounded and give themselves to flight. Slaughter everywhere. Three leading Haedui are captured and taken to Caesar: Cotus, the cavalry commander who had quarreled with Convictolitavis at the most recent elections, and Cavarillus, in charge of infantry after Litaviccus' defection, and Eporedorix, leader of the Haedui in war with the Sequani before Caesar arrived.

68. His cavalry in flight, Vercingetorix took his forces, still arranged before the camp, and marched for Alesia, a Mandubii town, and ordered the baggage brought quickly from camp to follow. Caesar took his baggage to a nearby hill, left two legions on guard, and followed as far as daylight allowed. Killing some three thousand enemy of the rear guard, he made camp next day before Alesia. Reconnoitering the city, seeing the enemy terrified because the cavalry—the part of the army they trusted most—had been routed, he urged his men to hard work and began building ramparts.

69. The town, prominently placed on a hilltop, seemed undefeatable except by siege.[24] Two rivers washed the foot of the hill on two sides. Before the town stretched a plain almost three miles long. On the other sides hills of similar height surrounded the town at a little distance. Gallic forces filled the whole space under the wall on the hillside facing the rising sun and had constructed a trench and stone wall six feet high. The fortification begun by the Romans had a circuit of nine miles. Camps were pitched in good places and twenty-three forts were constructed there, in which detachments were placed by day

[24] Alesia stood southeast of Paris in Burgundy on the way to Dijon, on a bluff rising 500 feet above the plain that lay mainly to the west, the town itself between the Ose and Oserain rivers. Caesar's double fortifications, to besiege the town on one side and to protect him from attacks from beyond on the other, were immense, daring, and effective.

in case of a sudden breakout. By night they were held by sentries and strong garrisons.

70. As work begins, cavalry fighting breaks out on the plain, a bit less, as we said, than three miles long with scattered hills. Both sides fight with extreme energy. When ours are sagging, Caesar sends in Germans and sets legions out in front of camp to deter sudden eruption of enemy infantry. Adding the legions' protection raises our men's spirits. Enemy fugitives crowding in obstruct each other and clog the narrow gates. The Germans press ferociously right up to the wall. Great slaughter. Some abandon horses to try to cross the ditch and climb the wall. Caesar orders the legions he set in front of the wall to advance a little. The Gauls behind the walls are no less frightened. Thinking we are advancing at them, they shout "to arms!" In fear some rush into town. Vercingetorix orders the gates closed so the camp would not be laid bare. The Germans retreated after killing many and capturing numerous horses.

71. Vercingetorix decides to send away the cavalry by night, before the Romans can complete their fortifications. As they go, he orders each to go to his own nation and collect for war everyone of age to bear arms. He describes his own merits to them and begs them take care for his safety and not hand over to enemy torture a man who had well served their common freedom. If they were not careful, eighty thousand chosen men would die with him. Making a reckoning, he had barely grain for thirty days but could endure a little longer by scrimping.

Giving these orders, he sends the cavalry out quietly toward midnight through a gap in our siege works. He orders all the grain brought to him and sets the death penalty for those who do not obey. He distributes to the soldiers the cattle the Mandubii had gathered in abundance. Grain he begins to measure out sparingly and gradually. He brings all the forces posted in front of town back inside. Thus he waits for help from Gaul and prepares to continue the war.

72. Learning this from refugees and captives, Caesar establishes this manner of fortification: He dug a trench twenty feet wide with vertical sides, so the trench's bottom was as wide as its top opening. The other fortifications he laid out four hundred feet from the trench, with this in mind, that because he had to enclose so large a space and the whole could not easily be surrounded with a ring of soldiers, he had to avoid unexpected or night onrushes of enemy hordes against his fortifications or having weapons thrown by daylight against our men as they worked. At that distance, he laid out two trenches fifteen feet wide and of equal depth, filling the innermost of them (on flat and low ground) with water diverted from the river. Behind them he built a wall and then rampart twelve feet high. To that he added breastwork and watchposts, with huge "antlers"[25] projecting where breastwork and rampart joined, to slow enemy ascent, and surrounded the whole work with towers eighty feet apart.

73. Then they had to gather lumber and grain to build such large fortifications. As a result, our forces were reduced with so many going far out from camp. Sometimes the Gauls tested our works and tried to break out from town by several gates in full force. So Caesar thought to add again to these works, to be able to defend them with fewer soldiers. Tree trunks or stronger branches were cut down, peeled, and sharpened at the tip, then continuous trenches five feet deep were dug. The stakes were set in them and tied from the bottom to resist being torn up, with the branches sticking up. There were five rows of them, connected and interconnected. Whoever entered

[25] These "antlers" were sharpened and probably forked stakes projecting in a row at the point where the slope of earthwork met the wall of breastwork.

one would entangle himself on the sharpest objects in the trench. These they called tombstones.[26]

In front of them—arranged in angled rows like a quincunx—were dug pits three feet deep, a little narrower at the bottom. Into these were placed rounded stakes thick as a thigh, fire-hardened and sharpened, protruding from the ground no more than four fingers' width. To strengthen and stabilize them, trampled earth a foot deep filled part of the pit, with the rest covered with fronds and shoots to hide the trap. Eight rows of this kind were dug, three feet apart. They called this a lily from its likeness to the flower. In front of these, stakes a foot long with iron hooks fixed in them were buried in the earth and distributed at moderate intervals all along. These they called spurs.

74. When this was done, following the most level ground possible and enclosing some dozen miles, he completed a second set of separate fortifications against an external enemy, so the garrisons by our fortifications would not be surrounded, if it came to it, even by huge forces; and to avoid being forced to leave camp while in danger, he orders them all to bring in thirty days' fodder and grain.

75. While this is going on at Alesia, a council called of Gallic leaders decides not to summon all who could bear arms (as Vercingetorix recommended) but a fixed number levied from each nation, to avoid a crowd too large to be managed or kept straight or regularly supplied. They ordered the Haedui and their clients, the Segusiavi, Ambarri, Aulerci Brannovices, and Blannovii to supply thirty-five thousand; an equal number from the Arverni along with the Eleuteti, Cadurci, Gabali, and

---

[26] The Latin word here, "cippi," was too colloquial for serious writing: here it evokes black humor. (The protruding branches were camouflage for the pitfall.) The "lilies" and "spurs" are similarly mordant.

Vellavii, who were used to being under Arverni rule; from the
Sequani, Senones, Bituriges, Santoni, Ruteni, and Carnutes,
twelve thousand; from the Bellovaci, ten; the same from the
Lemovices; eight thousand from the Pictones, Turoni, Parisii
and Helvetii; the Suessiones, Ambiani, Mediomatrici, Petro-
corii, Nervii, Morini, and Nitiobriges, five thousand; Aulerci
Cenomani, the same; Atrebates, four thousand; Veliocassi,
Lexovii, and Aulerci Eburovices, three; Rauraci and Boii, two;
and thirty thousand from all the nations that border the ocean
and are called habitually Armorican, including Curiosolites,
Redones, Ambibarii, Caletes, Osismi, Veneti, and Venelli.

Of these, the Bellovacii did not supply their number, saying
they would fight the Romans in their own name and way and
obey no one else's commands; but at Commius' request, they
sent two thousand out of friendship.

76. As we said, Caesar had found the assistance of this Commius reliable and helpful in earlier years in Britain. For these
services, he had exempted his state from tribute, restored their
laws, and subjected the Morini to Commius.[27] But the enthusiasm in all Gaul for claiming their freedom and recovering
their former martial glory was enough to erase kindness and
friendship from memory.

Everyone worked with heart and hand for this war. Eight
thousand cavalry[28] and about 250,000 infantry were collected
and reviewed in Haedui territory, counted up, and assigned
commanders. Supreme command is given to Commius of the
Atrebates, Viridomarus and Eporedorix of the Haedui, and
Vercassivellaunus the Arvernian (Vercingetorix's cousin). They

[27] Commius, heard of first in Britain, 4.21 and later. The Atrebates had been tribu-
tary to some other nation, and here C. frees them from that and gives them the
Morini as their own tribute-paying client.

[28] In 7.64 the number was 15,000.

are assigned a select few from these states with whose advice to manage war. Eager and full of confidence, they all set off for Alesia. Not one of them thought the mere sight of such an army could be endured, especially in a two-headed battle, when in fighting off a sally from the town, such huge forces of cavalry and infantry could be seen outside.

77. The people besieged in Alesia, after the day when they expected help to arrive had passed and all their grain was consumed, unaware what was happening among the Haedui, met to discuss what would come of their fortunes. Various opinions were offered there. Some commended surrender, others, while strength lasted, a breakout. The speech of Critognatus should not be omitted, for his unique and wicked cruelty.[29] Born of the noblest Arverni and held in high regard, he says:

"I will say nothing of those who say 'surrender,' meaning vile servitude. I do not regard them as citizens, nor should they be invited to council. Let me address those who approve a breakout. You all agree the memory of our former courage lives in their sentiment. It's softheadedness, not courage, to be unable to bear deprivation a while. Men offering themselves voluntarily to death are easier to find than men who endure suffering calmly. I might approve this sentiment (their prestige means so much to me) if only life were at risk. But in choosing a course, look at all of Gaul, here summoned to our aid.

"If eighty thousand men are killed in one place, what spirit do you think our neighbors and kinsmen will show if they are forced to fight almost over our very corpses? Do not deprive of your assistance these men who have despised their own danger to save you. Do not overthrow all Gaul and subject it to

---

[29] This is the longest quoted speech in Caesar and it comes, remarkably, not from the leader of the revolt, Vercengetorix, but from a character otherwise unknown. We have moved several weeks into the future from the previous paragraph.

perpetual slavery by your foolhardy recklessness or feeble spirits. Just because they have not arrived in time, do you doubt their loyalty and character? What? Do you think the Romans drill on the outer walls daily just for exercise? If their messengers cannot reach you because every approach is blocked, use the Romans as witnesses of their approach. Terrified by it, they work night and day.

"So what is my advice? Do what our ancestors did in the war (hardly equal to this one) with the Cimbri and Teutones. Driven into towns and forced by similar need to sustain life on the corpses of those whose age made them useless for fighting, they never surrendered. If we did not have their example, I would still think it beautiful to establish our own and hand it on to posterity in the name of liberty. What war was ever like that? Ravaging Gaul and bringing huge disaster, the Cimbri finally left our land and headed elsewhere. They left us our rights, our laws, our farms, and our freedom. What do the Romans seek or want, driven by envy, but to settle in the farms and cities of a people they know are famed and powerful in war and to impose endless slavery on them? They fight wars for no other reason. If you do not know what goes on in distant nations, look nearby at a Gaul reduced to a mere province, its rights and laws transformed, bowing to their axes, oppressed in endless slavery."

78. When all was said, they decide that those useless (owing to health or age) should leave the town and that they should try everything before stooping to Critognatus' plan. But they would still follow it, if circumstances required and help was delayed, rather than endure terms of surrender and peace. The Mandubii, who had let them into the town, are required to leave with their children and wives. When they reached the Roman fortifications, they wept and prayed to be taken in and

fed as slaves. But Caesar put out guards on the ramparts and forbade their admission.[30]

79. Meanwhile Commius and the other leaders entrusted with supreme command arrive at Alesia with all their forces, take an outer hill almost a mile from our fortifications, and set down. Next day they bring out cavalry and fill the whole plain, which we said was two and a half miles long, and stationed infantry a little way off, hidden on higher ground. From the town of Alesia, there was a view of the field. Seeing their supporters, they rush together, congratulating each other and raising everyone's spirits in rejoicing. They brought troops out before town and set down, covering the nearest trench with frames and filling in with earth, making ready for sorties and every other contingency.

80. Caesar distributes his whole army to the two sides of the fortifications.[31] When need arose, everyone would hold and know his position. He orders the cavalry from camp and joins battle. There was a view down from the whole encampment, which held a long ridge. All the soldiers watched intently for the fight's outcome. The Gauls had scattered archers and light-armed soldiers among the cavalry, to assist their own men if they pulled back and to resist our cavalry's onrush.

Some of our cavalry, wounded by the unexpected attack, left the fight. Since the Gauls were sure their men were better fighters and saw our men hard pressed by their numbers, both the ones inside their fortifications and those who had gathered to help them roused their spirits with shouts and howls. The action took place in sight of all, so neither fine nor foul deed could be concealed, with both sides roused to courage by love of praise and fear of shame. While they fought from noon to

---

[30] Dio 40.40 has them trapped between the lines and starving to death.
[31] Outward-facing and inward-facing.

sunset with victory uncertain, the Germans on one flank, forming up in troops, attacked the enemy and drove them back. As they were driven into flight, the archers were surrounded and killed. So on the other flanks our men chased them in retreat all the way to their camps and gave them no chance to regroup. Those who had come out of Alesia went back sadly to town, almost despairing of victory.

81. After a day making a great many hurdles, ladders, and grappling hooks, the Gauls leave camp quietly at midnight and come to the fortifications on the plain. Suddenly raising a shout, so those besieged in town would know of their arrival, they begin to throw down hurdles, harass our men on the rampart with slings, arrows, and stones, and ready the other means of assault. When he hears the shout, Vercingetorix gives signal to his men by trumpet and leads them from the town. Our men come to the walls, each to his place assigned days before. They intimidate the Gauls with slings for one-pounders, stakes arranged on the works, and lead shot.[32] Darkness impedes vision and many are wounded on each side. Many javelins are thrown by the catapults. But Mark Antony and the legate Gaius Trebonius, who had charge of defense here, sent men taken from the farther outposts to where they knew ours were hard pressed.

82. As long as the Gauls were farther from the walls, they did more with their many and various missiles. After drawing closer, some fell unawares on stakes, others were run through by falling in ditches or died struck through by javelins from the wall and towers. With many wounds on all sides and no breach in the fort, as daybreak approached they feared they would be surrounded by an attack from the camp on higher

[32] The slings gave distance and momentum to larger stones, the stakes slowed enemy onrush, and the smaller but denser lead shot were also propelled by slings.

ground against their exposed flank, and so returned to their own side. The ones inside the town, bringing out the things Vercingetorix had readied for their sally, spent too long filling up the first trenches before realizing their men had withdrawn without getting near the fortifications. So they left the work unfinished and returned to town.

83. Driven back with great losses twice, the Gauls consider what to do. They summon local experts to learn how the upper camp was placed and fortified. A hill on the north, too large around for our men to incorporate in their works, made for camp on sloping and disadvantageous ground. Legates Gaius Antistius Reginus and Gaius Caninius Rebilus held it with two legions. Reconnoitering the land with scouts, enemy leaders select sixty thousand from the nations with the greatest reputation for courage. They decide secretly together what to do and how, choosing the attack time for around noon. They place Vercassivellaunus from the Arverni in charge, one of the four generals, a relative of Vercingetorix. He led them from camp at first watch, completing the journey by dawn, hidden behind the hill. He ordered his men to rest from the night's work. Nearing noon, he makes for that camp we mentioned. Simultaneously, cavalry approached the fortifications on the plain and the other troops began to show themselves outside camp.

84. Vercingetorix sees his men from the citadel of Alesia and comes out of the town. He brings out hurdles, poles, sheds, sickles—everything needed for a sally. They fight everywhere at once, trying everything. Wherever seems weakest, there they swarm. Roman forces are stretched over extensive fortifications, so it's hard to respond on several fronts. The shouting behind the fighters does a lot to frighten our men, because they see their danger hanging on the courage of others. What men can't see upsets their minds most.

85. Caesar finds a good place to see what is happening everywhere. He sends help to troops where they are struggling. Both sides think this is the best time to fight. The Gauls: if they don't break through, all hope is lost; the Romans: if they prevail, they will see all their labors ended. The greatest struggle is at the upper lines, where we said Vercassivellaunus was sent. The sloping ground has a great effect. Some hurl spears, others cover their approach under a tortoise. Fresh troops step in for weary ones. The earthwork heaped up at the wall gives the Gauls an approach and covers what the Romans had hidden in the ground. Weapons and strength begin to fail our men.

86. Knowing this, Caesar sends Labienus with six cohorts to relieve the hard-pressed. If they cannot hold, he orders him to pull the cohorts back and fight their way out—but only if necessary. He goes round urging the rest not to give way. He tells them the profit of all their former fighting will come down to this day and hour.

The Gauls inside despair in face of the huge fortifications on the plains and try to climb to the top, bringing the equipment they had prepared. They drive off the men on the towers with a shower of spears, then fill the ditch with earth and hurdles, tearing open the rampart and breastwork with hooks.

87. With some cohorts Caesar first sends young Brutus, then the legate Gaius Fabius with others, and then last, when the fighting is hot, brings fresh troops himself to help. Renewing the fight and driving back the enemy, he makes for where he had sent Labienus, taking four cohorts from the closest tower and ordering part of the cavalry to follow and the rest to circle the outer walls and attack the enemy from behind. Labienus, unable to hold off the enemy from behind ramparts or ditches, gathers eleven cohorts that chanced to be nearby,

pulled from other defenses, and reports to Caesar what he thinks should be done. Caesar hurries to join in the battle.

88. Recognizing him by the distinctive colored garment he used in battles[33] and seeing the cavalry squads and cohorts he had ordered follow him (the downhill slopes were in clear view from the heights), the enemy join battle. Shouting on both sides, then a general shout along the ramparts and all the fortifications. Our men discard javelins and fight with swords. Suddenly the cavalry appear behind the Gauls and the other cohorts approach. The enemy turn tail: our cavalry greet them. Great slaughter. Sedullus, general and chief of the Lemovici, is killed. Vercassivellaunus of the Arverni is captured alive as he flees. Seventy-four military standards are brought to Caesar. Out of so many, a few make it to their camp alive. Seeing from town the slaughter and flight, the Gauls despair and withdraw troops from the walls. This news led to general flight from the Gallic camps. If our men were not weary from the day's struggles and reinforcements, the whole enemy host could have been destroyed. Sent out at midnight, cavalry pursued their rear guard, capturing and killing a great many. The rest flee to their home territories.

89. Next day, Vercingetorix calls a council to say he had entered the war not out of personal need but for the liberty of all. Forced to yield to fortune, he offers himself to them, either to die to placate the Romans or to be handed over alive. They send legates about this to Caesar. He orders weapons surrendered and leaders handed over. He sits in the fortifications before his camp and there the leaders are handed over. Vercingetorix is surrendered, arms are laid down. Setting aside the Haedui and Arverni (hoping to use them to win over their

---

[33] The Roman general with his army wore a great cloak, often but not always "purple" in color, but always distinctive and visible.

nations), he gives the captives to his army as slaves, one to each soldier.

90. With this all done, he marches to the Haedui and takes back control of the nation. Legates sent there from the Arverni promise to do as he commands. He orders a great number of hostages. He gives back about 20,000 captives to the Haedui and Arverni.

He orders Titus Labienus to make for the Sequani with two legions and cavalry, assigning Marcus Sempronius Rutilus to him. The legate Gaius Fabius and Lucius Minucius Basilus he stations with two legions among the Remi, to avoid any disaster from the nearby Bellovaci. He sends Gaius Antistius Reginus to the Ambivareti, Titus Sextius to the Bituriges, and Gaius Caninius Rebilus to the Rutheni, each with one legion. He establishes Quintus Tullius Cicero and Publius Sulpicius at Cabillo and Matisco[34] among the Haedui on the Sâone, to obtain grain supply. He decided to winter at Bibracte. When his report arrives, a supplication of twenty days is decreed at Rome.

[34] Châlon-sur-Sâone and Mâcon.

EIGHTH COMMENTARY

51–50 BCE

From here, we leave Caesar's words behind to conclude the story of his years in Gaul. He took up the pen and his characteristic style again himself later to tell the story of his struggle for power with Pompey and others in his commentaries on the civil war, though that work as well had to be completed by other hands. He wrote when he could and he wrote for political purpose. Was the winter of 52–51 the moment at which the seven commentaries we have from Caesar's hand were compiled and disseminated? Those who argue that the whole work was published at once need to find a way to explain the choice to publish *then*. If Caesar was indeed working year-by-year, then what needs explaining is only the failure to produce commentary a year later, at the end of 51.

What we have in this eighth commentary, covering the two last years Caesar spent in Gaul, comes from the hand of Aulus Hirtius. Hirtius was a loyal Caesarean, legate with Caesar in Gaul from 58 onwards, faithful through the civil wars until Caesar's death. He had been nominated consul by Caesar for 43 with Gaius Pansa and duly took office for that year. He interpreted his loyalty to Caesar's memory as requiring him to pitch in with Octavian and Pansa against Mark Antony, and he lost his life in the successful battle against Antony at Modena in April 43. (Suetonius reports a series of scandalous rumors about Octavian's youthful affairs with men, including Caesar himself—that accusation came from Mark Antony—, followed by an encounter in Spain with Hirtius, who supposedly paid him 300,000 sesterces for his favors.)

Hirtius wrote his commentary on the last years of the Gallic war and another on Caesar's war at Alexandria after Caesar's death. (Others probably wrote the surviving accounts in the same vein of Caesar's fighting in Africa and Spain.) Years had elapsed since the events recounted and it is unlikely that Hirtius had intended in the moment to write such an account. Accordingly, whatever materials he had to draw on (any by Caesar himself?), his account is less precise and accurate than those of the earlier commentaries written by the greater writer closer to the time of events.

Indeed, the translator of the *Gallic War* is put in a perplexion by Hirtius. To read with the care a translator must makes the shift into this eighth commentary a startling moment. The lucidity, crispness, and narrative speed of Caesar's prose have become familiar by now. Hirtius, by contrast, writes sludge. I have resisted the temptation to clean him up and have added a few notes to reassure the reader that particularly slovenly passages are in fact translated here as accurately as possible.

When Hirtius wrote, of course there would be an audience for the authorized Caesarean view of the events he describes, but it is also worth recalling that sometime not long after Caesar's death, the newly sharpened pen of Sallust would also begin telling stories of the world Caesar lived in and made. His style was taut and effective, his perspective jaundiced even if essentially loyal to Caesar, and his method indirect. Though his mainly lost *Histories* ranged more widely, his famous surviving essays tell constrained stories (the revolt of Catiline, the war with Jugurtha decades earlier) in order to make their political point. Sallust was clearly idiosyncratic. Hirtius gives us the official version, the authorized Caesarean story. He owns up to his authorship, but absent a few short passages, what he has written could have been passed off as a clumsy imposture, an attempt at Caesarean style and content that might almost fool a few. Remarkably, he recounts some episodes of the preceding year that Caesar omitted in his seventh commentary, leaving us to wonder what else Caesar had omitted over the years.

He acknowledges authorship in a letter to Balbus that appears in all the manuscripts at the beginning of this commentary. We have met Cornelius Balbus before, born in Cadiz, made a Roman citizen and given a Roman name for service to Pompey, then a supporter of Caesar without losing Pompey's friendship. He was rich and influential and envied, hence the factitious legal case in 56 BCE for which the speeches of Pompey, Crassus, and Cicero (his *pro Balbo* survives) got him acquitted. In the civil war and after, he was closer still to Caesar, then to Octavian, leading to his consulship (the first for a "naturalized citizen") in 40. He kept his own account of his times (since lost) and here intervenes to ensure completion and preservation of Caesar's commentaries.

This commentary comprises two years' narrative. Hirtius explains: "I don't think I need to do this, especially because the following year (the consulship of Paulus and Marcellus) has nothing of importance happening in Gaul. I've decided to write a bit more and attach it to this commentary so readers will know where Caesar and his army were at this time." Hirtius also had to stitch together his ending with the beginning of Caesar's commentaries on the civil war, but we are not quite sure how he did that because the end of this commentary seems broken off before Hirtius' own conclusion. What we have here ends as Caesar returns to Cisalpine Gaul at the end of 50. It was there that he monitored the deteriorating situation in Rome, welcomed the fleeing tribunes Antony and Cassius Longinus, and made his decision to go to Rome. His first commentary on the civil war begins similarly in mid-narrative, in the very first days of the year 49, when Lentulus had taken office as consul, and just before the flight of the tribunes.

Gaul in 51 was exhausted but not yet at rest. The great rebellion was over, but insurgencies continued. In January, the Bituriges, though Caesar had been victorious at their capital of Avaricum only the previous spring, took up arms again, but were quickly disposed of. Caesar returned to Bibracte, a more central location, pulling together six legions, but then the Carnutes and Bellovaci revolted briefly. In the course of this spring and summer, patiently and obsessively, he brought the central and northern tiers of Gaul to sullen acceptance.

Then he turned his attention south to unrest led from the Cadurci and Senones people and laid siege to the rebel hill fortress of Uxellodunum, about two hundred miles south of the Bituriges. The siege was short and successful and many captives were taken. Caesar ordered that the fighters among the prisoners all be mutilated: their hands were cut off. This was a sentence of either painful death (infected wounds in the circumstances were likely) or burdensome life.

In what could have been a summative mood, Caesar left the site of that massacre for his first visit to Aquitaine in the southwest and to the Roman city of Narbonne inside the province borders. He then circled back north at the end of the year to winter himself at Arras among the Belgae and to be within reach of all his legions, spread in camps from two among the Haedui, then north into the familiar contested territory of the Treveri and others, in the process coming back in contact with Labienus and Antony. Antony, he found, had even captured the mercurial and impressive Commius of the Atrebates.

ROME IN 51

At Rome, the year 51 challenged Caesar and foreshadowed the contest to come. Marcellus and Rufus were consuls, Marcellus in the lead. He maintained a steady barrage of harassment designed to put Caesar in his place. He was perhaps less obstreperous than Cato would have been had he won the election for this year, but the drumbeats of opposition were growing louder. Early in the year he took steps to abrogate the citizenship Caesar had conferred on the people of Comum on Lake Como in northern Italy and as a sign of his action ordered a visitor from there to be flogged. Caesar had surely taken his authority further than was prudent, and Cicero's best intervention claimed merely that the abused visitor was a magistrate of his city, on the idea that magistrates in towns with "Latin rights" but not automatic citizenship acquired citizenship as individuals by right of office.

More troubling was Marcellus' argument that Caesar's great victory in 52 over Vercingetorix showed that his job in Gaul was done and so he and his army should come home. Suppressing insurgents in this year, necessary or unnecessary for military reasons, meant Caesar was showing that he was still needed in Gaul till the end of his term.

Pompey was not unhappy to see Caesar the subject of this harassment but prudently decided to hold off until early in 50 any decision on recall. Pompey's program through these last years of Caesar's time in Gaul shows hesitation and deferral of decision, a desire to see Caesar constrained but an unwillingness to take active steps himself to constrain him. In light of what happened after Caesar returned, it's fair to conclude Pompey missed his chance.

In July the consular elections for 50 brought in another Marcellus (married to the older sister of the young Octavian) and Aemilius Paulus (brother of the future triumvir Lepidus). They did not portend well for Caesar. By fall, it was clear that Caesar's rivals, enemies, and many sometime friends were coalescing to resist his return to active Roman public life after almost a decade away.

IN THE CONSULSHIP OF
SULPICIUS RUFUS AND
CLAUDIUS MARCELLUS

PREFACE

Compelled by your continual urgings, Balbus, since my daily refusals seemed only an apology for my laziness, not an excuse based on difficulty, I have undertaken a challenging task. To our Caesar's commentaries on his deeds in Gaul, since his earlier and later works were not linked, I have attached a final book and I have brought his last unfinished one on events at Alexandria down to the end not of civil war, to be sure—no end in sight—but of Caesar's life. I would like readers to know how unwillingly I undertook this writing, so I can elude charges of folly and arrogance for inserting myself into the midst of Caesar's writings. Everyone agrees there is nothing, however painstakingly finished, whose elegance is not outdone by these commentaries. They were published so writers would not lack for knowledge of great events, but they are so universally praised that they seem to have deprived authors of material, not supplied it.

We are more amazed by this than anyone. For others know how well and correctly they were composed, but we know how quickly and easily. Caesar possessed immense ease and elegance in writing, along with extremely precise skill at explaining his plans. I did not even participate in the Alexandrian and African wars. Though I know something of them from Caesar's conversation, we pay attention differently to fresh and wonderful tales from how we listen to things to which we will have to testify.

But now while I gather every excuse not to be compared with Caesar, I risk the very charge of arrogance merely for thinking I *could* be compared with Caesar in anyone's eyes! Farewell.

1. All Gaul was beaten. Caesar, with no break in fighting from the summer before, wanted his soldiers to recover quietly from their efforts in winter quarters, but several nations then were reported renewing war plans and framing conspiracies. A plausible explanation was advanced, that the Gauls all knew they could not resist the Romans with massed forces in one place, but if several nations made different simultaneous attacks the army of the Roman people would not have strength or time or forces to pursue all. No one nation should refuse the risk of loss if in the interval the others could assert their liberty.

2. To keep from proving the Gauls right, Caesar put quaestor Mark Antony in charge of winter quarters. With a cavalry guard he sets out from Bibracte the day before the January Kalends (31 December) for the thirteenth legion, which he had stationed not far from the Haedui in Bituriges territory, and joins it with the eleventh legion, which was nearby. Leaving two cohorts to guard the baggage, he leads the rest of the army to the richest part of Bituriges country. With spreading lands and numerous towns, they could not be kept in check by a single legion in quarters from preparing for war and making conspiracies.[1]

---

[1] This prosperity and readiness survived the burning of more than twenty of their "cities" the year earlier at Vercingetorix's order (7.15).

3. Caesar's sudden arrival meant—as it had to for scattered, unready people—that farmers living free of care were run down by cavalry before they could flee to towns. For even the common signal of enemy invasion—usually inferred from burning farmhouses—was taken away by Caesar's order, so they would not be short of grain and fodder if they wanted to go farther nor would the enemy be terrified by fires. Many thousands were captured. Those of the frightened Bituriges who could fly from the Roman arrival fled to neighboring nations, trusting in private connections or other alliances. Pointless. For Caesar by great marches appears everywhere and gives no nation room to think of others' safety more than their own. By his speed he kept old friendships and invited those hesitating in terror to consider truce terms. When he proposed terms, the Bituriges, thinking Caesar's mercy gave them a path back to his friendship and that neighboring nations had given hostages without being punished and were welcomed into alliance, did the same.

4. As reward for their effort and endurance, for staying diligently on post in winter days on hard roads and insufferable cold, Caesar promises two hundred sesterces each to soldiers and as many thousand to centurions, instead of plunder.[2] Returning the legions to quarters, he returns to Bibracte on the fortieth day. While he was hearing cases there, the Bituriges send representatives to him asking help against the Carnutes, whom they complained were waging war on them. Hearing this, although he had not been in quarters more than eighteen days, he takes the fourteenth and sixth legions from camp on the Saône—it said in the last commentary he had put them there to regulate the grain supply. So with the two legions he sets out to pursue the Carnutes.

[2] The amounts must be garbled: centurions would normally get double the share of a common soldier, not a thousand times as much.

5. When news of the army reached the enemy, the Carnutes, instructed by the sufferings of others, desert the villages and towns where they lived in small farmhouses thrown up out of need to endure the winter (for they had lost several towns in defeat) and scatter and flee. Caesar does not want his soldiers to have to suffer the terrible storms breaking out in that season, so makes camp in Cenabum, a town of the Carnutes, and protects the soldiers, quartering some in Gallic houses, some in houses built with straw roofs hastily gathered. He sends cavalry and auxiliaries in all directions wherever it was said the enemy had gone. Not a mistake, for our men usually came back with great booty. The Carnutes, overcome by the harsh winter and fear of danger, not daring—once driven from their homes—to stay in one place for long and unable to hide in protecting forests during bad storms, scatter to neighboring states, while many of them go missing.

6. Caesar thought it enough, in the toughest season of the year, to dispel the gathering forces so no war could begin. Confirming as far as possible that no great war could be gotten together that summer, he placed Gaius Trebonius in quarters at Cenabum with the two legions he had kept with him. He ascertained from regular embassies of the Remi that the Bellovaci, who lead all Gauls and Belgae in martial glory, and the nations nearby were gathering an army under Correus of the Bellovaci and Commius of the Atrebates. They collected them in one place so the whole mass could invade the Suessiones, tributaries of the Remi. Caesar thought not only his reputation but even his safety required that no disaster befall allies who had served the republic well and so he called the eleventh legion from quarters again. He sent a letter to Gaius Fabius to lead the two legions he had to Suessiones country and summoned from Labienus one of his two legions. So as the situa-

tion of camps and the needs of war allowed, by his own constant effort he imposed the burden of expeditions on the legions by turns.

7. Gathering these forces, he sets out against the Bellovaci, making camp in their country and sending cavalry squads in all directions to capture men from whom he could learn the enemy's plans. The cavalry do their job, reporting they found few people in farmhouses. They were not left behind to farm (thorough emigration had occurred everywhere) but sent back to spy. When Caesar asked them where the mass of Bellovaci was and what was their plan, he discovered that all Bellovaci who could bear arms had gathered in one place, along with Ambiani, Aulerci, Caleti, Veliocasses, and Atrebates. They had chosen high ground for camp in a forest surrounded with marshes and had sent all their baggage deep into the woods.

Several leading citizens were responsible for the war, but the mass obeyed Correus especially, for they knew he hated the name of the Roman people intensely. A few days earlier, Commius of the Atrebates had left camp to bring support from Germans who were nearby in immense numbers. The Bellovaci had decided by agreement of all the leaders and the keen enthusiasm of the people that if, as was reported, Caesar was coming with three legions, they would give him battle rather than be forced to fight his whole army later in worse and harsher conditions. If he brought a larger force, they would stay where they were, using ambushes to prevent the Romans from finding fodder (which was scant and scattered because of the season) and grain and other supplies.

8. When Caesar learned this from many witnesses, all in agreement with each other, and saw that the plans in play were full of prudence and not just impetuous barbarism, he decided to work every way to bring the enemy to battle despising our

small force. He had uniquely courageous veteran legions, the seventh, eighth, and ninth, as well as the eleventh chosen from youth of great promise, eight years in service but in comparison with the others not yet claiming a reputation for experience and courage. He summoned his council to encourage the mass of soldiers by reporting everything he had been told. To see if he could bring the enemy to fight with three legions, he arranged his line so the seventh, eighth, and ninth legions marched ahead of all the baggage, then after the line of all baggage (there was not much, as is customary on marches) he brought the eleventh, so the enemy would not be surprised by seeing a greater force than they were looking for. Thus he makes his army almost a marching square and brings it into enemy sight sooner than they expected.

9. When the Gauls—whose confident plans had been reported to Caesar—suddenly see our legions marching resolutely as if aligned for battle, they bring their force out from camp and do not leave the high ground. Perhaps they feared battle or were startled by our arrival or were just watching for our plan. Caesar, though preferring to fight, is still surprised by the great mass and pitches camp against enemy camp with a valley deeper than wide between them. He orders camp to be protected by a rampart twelve feet high, then a breastwork to be built proportionate to its height and a double trench dug fifteen feet deep with straight sides. Towers were raised three stories high, joined by connecting covered bridges, whose fronts were protected by wicker breastwork, in order to defend against the enemy with a double trench and a double row of fighters, one from the bridges, safer for their height and allowing spears to be thrown farther and more daringly, the other, set in the trench nearer the enemy, protected from falling weapons by the bridges. He put taller gates and turrets at the entrances.

10. The fortification served two purposes. He hoped the size of the works and his show of fear would raise enemy confidence, but he also saw that when we had to go farther for grain and fodder, with this fortification the camp could be defended by a small force. Meanwhile, frequent skirmishing occurred among small bands from the two camps across the marsh. Sometimes our Gallic or German allies crossed the marsh and chased the enemy fiercely, or again the enemy crossed and pushed our men farther back. It happened on the daily foraging (it had to happen), looking for fodder in the few scattered farmhouses, that foragers would be surrounded by enemy in difficult country. Even if this brought our men only modest losses of cattle and slaves, it also encouraged foolish hopes in the barbarians, the more so because Commius—I said he had gone to summon German auxiliaries—had arrived with cavalry. Even with no more than 500 of them, the barbarians were still full of themselves over the Germans' coming.

11. Caesar observed the enemy for several days keeping to their camp, which was protected by marshes and by its site, and so unable to be attacked without a ruinous battle, in a place that could not be walled around except by a larger army. He writes to Trebonius to summon the thirteenth legion, wintering among the Bituriges with legate Titus Sextius, to come as quickly as possible with a total of three legions by forced marches. He sends by turns cavalry of the Remi, Lingones, and other nations—he had demanded a huge number—to guard the foragers, who might face sudden enemy attack.

12. Days went on and attention faded with routine, as often happens over time. The Bellovaci lay ambush in the woods with an elite infantry band, observing our cavalry's daily patrols. Next day they send their cavalry to lure ours out into a trap and then attack when they were surrounded. This bad luck

struck the Remi, to whom that day's duty had fallen. Suddenly spotting enemy cavalry and sneering at their inferior numbers, they chased them eagerly and were surrounded by infantry on all sides. Unnerved by this, they retreated more rapidly than cavalry usually do, losing Vertiscus, a tribal chief and cavalry commander. Scarcely able to sit a horse at his age, in the Gallic way he would not excuse himself from command for age nor wish them to fight without him. The enemy's spirits were inflamed and stirred by battle success, with a prince and commander of the Remi killed, while ours were cautioned by the loss to set their posts in more carefully scouted places and to pursue withdrawing enemies prudently.

13. Daily skirmishes in sight of both camps continued where the marsh could be forded and crossed. In this contest, the Germans Caesar had brought across the Rhine to fight alongside cavalry bravely crossed the marsh, killed a few resisters, and stubbornly pursued the remaining mass. They terrified not only the ones overcome hand-to-hand and those wounded at a distance but even those supporting from farther away—all fleeing disgracefully, making no end of their running until they had abandoned high ground and retreated to camp—and some even fled farther away in shame. Their whole army was so unsettled in this danger that one could scarcely tell whether they were more insufferable after a trivial victory or more cowardly after slight mischance.

14. After several days spent in camp, the Bellovacan leaders learned of the approach of the legions and legate Gaius Trebonius. Fearing a siege like that of Alesia they send away by night everyone up in years or weaker and unarmed, and all the remaining baggage besides. They lay out a confused and muddled line of march (even light-armed Gauls are usually followed by a swarm of wagons), then dawn overtakes them and they

draw up forces in front of camp so the Romans would not begin
to pursue them before the baggage train had gotten very far.
Caesar did not want to attack defenders by climbing such a hill
nor miss a chance to move his legions to where the barbarians
could not leave safely without our soldiers harassing them. Seeing the camps separated by a marsh difficult to cross (that
would slow pursuit) and again seeing a ridge across the marsh
almost reaching the enemy camp—separated from it by a narrow valley—he lays bridges across the marsh, crosses the legions, and quickly comes to a plateau atop the ridge, protected
on both sides by downslopes. He forms the legions and marches
to the end of the ridge and sets out the army there, where catapults could hurl spears into the enemy's formations.

15. The barbarians relied on the lay of the land and stayed
at battle positions. They couldn't refuse battle if the Romans
attempted the hill but didn't dare send out their forces in small
numbers, because dispersal would produce chaos. Seeing their
stubbornness, Caesar draws up twenty cohorts, surveys a camp
on that site, and orders it fortified. When work is done, he lines
up the legions before the rampart and sets cavalry on post with
horses on tight rein. When the Bellovaci saw the Romans ready
to pursue them and could not safely stay the night or longer
there, they made this retreat plan: taking bundles of straw and
branches (abundant in their camp), they handed them along,
placing them before their line; at a signal at the end of the day,
they set them ablaze all at once. The spreading flame swiftly
hid their whole force from Roman sight. As this happened the
barbarians fled, running flat out.

16. Caesar, even if he could not observe the enemy retreat
for the fire in the way, suspected the stratagem meant flight.
He advances the legions and sends cavalry squads in pursuit.
Fearing ambush if the enemy stopped there and tried to lure

our men into a bad place, he advances slowly. The cavalry were leery of entering smoke and thick flame and, if they ventured boldly, they could scarcely see the front ends of their own horses, so they gave the Bellovaci easy opportunity to retreat. So, cunning and fearful as they fled, the enemy advanced without losses almost ten miles and pitched camp in a well-protected place. Sending out cavalry and infantry repeatedly on ambush from there, they brought great losses to Roman foragers.

17. While this was happening too often, Caesar finds out from a captive that Correus, the Bellovacan leader, had chosen six thousand of the bravest infantry and all told a thousand cavalry to place an ambush where he thought the Romans would send men after grain and fodder. Knowing this, he brings out more legions than customary and sends cavalry ahead, the usual way he usually sent a guard for foragers.[3] Among them he inserts light-armed auxiliaries and he comes as close as he can with the legions.

18. The Gauls in their ambushes had chosen for this action a plain no more than a mile each way, protected all around by thick woods and a deep river, and they surrounded it with ambushes like hunters. Scouting the enemy's plan, our men were battle-ready in weapons and spirits, refusing no combat—they had the legions backing them. When they arrived as cavalry squads, Correus thought he had been offered his chance for action. First he showed himself with a small band and attacked the nearest squads. Ours withstand the assault from ambush firmly and do not crowd together—that often happens in cavalry battle out of fear, with losses taken just because of the crowding.

---

[3] "usual . . . usually": an accurate rendering of Hirtius' thoughtless repetition.

19. Our squads fight a few at a time and do not let themselves be surrounded. Then the rest of the enemy break out of the woods fighting, led by Correus. The contest was intense across the field, beginning evenly for a long time. Then gradually from the woods a full infantry line emerges, forcing our cavalry to withdraw. Light-armed infantry quickly come up to help—I said they were sent ahead of the legions—and they fight relentlessly amidst our cavalry. Fighting went on evenly a while longer, then gradually, as happens in battle, the ones who had resisted the first ambush attack become stronger just because their prudence suffered no ambush losses.

Meanwhile the legions draw closer with frequent messengers reaching our men and the enemy at the same time, saying that the general is near with forces ready for battle. Hearing this, our men fight keenly, relying on support from the cohorts. (If they acted slowly, they would appear to share victory's glory with the legions.) Enemy morale collapses and they take flight by different routes. Pointless: wanting to trap the Romans in a tight spot, they were themselves snared by it. Beaten and routed at last, losing most of their forces, they flee in disarray, some seeking the woods, some the river—energetically chased down and killed as they fled by our men. Unvanquished meanwhile in disaster, Correus could not be made to seek the woods or accept our men's invitation to surrender, but by fighting heroically and wounding many he forced our victorious men, roused by rage, to hurl their weapons at him.

20. Afterwards, Caesar coming upon the fresh traces of battle assumes the enemy, learning of such a disaster, would abandon their camp site, said to be no more than about seven miles from the killing field. Though he sees the river crossing obstructed, still he crosses his army and goes on. But the Bellovaci and other nations quickly hear from a few wounded refu-

gees, who had escaped fate in the woods, that all had gone badly: Correus was killed and the cavalry and strongest of the infantry were lost. Thinking the Romans were about to appear, they call council hastily with a trumpet blast, and ambassadors and hostages are sent to Caesar.

21. Everyone agreed to this plan, so Commius of the Atrebates fled to the Germans from whom he had drawn help in the war. The rest send ambassadors to Caesar straightaway, asking him to accept as their punishment what they were sure his mercy and kindness would never have inflicted on them if he had been able to impose it on them at full strength without battle. Bellovacan resources had been devastated in the cavalry battle, many thousands of choice infantry had died—scarcely had messengers escaped slaughter. But they had gotten this benefit out of that battle, for all the disaster, that Correus, instigator of war and rouser of rabble, had been killed. When he was alive, the senate had never had as much power as the clueless populace.

22. Caesar reminds the ambassadors in their pleading that the Bellovaci and other Gauls had undertaken war the same season last year, with the Bellovaci stubbornly persisting in their purpose most of all, not brought to their senses even by the others' surrender. He knew and understood they could easily blame the dead for the fault. But no one was powerful enough to rouse and wage war with a feeble band of plebeians if princes were unwilling, if the senate resisted, if all good men shied away. But he would still settle for the penalty they had brought on themselves.

23. The following night the ambassadors take his answer to their people and prepare hostages. Ambassadors of other nations rush in to watch what came of the Bellovaci, giving hostages and doing Caesar's bidding, except for Commius,

whose fear kept him from trusting his safety to anyone's oath. The year before Titus Labienus, while Caesar was hearing cases in Cisalpine Gaul, discovered Commius canvassing nations and forming a conspiracy against Caesar. Labienus thought he could punish this disloyalty without treachery.[4] He did not think Commius would come to his camp if called and did not want to put him on guard by trying, so he sent Gaius Volusenus Quadratus to arrange his murder while appearing to parley. He gave him chosen centurions suitable for the task.

When they came to parley and Volusenus took Commius' hand as agreed, a centurion was either troubled by the unusual task or quickly thwarted by Commius' retinue and was unable to kill the man. But he struck him heavily on the head with the first blow of his sword. With swords drawn on both sides, both parties thought of flight more than fight, ours thinking Commius was fatally wounded, the Gauls fearing worse than the ambush they had seen. After this Commius is said to have decided never to come within sight of any Roman again.

24. Conquering such warrior nations, Caesar saw no nation left that could launch a war of resistance, but as some were leaving their towns and fleeing their farms to escape Roman rule he decided to send his army in several directions. He keeps with him quaestor Mark Antony and the twelfth legion. Legate Caius Fabius and twenty-five cohorts he sends to the farthest corner of Gaul, because he heard some nations were in arms there and he thought it wasn't enough that legate Caius Caninius Rebilus, who was there, had two legions not quite at strength.[5] He calls Titus Labienus to join him, and the

---

[4] This encounter occurred about the time of the events in 7.75–76, but Caesar did not mention it.

[5] In 7.90 Caesar said Rebilus had one legion with him—probably in the far south of Gaul bordering the Roman province. If there were now two, then the weakness

fifteenth legion with him in winter quarters he sends to Gaul of the togas[6] to protect colonies of Roman citizens, to prevent any loss from barbarian incursion such as happened the summer before to the people of Trieste, overrun by their sudden attack and brigandage.

He himself goes to waste and pillage Ambiorix's lands. He had despaired of bringing the terrified fugitive under his control, but thought it appropriate for his reputation to leave that land so stripped of citizens, farmhouses, and livestock that Ambiorix would be unable, hated by his own people—if fortune left any there—to return to his nation after all these disasters.

25. After sending legions and auxiliaries all over Ambiorix's territory, laying waste everywhere with slaughter, fire, and plunder, killing or capturing a huge number of people, he sends Labienus with two legions against the Treveri, a state close to Germany and thus tested by daily wars, differing little in manners and ferocity from the Germans, obeying orders only when compelled by an army.

26. Meanwhile legate Gaius Caninius heard from messages and messengers from Duratius—a constant friend of Romans though some of his people had rebelled—of a great many enemy gathering among the Pictones and so he marches to the town of Lemonum.[7] On arriving and learning reliably from captives that Duratius was trapped and besieged in Lemonum by thousands of men led by the Andean Dumnacus, he made

---

arose from battle depletion of the one and the addition of a second full of raw recruits from the province.

[6] Togas because the people south of the Po had received Roman citizenship as a result of the Social War a generation earlier; Caesar himself had not used the term in the earlier commentaries. This generosity, of course, had the effect of sending a legion closer to Rome if the occasion ever arose to intimidate, threaten, or attack Caesar's enemies there.

[7] Poitiers.

camp in a strong position, for he was unwilling to engage the enemy with his weakened legions. Dumnacus, realizing Caninius was near, turned all his force against the legions, setting to attack the Roman camp. Wasting several days on this siege, at great loss to his side but still unable to breach any part of the fortifications, he went back to besieging Lemonum.

27. Just then legate Caius Fabius accepts the submission of several states, sealing loyalty with hostages. From letters of Caninius he learns what is happening among the Pictones. With this knowledge he leaves to assist Duratius. Dumnacus, hearing of Fabius' approach, loses hope of safety, having at the same time to resist a Roman army outside and watch and fear his townsmen. Suddenly he leaves the place with his army and thinks he will not be safe until he crosses his army over the Loire—needing a bridge to cross because of its size. Fabius, before he came in sight of the enemy or joined Caninius, instructed by people who knew the region, believed that the terrified enemy would most likely head where they were in fact heading. So he makes for the same bridge with his army and orders the cavalry to go as far ahead of the legions' line as they could and still make it back to the same camp without exhausting the horses. Our cavalry pursued as ordered, breaking Dumnacus' line and attacking frightened fugitives baggage-laden on the march. They take great plunder and kill many. The matter well settled, they return to camp.

28. Next night Fabius sent out cavalry ready to fight and delay the enemy march until his arrival. Following his orders, cavalry commander Quintus Atius Varus, a man of distinctive spirit and shrewdness, encourages his men to pursue the enemy column, setting some cavalry squads in good positions and giving battle with the rest. Enemy cavalry fight with spirit as their infantry halt in order to come to assist their cavalry

against ours.[8] The battle is hotly fought. Our men despise yesterday's beaten enemy and know the legions are following
them. Ashamed to yield and eager to finish the battle themselves, they fight the infantry bravely, while the enemy, thinking no more forces could arrive (from what they had seen the
day before) seemed to have gained a chance to destroy our
cavalry.

29. After a spell of intense fighting, Dumnacus arranges his
line to support the cavalry, when suddenly our tight-formed
legions come in view before the enemy. The barbarian squads
recoil at the sight; the infantry are terrified. Breaking up the
baggage train, they flee headlong and shouting in all directions. Our cavalry, fresh from fighting off their fierce resistance, rejoice in happy victory, raising shouts on all sides, and
then surround the retreating forces, killing there as many as
their horses had strength to chase and their right hands
strength for killing. More than twelve thousand men, some
still armed, some casting aside weapons out of fear, were killed
and all the baggage captured.

30. After this rout, news arrives of Drappes of the Senones.
When Gaul first revolted, he gathered ruined men from everywhere, incited slaves to flee, collected refugees and bandits
from every state, then harassed Roman baggage and supplies.
Now he collected no more than two thousand refugees from
this rout to attack the province, plotting with Lucterius the
Cadurcan, whom we learned in the previous commentary had
wanted to attack the province at the outset of the revolt.[9] The
legate Caninius makes after them with two legions to keep the

---

[8] The Gauls were marching with infantry ahead and cavalry bringing up the rear;
the real engagement begins when the infantry stop and turn to support the cavalry.

[9] 7.7; but this episode with Drappes was not mentioned by Caesar.

damage or just the panic in the province from turning into a great disgrace because of the pillaging of the ruined men.

31. Gaius Fabius sets out with the rest of the army[10] for the Carnutes and the other states whose forces he knew were worn down in the battle with Dumnacus. He was sure they would be more submissive after their fresh disaster, but if he gave them space and time, Dumnacus could rouse them. Fabius thus achieves the greatest swift success in retaking these peoples. The Carnutes, often harassed but never speaking of peace, give hostages and surrender, while other nations by the ocean in farthest Gaul (the ones called Armoricans), influenced by the Carnutes' prestige, immediately obey orders on the arrival of Fabius and the legions. Dumnacus, exiled from his country, alone and astray and hiding out, has to head for the most remote Gallic lands.

32. Drappes and Lucterius knew Caninius and the legions were near and thus they were unable to enter the province without certain destruction at the hands of the pursuing army. Nor could they roam free for brigandage, so they halt in the territory of the Cadurci. Since Lucterius had been powerful there once in settled times and always had considerable influence among those barbarians as the source of new schemes, with his own and Drappes' troops he seizes the town of Uxellodunum—exceedingly well protected by its site and formerly a dependency of his. He adds the townsmen to his forces.[11]

33. Caninius arrived soon thereafter and saw the town protected all around by sheer rocks, making it difficult for armed men to ascend, even unopposed. He also saw the townsmen

[10] What rest of what army? Hirtius often forgets to mention important facts, such as the joining up of Caninius' and Fabius' forces implied here as they separate.

[11] Probably Puy d'Issolu, north of Toulouse. The description is not *quite* right, but Hirtius is even weaker on geography than Caesar was.

had much baggage. If they tried to slip away quietly with it they could not outrun our cavalry or even our legions. He divided his cohorts three ways and made three camps on high ground, beginning to lead a rampart around the town gradually, as far as the size of his forces allowed.

34. When the townsmen noticed this, they were troubled by wretched memories of Alesia, fearing a similar outcome from the siege—Lucterius most of all. He had experienced that danger and cautioned that they had to plan for grain, so they all agree to leave some troops behind and go out light-armed to bring in grain. Approving that plan, next night they leave two thousand armed men behind while Drappes and Lucterius lead the rest out of the town. Over the next few days they collect a considerable quantity of grain in Cadurci territory, where some tried to help them with grain while others simply could not stop them taking it. Sometimes they come to our camps with night raids. So Gaius Caninius puts off surrounding the town with fortifications, worried he could not protect it all when done and might disperse weakened garrisons in too many places.

35. With a large supply of grain in hand, Drappes and Luc-terius camp no more than ten miles from town, from there to take the grain little by little into town. They divided tasks between them: Drappes remains on guard in camp with some troops; Lucterius takes a line of pack animals toward town. Setting guards there, he starts about the tenth hour of night to bring grain to town by narrow woodland paths. When camp guards heard the noise and scouts who had been sent out reported what was happening, Caninius quickly attacks the grain-bearers with armed cohorts from the nearest posts just on daybreak. Frightened by sudden misfortune, they fled to their guard posts. Seeing this, our men go straight at the armed

men and allow none to be taken alive. Lucterius escapes with
a few men but does not return to camp.

36. Successful, Caninius learned from captives that some of
Drappes' forces were camped about ten miles away. Hearing
this from several sources, he realized that with the other general put to flight, the rest would be terrified and easily overcome. He thought it great luck that no refugee from the slaughter had reached camp to report to Drappes the disaster they had
suffered. Seeing no danger in trying, he sends all his cavalry
and German infantry—all swift men—ahead toward the enemy
camp. He divides one legion in three camps and takes another
with him without its baggage. Nearing the enemy, he hears
from scouts sent ahead that in camping, as is barbarian custom, they abandoned high ground and set down by the river-
side; and that the Germans and the cavalry had attacked them
unawares and begun battle. Hearing this, he brings his legion
forward armed in formation. Suddenly then from everywhere
when signal is given they take the high ground. When this
happens, the Germans and the cavalry spot the legionary standards and fight vigorously. The cohorts immediately attack
from all sides, killing or capturing everyone and taking immense booty. Drappes himself is captured in that battle.

37. With that successfully accomplished with hardly a
wounded soldier, Caninius returns to besieging the townspeople. With the enemy outside destroyed—fear of which had
kept him from dividing his forces before and surrounding the
townsmen with fortification—he orders works undertaken on
all sides. Next day Gaius Fabius arrives with his forces and
takes up besieging part of the town himself.

38. Meanwhile, Caesar leaves quaestor Mark Antony with
fifteen cohorts among the Bellovaci, to keep the Belgae from
any chance of plotting anew. He visits the other states, orders

numerous hostages, and calms the fears of all with his encouragement. When he got to the Carnutes, in whose state (as Caesar described in an earlier commentary) the war originated, he noticed they were particularly fearful out of consciousness of what they had done, so to free the nation quickly from fear he ordered Gutuatrus, as leader of that uprising and proponent of war, be handed over for punishment.[12] Though he did not trust himself to his own people, soon with cooperation from all he was found and brought to camp. Against his nature, Caesar is forced to punish him by a great throng of soldiers, who blamed this one for all the dangers and losses endured in the war, so he was beaten lifeless and beheaded.

39. There Caesar learned from regular letters of Caninius about what had been done with Drappes and Lucterius and what the locals were thinking. He sneered at their small numbers, but judged that their stubbornness merited a substantial punishment. Then the rest of Gaul would not think they needed only bravery and not strength to resist Rome and so would not follow their example and take advantage of their location to assert their liberty. He knew that all Gauls knew there was one summer left to his governorship, so if they could hold out that long, they would fear no further danger. He left legate Quintus Calenus to follow with two legions by normal marches while he made for Caninius with all his cavalry as fast as possible.

40. When he reached Uxellodunum ahead of all expectations, he found the town surrounded by fortification. There was no way to pull back from siege, but he knew from deserters that the townsfolk had abundant grain supply, so he began to

---

[12] Caesar in 7.3 called him Cotuatus. Some have argued that the word *gutuater* (attested in a few later Gallic inscriptions) denotes a kind of Gallic priest, perhaps a druid.

try to keep the enemy from water. A river divided the lower valley that almost surrounded the hill, steep on all sides, on which Uxellodunum sat. The nature of the place kept him from diverting it, for it passed at the very foot of the hills in such a way that no trench-digging could lead the water off in any direction. The townsfolk's descent to it was steep and difficult, so they could not approach the river without risk of injury and death when our men made a stand, nor could they make their way back up the difficult ascent. Seeing this difficulty, Caesar stationed archers and slingers and, at some of the easiest paths, catapults to keep them from the water of the stream.

41. Then all their water-bearers gathered in one place, under the town wall, where a sizeable spring of water broke out on the side where for about three hundred feet the river did not encircle the camp.[13] Everyone wanted to keep them from this spring, but Caesar alone saw how. With great effort and constant fighting he began to drive forward sheds against the mountain and build an earthen ramp. The locals run down from above and fight in safety from just out of reach, wounding many of our men making their way up, but our soldiers are not stopped from pushing forward the sheds and overcoming the challenges of the position with hard work. At the same time, they worked tunnels toward the rivulets and the source of the spring, and could do this without danger and without the enemy noticing. The ramp is built up sixty feet high, and on it they place a tower of ten stories, not actually reaching the top of the wall (that could not be done by any works), but enough to be higher than the spring. When spears were hurled by catapults from there toward the approaches to the spring and the townsmen could not get water safely, then not only the

---

[13] Hirtius is muddled again, either in his writing or in his knowledge of the site or both, and best efforts to identify the place have not been very persuasive.

cattle and beasts of burden but even a great many of the enemy were laid low by thirst.

42. Terrified by this threat, the townsmen fill barrels with tallow, pitch, and scrap lumber, set them afire, and roll them down on our works, fighting hard at the same time to use the dangers of battle to keep the Romans from putting out the fire. A great blaze erupts right in the works, for whatever they threw down the steep slope was caught by the sheds and ramp, swallowing up what got in its way. Our soldiers, on the other hand, though hard pressed in a dangerous kind of fight on uneven ground, still endured everything bravely. The action took place on high ground in plain view of our army, with great shouting on both sides. Everyone threw himself against enemy weapons and flames as visibly as he could, the better for his courage to be known and recorded.

43. When Caesar sees a number of his men wounded, he orders cohorts from all sides of town to climb the mount and raise a shout as if they were seizing the walls. The townsmen were terrified by this and unsure what was going on elsewhere, so they call their armed men back from attacking our works and deploy them on the walls. So our men, when that fight was over, quickly douse or tear down the parts of the works that were in flames. The townsmen continued to resist fiercely even after losing so many to thirst, finally the spring's streams were cut and turned aside by our tunneling. When this happened, the ever-flowing spring dried up quickly and made the townspeople so desperate for their safety that they thought it had happened not by human cunning but by the will of the gods. They were compelled to surrender.

44. Caesar knew everyone was aware of his mild temperament and did not fear anyone thinking he acted harshly out of

cruelty.[14] But he could not foretell the outcome of his strategy if many people in different places joined in plans of this sort, so he decided to intimidate the rest with exemplary punishment. He cuts the hands off all who had borne arms and lets them live so the punishment for wrongdoing would be well attested. Drappes, whom I said Caninius had captured, perhaps out of grief and shame for his chains or else fearing worse punishment, fasted a few days and so perished. At the same time, Lucterius—I wrote that he fled the battle—fell into the power of the Arvernian Epasnactus. He had moved on frequently, trusting himself to the loyalty of many but feeling he could safely stay nowhere for long, as hostile as he had to think Caesar was. The Roman people's great friend Epasnactus the Arvernian had no hesitation leading him to Caesar in chains.

45. Labienus meanwhile fights a successful cavalry battle in Treveri country, killing numerous Treveri and Germani, who refused no one help against the Romans. He takes their chiefs into his power alive, including Surus the Haeduan, exceedingly noble for ancestry and courage, the only one of the Haedui still in arms.

46. Knowing this, Caesar saw and judged that things were going well everywhere in Gaul. While Gaul had been beaten and subjugated in the preceding summers, he had never visited Aquitaine, but partially subdued it by sending Publius Crassus, so he set out with two legions to spend the summer's end there. This he accomplished as quickly and successfully as other things. All the Aquitanian nations sent Caesar legates

---

[14] This is not *mere* humbug: Cicero said as much of him in a letter (*ad Fam.* 6.6.8). The bloodthirst of combat and the massacres by his troops never diminished *his* reputation for mildness when presented with the opportunity to make a calm strategic choice.

and gave him hostages. Once this was done, he set out for Narbo with a cavalry guard, sending legates to take the army to winter quarters. He placed four legions in Belgium with legates Mark Antony and Caius Trebonius and Publius Vatinius; two legions he sent among the Haedui—whose prestige he knew was the highest in all Gaul; two he set among the Turones on their border with the Carnutes, to control the whole region down to the ocean; the two remaining he put among the Lemovices not far from the Arverni, so there would be no part of Gaul without an army.[15]

He spent a few days in the province himself, reviewing all the courts, hearing public disputes, and rewarding the worthy. He had an excellent opportunity of discovering each one's attitude toward the Roman people in the Gallic uprising, which he had endured with the loyal support of the province. With all this accomplished he took himself to the legions in Belgium and wintered at Nemetocenna.[16]

47. There he finds out that Commius of the Atrebates fought a battle with his cavalry. For when Antony arrived in winter quarters and the nation of the Atrebates remained loyal, Commius, after the wounding we mentioned above, was always ready to exploit every whim among his people, so the ones looking for war would not be without a guide and leader in arms, while the state was still obeying the Romans. Together with his cavalry he supported himself and his people by brigandage, haunting the roads and intercepting much of the supplies being taken to the Roman winter quarters.

48. The cavalry commander C. Volusenus Quadratus was assigned to Antony, to winter with him. Antony sends him to

[15] By counting we infer that he took one more legion back to Cisalpine Gaul with him.
[16] Arras.

pursue the enemy cavalry. Volusenus combined his singular courage with great hatred for Commius and so did as he was ordered more readily. Setting ambushes and attacking his cavalry repeatedly, he had achieved battlefield successes. Finally, when the fighting was hot and Volusenus himself pursued Commius stubbornly, taking along a few of his men, trying to cut him off, his enemy Commius in headlong flight drew Volusenus on too far, suddenly calling on the loyalty and assistance of all his men not to leave his wounds, so perfidiously inflicted, go unpunished. He turns his horse away from his men and lets himself go heedlessly after the prefect. All his cavalry do the same and cause our few men to turn in flight. Commius brings his horse, spurred to fury, alongside the horse of Quadratus and with his lance turned he drives it through the middle of Volusenus' thigh with great force.

With the prefect injured, our men do not hesitate to make a stand, turning their horses and driving back the enemy. When this happens, many of the enemy, driven back by our side's great onrush, are wounded. Some are run down in flight, some are cut off. The leader avoided this evil by the speed of his horse. And so the battle was a success, but the prefect was so gravely wounded that he was taken back to camp almost in peril of his life. Commius, on the other hand, either had assuaged his grievance or perhaps just lost most of his men. He sends representatives to Antony, swearing to go where he was told and do what was commanded, and he gives hostages. He asks one concession to his fears—that he not have to come within sight of any Roman.[17] Antony thinks this demand arises from an understandable fear and so grants the request and accepts the hostages.

[17] He swore this already at 8.23 (when the wounds "so perfidiously inflicted" mentioned above were received).

EIGHTH COMMENTARY
(CONTINUED)

50 BCE

Hirtius' account of this last year in Gaul includes no material business there. The follow-on demonstrations of authority from 51 had been effective. At the end of the year, Caesar apportioned his army to maintain Roman authority whatever might come. Half the remaining troops were among the Belgae, the other half centrally positioned and, as it happened, among the Haedui. The Haedui had no real choice but to smile and accept the honor of hosting Rome's finest soldiers. Bear in mind that the settlement in 52 of the great rebellion had let the Haedui off the hook for their betrayals and failings. The message to them was clear: resistance may or may not be futile, but it is certainly unprofitable. Cooperation was to be profitable. Rome did not always end its conquests with so flagrant a purchase of elite support, but there was almost always some element of reward for submission.

Caesar left Gaul at the usual season to find his future from headquarters in Cisalpine Gaul. His enemies had been busy.

The clearest step the established order took against Caesar this year was thinly veiled. Rome still wanted, several years after Crassus' death, to prepare to fight the Parthians, and when a scare was promoted in May 50, Pompey and Caesar were each asked to supply a legion to hold in readiness for that purpose. But Pompey met that request by agreeing to supply the legion he had supposedly loaned to Caesar some time before. In other words, the request of one from each was effectively a move to strip two from Caesar. No surprise, when the legions reached Italy, there was no move to send them on to Parthia. Pompey kept them in Capua south of Rome, ready for when he would need them. If there was a plus for Caesar in this transfer, it lay in the attitude of those troops toward Pompey and Caesar. They respected Caesar; they knew they were supposed to respect Pompey.

Caesar had his own strength now, in the vast wealth plundered from Gaul during his time there. He was able to give Lucius Aemilius Paullus, running for consul in 50, nine million denarii, which finished funding the construction of the Basilica Aemilia in the Forum. Scribonius Curio had been a friend to all, but when Caesar paid off his 2.5 million denarii in debts in 50, he became a loyal supporter to Caesar (earning for his pains death in battle in Africa fighting for Caesar in 49). In March of 50, then as tribune, Curio vetoed any discussion of replacing Caesar. Not only were these two purchases important in themselves, but they also reminded many others of what was possible for those who supported Caesar. Long years back from the wars left Pompey without disposable wealth on this scale.

In the late spring, Pompey fell ill at Naples for several weeks, but he recovered to general rejoicing. Plutarch later would describe this as a moment of overbearing confidence for Pompey, quoting him as claiming that he could stamp his foot on the ground and Italy would pour forth whole armies to support him.

Caesar was well informed about Rome's events and rumors, and during this summer sent his legate Mark Antony back to Rome to stand for election as augur and as tribune. He was successful in both campaigns, notably defeating the vehement anti-Caesarean Ahenobarbus in the contest for the augurate. But Caesar's candidate for consul, Sulpicius Galba, was not successful. The successful ones were both bad news for Caesar: another Marcellus, brother of the one from 51, and Cornelius Lentulus Crus. Some suspected Caesar might have his hooks into Lentulus, but in fact his only support in 49 would come from three praetors (one of them was the Lepidus who would join the second triumvirate with Antony and Octavian) and the two tribunes, Antony and Cassius.

Crisis loomed over whether Caesar would be allowed to run for consul for the year 48 during the summer of 49 without giving up his troops and returning to the city. By August the word on the street was that Pompey had finally and firmly decided to oppose that permission and that Caesar had decisively refused to comply. Would he, the street asked, swoop back toward Rome to defend Curio and tribunal authority?

As the year ended, alarm grew. On 1 December, Cato proposed that both Caesar and Pompey should dismiss their armies and present themselves as citizens at Rome. That proposal sounded good to many and drew an overwhelming vote in the senate, but the consul Marcellus used senate procedure to prevent its actual passage and confirmation. Curio's term as tribune ended on 9 December (as Antony and Cassius took office) and he fled for safety to join Caesar in Ravenna. Caesar's forces were gathering: he now had three legions south of the Alps. Even the officially sacrosanct tribunes, however, might not feel safe much longer.

Caesar speaks for himself about this crisis in the opening pages of his commentaries on the civil war. What was anyone else thinking? We have a document that presents itself as a letter from Sallust to Caesar that some scholars date to this moment of crisis, offering Machiavellian advice. The oligarchs must be faced and broken. The Roman people must be remade by the admission of large numbers of new citizens. The old order could not go on.

In the first days of January, Curio returned to Rome with a letter from Caesar described by the Cassius Dio (41.1) thus:

> As to the letter, it contained a list of all the benefits which Caesar had ever conferred upon the state and a defense of the charges which were brought against him. He promised to disband his legions and give up his office if Pompey would also do the same; for while the latter bore arms it was not right, he claimed, that he should be compelled to give up his and so be exposed to his enemies.

It was too late. The senate was unmoved. On January 7, they passed the *senatus consultum ultimum*, "the senate's ultimate decree" granting the consuls virtually unrestricted authority to take whatever steps they judged necessary to defend the republic. Caesar was ordered to disband his army. Now it was time for the tribunes Antony and Cassius, powerless to help further, to flee to Caesar.

On the night of January 10, Caesar's troops crossed the tiny river Rubicon that formed the boundary between home and abroad. Caesar's colleague Asinius Pollio wrote an account of that night twenty years later, famously taken up a hundred years after Caesar by the poet Lucan (who hated him), and turned into the familiar and dramatic story of Caesar at the head of his troops pausing to reflect, then plunging across the stream on horseback to pursue his fortune. It was still later that other writers gave Caesar his famous line—"the die is cast!" The die was indeed cast, however little truth there is to the familiar story.[1]

[1] I am grateful to Professor Robert Morstein-Marx for sharing unpublished work that shows we have no reason to think that getting across that bit of water was in any way dramatic. It was unmistakably important that Caesar began to move south with his army, but it was not (as most moderns claim) actually illegal. Much remained uncertain, but Caesar was still looking for a peaceable resolution to the crisis. The dreary breakdown of negotiations with Pompey and Pompey's decision to flee Italy later in January 49 are what made civil war inevitable.

IN THE CONSULSHIP OF
AEMILIUS PAULLUS AND
CLAUDIUS MARCELLUS
THE LESSER

I know Caesar put together individual commentaries for individual years. I don't think I need to do this, especially because the following year (the consulship of Paulus and Marcellus) has nothing of importance happening in Gaul. I've decided to write a bit more and attach it to this commentary so readers will know where Caesar and his army were at this time.

49. While Caesar was wintering in Belgium, he had this one purpose, to keep the nations there friendly and give none pretext or hope for taking up arms. He wanted nothing less than to have the need to fight a war pressed on him as he neared the time of his departure, to leave behind a war that all Gaul could readily take part in without immediate danger as he was leading his army away. And so he greeted all the nations respectfully, bestowed great gifts on their chiefs, and imposed no new burdens, thus keeping a Gaul wearied by so many defeats in battle the more easily at peace on better terms of obedience.

50. When winter ended, against his usual habit he made for Italy by the longest possible marches, to call on the mu-

nicipalities and colonies to which he had commended the candidacy for the priesthood of his quaestor Mark Antony.[2] He was glad to exert his influence on behalf of a man so close to him whom he had sent on ahead to declare his candidacy, especially against the plotting and power of a few men who wanted to uproot the influence Caesar had as he retired by defeating Antony. Though he heard on the way before reaching Italy that Antony had been made augur, he still thought the case no less strong for visiting the municipalities and colonies to thank them for offering their loyalty en masse to Antony, and at the same time to press his own candidacy for the office of the following year, especially because his enemies were boasting that Lentulus and Marcellus had been made consuls to strip Caesar of his honor and dignity, taking the consulship away from Servius Galba, though he had much more influential support but had been joined to Caesar by friendship and service as a legate.[3]

51. Caesar's arrival was greeted by all the municipalities and colonies with unbelievable honor and love. This was the first time he came to them after the war with all Gaul. Nothing imaginable was left undone for the decoration of all the gates, roads, and places where Caesar would go. The whole population, including children, went out to meet him, victims were sacrificed everywhere, forums and temples were full of couches spread with covers, so you could anticipate the rejoicing of the universally admired triumph. Such was the great extravagance of the rich and the enthusiasm of the poorer folk.

---

[2] Antonius was elected to his priesthood in September 50.
[3] I reproduce the baggy shapelessness of an 82-word sentence in 106 of my own.

52. When he had passed through all the regions of Gaul of the togas, he returned to the army at Nemetocenna with the greatest speed. Summoning the legions from all the winter quarters to Treveri territory, he went there himself to review the army.[4] He put Labienus in command of Gaul of the togas, to encourage their support for his candidacy for the consulship. He himself set out on marches long enough to offer a healthy change of air. Once there, though he heard frequently that Labienus was being enticed by his own enemies and he was informed that the plotting of a few was seeking to use senatorial intervention to take away part of his army, he still believed none of what he heard about Labienus and could not be induced to act in any way against the authority of the senate. He judged that his case would be easily won through the free choice of the conscript fathers.

For Curio, a tribune of the people, had undertaken to defend the cause and reputation of Caesar and regularly promised the senate that if anyone suffered from fear of Caesar in arms while Pompey's lording it over the forum with his own forces was itself a source of no little fear, then both could give up their weapons and dismiss their armies. With that the city would be free and autonomous. He did not merely promise this, but even tried to obtain a senatorial decree through voting. The consuls and Pompey's friends succeeded in blocking that proposal and so dismissed the idea by delaying.

53. This was considerable evidence for the position of the senate as a whole, consistent with what they had done before. Marcellus in the preceding year, when he was impugning the standing of Caesar, violating the law of Pompey and Crassus,

---

[4] This was a great show, well north toward the Rhine, designed to leave a lasting impression of the size and power of Roman armies.

brought prematurely to the senate a bill on the provinces of Caesar, and when the debate was over Marcellus went to make a division, seeking every advantage for himself out of jealousy toward Caesar, but a crowded senate went entirely over to the other side. The spirit of Caesar's enemies was not broken by this, but they were warned to come up with greater compulsions by which the senate could be made to approve what they had determined to do.

54. Then there was passed a decree of the senate to send one legion from Pompey and another from Caesar to the Parthian war. It was not at all unclear that the two legions were to be taken from only one of them. For Pompey contributed the first legion he had sent to Caesar, made up by a draft in Caesar's province, as if it were from his own number. So Caesar, without any doubt as to his opponents' intentions, gave the legion to Pompey and in his own name orders the fifteenth legion, which he had in nearer Gaul, to be handed over according to the senate's decree.[5] In its place he sends the thirteenth legion into Italy to watch the stations from which the fifteenth was removed. He assigns winter quarters to the army: Trebonius he places in Belgium with four legions, Fabius with the same number he moves to the Haedui. He thought Gaul would be safest if the Belgae, the bravest, and the Haedui, the most respected, were held in check by armies. He himself left for Italy.

55. When he arrives there, he learns that the two legions he had sent, which by the senate's decree should have been sent to the Parthian war, had been handed over by the consul Marcellus to Pompey and kept in Italy. Though from this there was

[5] Plutarch *Pompey* 56 says that Caesar gave the departing fifteenth legion such generous gifts that he knew they would remain loyal to him.

no doubt what was being planned against Caesar, still Caesar decided to endure everything as long as there was some hope left of legal debate rather than war. He makes his way . . . [6]

[6] The last word, *contendit*, appears only in a few manuscripts, but is precious evidence that the text is broken off. Other scribes preferred to end with a complete sentence and so omitted the word. We end as the book stands late in 50 BCE, while Caesar's own account of the civil war begins in the first days of 49. A few paragraphs are likely missing.

AFTER WAR, AFTER GAUL

Did a million people die in this war for Gaul? That's the estimate of Pliny the Elder a little over a century later. A huge loss to the human race, he said, even if Caesar had no alternative. He thinks Caesar had a conscience guilty enough to keep him from mentioning casualties at all in his account of the civil wars. (In Gaul, he was not so shy.) I tried to make my own count of casualties and slaughter, and gave up in despair at the sketchy, inconsistent, and vague evidence Caesar provides. Instead, I have tried in my introductions and notes to make sure the reader attends to the corpse-heaping, blood-running, terror-shrieking battlefields that appear so matter-of-factly on these pages. In the end, the most appalling part of the story is precisely the calm, matter-of-fact treatment of episodes beyond ghastly to imagine.

Caesar brought many to their deaths, he plundered the region for its wealth, and he lived to kill again in the brutal civil war that followed. When his friends and colleagues came to kill *him*, it was not for his crimes but for his success and his future imagined successes. Claiming all of "Gaul" for Roman sway was self-evidently a good thing for Rome.

Caesar himself, of course, went on to batter his enemies into submission, in a war that ranged across the breadth of the Mediterranean, from Greece to Egypt to north Africa to Spain. He was consul with silent partners in 48 and 46, sole consul in 45, and then consul with Mark Antony in 44. "He doth bestride the narrow world like a colossus, and we petty men walk under his huge legs and peep about to find ourselves dishonorable graves"—thus Shakespeare's Cassius at the moment of plotting, not far from the truth.

Roman rhetoricians liked to train their students by making them argue famous historical decisions: Agamemnon thinks about whether to sacrifice Iphigeneia, that sort of thing. Should Caesar have been assassinated? The case in favor was powerful and obvious: he sought too much power, entailing the downfall of the established order. So he was killed and his nephew prevailed, creating a regime that was as much like the established order as possible, with new winners and new losers. Twenty centuries later the Prince in Lampedusa's novel *Il Gattopardo* (*The Leopard*) would famously observe that "if we want things to stay the same, things will have to change." Augustus was practicing what Italians call "gattopardismo" long before. The assassination, in short, made no difference except to ensure the killing of many and the destruction of the assassins. Stabbed to death at the foot of Pompey's statue in the senate's meeting place in Pompey's theater, Caesar still prevailed. (Suetonius says that the senate decreed that it would not again meet on March 15 and ordered the assassination site walled up in perpetuity.)

And they made him a god. The "emperors" who succeeded him were in the main deified themselves, and Rome persisted. Few today would think Caesar an actual god, but his standing as the kind of larger-than-life figure to whom adverse judgments do not stick is secure. His nephew was not half the Caesar he was, but made the excellent decision to live on to a ripe old age, so far outlasting his enemies that he left a regime (57 years after he began to grasp for it) cloaked in inevitability. It is conventional to lament the decline and fall of the Roman empire; better we should be astonished it lasted so long.

Caesar holds sway still, of course, especially over these pages. It is a book cool, controlled, and calm. Even if it is sometimes more elaborate than one might expect, it leaves an impression of laconic brevity. It is notable for all that it does not say, about the political context at Rome but even among the Gallic nations, and about the logistics of the army and its hangers-on. Most of all, it presents in plain view a series of ghastly slaughters recounted with no sign of regret or bad conscience, and none but the slightest mention of the vast plunder that accompanied the slaughters. A quartermaster's full account of the war and its ramifications would make a very different book, rich in fascinating detail we are denied.

But that choice to hold a tight, narrow focus is in the end a literary choice. Cool, focused, unhurried: the narrator of all but the last commentary is in his lofty, detached third-person voice himself the real hero of the story. We see the Gallic world through his eyes—or rather see what he wants us to see of the Gallic world—and so we all *become* Caesar, an audience subsumed in the self-aggrandizing statesman. It seems natural that he has been read in so many classrooms over the centuries since, natural that we are thus complicit with him. Those who refuse to read him have a point. But would it be really any better if he were banned from classrooms and read in guilty secret by rebellious students?

In the end, this book is brilliant and beautiful and a vehicle still carrying passengers on its mission of conquest and colonization in Gaul, of domination in Rome and the whole Mediterranean beyond. So, gentle reader, there is a way in which, as you put down this volume, you have become Caesar. Have a care what you make of yourself next.

Three Meditations on Caesar,
His War, and His Book

JOSEPH CONRAD, *HEART OF DARKNESS*

"And this also," said Marlow suddenly, "has been one of the dark places of the earth." . . . His remark did not seem at all surprising. It was just like Marlow. It was accepted in silence. No one took the trouble to grunt even; and presently he said, very slow—"I was thinking of very old times, when the Romans first came here, nineteen hundred years ago—the other day. . . . Light came out of this river since—you say Knights? Yes; but it is like a running blaze on a plain, like a flash of lightning in the clouds. We live in the flicker—may it last as long as the old earth keeps rolling! But darkness was here yesterday. Imagine the feelings of a commander of a fine—what d'ye call 'em?—trireme in the Mediterranean, ordered suddenly to the north; run overland across the Gauls in a hurry; put in charge of one of these craft the legionaries—a wonderful lot of handy men they must have been, too—used to build, apparently by the hundred, in a month or two, if we may believe what we read. Imagine him here—the very end of the world, a sea the colour of lead, a sky the colour of smoke, a kind of ship about as rigid as a concertina—and going up this river with stores, or orders, or what you like. Sand-banks, marshes, forests, savages,—precious little to eat fit for a civilized man, nothing but Thames water to drink. No Falernian wine here, no going ashore. Here and there a military camp lost in a wilderness, like a needle in a bundle of hay—cold, fog, tempests, disease, exile, and death—death skulking in the air, in the water, in the bush. They must have been dying like flies here. Oh, yes—he did it. Did it very well, too, no doubt, and without thinking much about it either, except afterwards to brag of what he had gone through in his time, perhaps. They were men enough to face the darkness. And perhaps he was cheered by keeping his eye on a chance of promotion to the fleet at Ravenna by and by, if he had good friends in Rome and survived the awful climate. Or think of a decent young citizen in a toga—perhaps too much dice, you know—coming out here in the train of some prefect, or tax-gatherer, or trader even, to mend his fortunes. Land in a swamp, march through the woods, and in some inland post feel the savagery, the utter savagery, had closed round him—all that mysterious life of the wilderness that stirs in the forest, in the jungles, in the hearts of wild men. There's no initiation either into such mysteries. He has to live in the midst of the incomprehensible, which is also detestable. And it has a fascination, too, that goes to work upon him. The fascination of the abomination—you know, imagine the growing regrets, the longing to escape, the powerless disgust, the surrender, the hate."

He paused.

"Mind," he began again, lifting one arm from the elbow, the palm of the hand outwards, so that, with his legs folded before him, he had the pose of a Buddha preaching in European clothes and without a lotus-flower—"Mind, none of us would feel exactly like this. What saves us is efficiency—the devotion to efficiency. But these chaps were not much account, really. They were no colonists; their administration was merely a squeeze, and nothing more, I suspect. They were conquerors, and for that you want only brute force—nothing to boast of, when you have it, since your strength is just an accident arising from the weakness of others. They grabbed what they could get for the sake of what was to be got. It was just robbery with violence, aggravated murder on a great scale, and men going at it blind—as is very proper for those who tackle a darkness. The conquest of the earth, which mostly means the taking it away from those who have a different complexion or slightly flatter noses than ourselves, is not a pretty thing when you look into it too much. What redeems it is the idea only. An idea at the back of it; not a sentimental pretence but an idea; and an unselfish belief in the idea—something you can set up, and bow down before, and offer a sacrifice to. . . ."

KENNETH REXROTH, "CLASSICS REVISITED XXXII, JULIUS CAESAR," *SATURDAY REVIEW*, JULY 30, 1966

Caesar was one of the most completely competent writers in all literature. It is impossible to doubt his meaning, if we have an ordinary grasp of the Latin language, but his style is nervous, full of surprises and deliberately odd. His syntax on the page looks like speech, but like Ernest Hemingway's, it is not talk that can be uttered. It is as formal, with its own special formulas, as that of Racine or Pope, who are also supposed to have written simply. Reading Julius Caesar, if you read Latin and have never read him as a child (a most unlikely contingency), is like riding a high-spirited horse, who for all his nerves is always completely under control. There is no prose just like his in any language. What he does with language, so he did with life. On every page of *The Gallic War* the simple, unambiguous nouns and verbs carom off each other like billiard balls. There are few adjectives and they serve mostly to fix the nouns in place. The adverbs are all active—they aim the verbs. Prose which exhibits so high a level of irritability, in the physiological sense, usually lacks unity of effect, subordination of parts to the whole—but not Caesar's. The rapid and complex movement of simple elements deploys on the page exactly as the battles it describes. He should be read as he wrote, at great speed. *The Gallic War* can be got through in two quiet evenings with port, biscuits, and a thick slice of Caerphilly, and that is the way it should be done. *The Civil War* can easily be read in a night.

MONTAIGNE, *ESSAIS* 2.10, "OF BOOKS"

But Caesar, in my opinion, particularly deserves to be studied, not for the knowledge of the history only, but for himself, so great an excellence and perfection he has above all the rest, though Sallust be

one of the number. In earnest, I read this author with more rever-
ence and respect than is usually allowed to human writings; one
while considering him in his person, by his actions and miraculous
greatness, and another in the purity and inimitable polish of his
language, wherein he not only excels all other historians, as Cicero
confesses, but, peradventure, even Cicero himself; speaking of his
enemies with so much sincerity in his judgment, that, the false co-
lours with which he strives to palliate his evil cause, and the ordure
of his pestilent ambition excepted, I think there is no fault to be
objected against him, saving this, that he speaks too sparingly of
himself, seeing so many great things could not have been performed
under his conduct, but that his own personal acts must necessarily
have had a greater share in them than he attributes to them.[1]

[1] Trans. William Carew Hazlitt.

Chronology

The principle that "life is one damned thing after another" seems on the evidence of quotation-hunters only to have been discovered in 1909, but should have been self-evident. To mitigate damnation, here is an outline of principal events relevant to Caesar's book.

146 BCE	Destruction of Carthage by Scipio the Elder and the end of serious rivalry to Rome in the western Mediterranean.
133 and 121 BCE	Assassination of Tiberius (133) and Gaius (121) Gracchus, senators who as tribunes advanced land-reform policies that infuriated the entrenched aristocracy.
107, 104, 103, 102, 101, 100, and 86 BCE	Consulates (the last terminated by death after only two weeks) of Gaius Marius, the first generalissimo—army reformer, successful commander, and effectively military dictator, with achievements surpassing all earlier leaders.
88, 82/81, and 80 BCE	Years of consulships (88 and 80) and dictatorship (82/81) of Lucius Sulla, who began as an officer of Marius and ended as his rival. His retirement at the end of 80 allowed restoration of a version of normal constitutional government.
70, 55, and 52 BCE	Consulships of Pompey, the first when he was years younger than the normal age for holding that rank. He rose to notice under Sulla, and his victories over Sertorius' rebels in Spain (76–71),

the rebel slave Spartacus (71), and king Mithridates of Pontus (61) garnered him an unprecedented three triumphs. It was Sulla who nicknamed him "the Great," a moniker he proceeded to earn.

63 BCE	The Catilinarian conspiracy crushed and its leaders executed by the consul Cicero.
59 BCE	Caesar's consulship.
58ff:	Caesar in Gaul.
58 BCE	Campaigns against the Helvetians and Germans led by Ariovistus; Cicero sent into exile.
57 BCE	Campaigns against the Nervii, while one of his generals is active in Britany and Normandy.
56 BCE	Caesar, Pompey, and Crassus meet at Lucca to collaborate on dominating the Roman world, creating the "first triumvirate"; relatively minor campaigns in northern Gaul.
55 BCE	Campaign against the Usipetes and Tencteri invading from across the Rhine; shows of force for Caesar across the Rhine and across the English Channel.
54 BCE	Caesar's second visit to Britain, then disaster when a legion and a half are destroyed in winter quarters.
53 BCE	Restoring order, recruiting additional troops.
52 BCE	Great Gallic revolt, nominally under Vercingetorix; battles of Avaricum, Gergovia, Alesia. Final score: Caesar 2, Vercingetorix 1.
51 BCE	Mainly quiet in Gaul, Caesar's attention diverted to Rome and the prospects for his return to another consular campaign.
50 BCE	Caesar's last year in Gaul, mainly quiet.
49 BCE	Caesar returns from Gaul; Pompey and his allies flee to Greece; civil war begins.
48 BCE	Battle of Pharsalus (August 9), death of Pompey (September 28) in Egypt.

46 BCE	Caesar's triumph at Rome for all his conquests.
44 BCE	Caesar murdered at the foot of Pompey's statue on the Ides of March
43 BCE	"Second triumvirate" arranged by Octavian, Antony, and Lepidus (November); proscriptions of their enemies, with the murder of Cicero (December).
31 BCE	Battle of Actium eliminates Antony and secures the regime of Octavian; he takes the name Augustus in 27 BCE, dies in 14 CE.

Acknowledgments

The first book written in Latin that I ever bought voluntarily (thus, not a textbook) was Edwards' old Loeb of the *BG*, my freshman year in college, at just the moment when I discovered that there were Latin authors (Caesar, Aquinas) that I could actually *read* and not merely disencrypt in the pedestrian classroom way. The magic of that moment, the discovery that reading Latin makes my head feel good, is with me to this day. The book I have still, a sacred relic. I began translating Caesar to tease and amuse myself at odd moments of distraction from administrative duties, found him rewarding and challenging, and so pressed on, convinced there would be a way to present the book as a work of literature and as the record of deeds deserving to be challenged.

Gibbon said of Augustine that his learning was too often borrowed, his arguments too often his own. I claim no unique learning or scholarly contribution here and have plundered the worthies of Caesarian scholarship unashamedly. Every third word should have a footnote, but this would be inappropriate in a translation meant for readers to enjoy, so I append here the books and articles I have read, with great admiration and gratitude.

* * * *

WORKS CONSULTED

The scholarly literature on Caesar is naturally vast. I list here the works to which I am particularly indebted, often for modest points of detail, often for much more. I stand on their shoulders, I crouch in their shadows, and I admire and proclaim their learning, insight, and wisdom.

Beckwith C. I. *Empires of the Silk Road*. 2009.

Bertrand, A. C. "Stumbling through Gaul: Maps, Intelligence, and Caesar's *Bellum Gallicum*," *Ancient History Bulletin* 11(1997) 107–22.

Bradley, K. *Slavery and Society at Rome*. 1994.

Canfora, L. "Cesare continuato," *Belfagor* 25(1970) 419–29.

———. *Julius Caesar*. 1999.

Coffee, N. "Caesar Chrematopoios," *Classical Journal* 106(2011) 397–421.

Collins, J. "Caesar as Political Propagandist," *ANRW* 1(1972) 922–66.

Connor, C. *Roman Bridges*. 1993.

Edwards, H. J. *Caesar: The Gallic War*. (Loeb edition) 1917.

Feeney, D. *Caesar's Calendar*. 2007.

Gaertner, J. and Hausburg, B. *Caesar and the Bellum Alexandrinum: an analysis of style, narrative technique, and the reception of Greek historiography*. 2013.

Garcea, A. *Caesar's De analogia. Edition, Translation, and Commentary*. 2012.

Gelzer, M. *Caesar: Politician and Statesman*. Trans. Peter Needham. 1968.

Goscinny, R., and A. Uderzo. *Asterix le Gaulois*. 1961. The "graphic novel" of Caesar's war in Gaul, in many volumes. Less inaccurate than one might expect and useful as a running ironic commentary on Caesarean imperialism. See also K. Brodersen, ed., *Asterix und seine Zeit: Die große Welt des kleinen Galliers*. 2001.

Goudineau, C. "Le *gutuater* gaulois: idéologie et histoire," *Gallia* 60(2003) 383–387; on the word, I follow him against Y. le Bohec, "*Gutuater*: nom propre ou nom commun?" *Gallia* 58(2001) 383–87.

Griffin, M., ed. *A Companion to Julius Caesar*. 2009.

Hammond, C. *Caesar: The Gallic War*. (Oxford World's Classics) 1996.

Kaster, R. *Cicero: Speech on behalf of Publius Sestius*. 2006.

Kemezis, A. "Caesar's Vesontio Speech and the rhetoric of mendacity in the late republic (Dio 38.36–46)," in *Cassius Dio: Greek Intellectual and Roman Politician*, Carsten Lange and Jesper Majbom Madsen, eds. 2016: 238–57.

Krebs, C. "Thucydides in Gaul: the siege of Plataea as Caesar's model for his siege of Avaricum," *Histos* 10(2016) 1–14.

Meusel, H. *C. Iulii Caesaris Commentarii de bello Gallico / erklärt von Fr. Kraner und W. Dittenberger*. 17th ed., 1913.

Millar, F. *A Study of Cassius Dio*. 1962.

Moscovich, M. J. "*Obsidibus traditis*: Hostages in Caesar's *De Bello Gallico*," *Classical Journal* 75.2(1979–80) 122–28.

Napoleon III. *Histoire de Jules César*. 1865–66.

Ortu, R., "*Praeda Bellica*: la guerra tra economia e diritto nell'antica Roma." (http://eprints.uniss.it/1594/1/Ortu_R_Articolo_2005_Praeda.pdf).

Osgood, J. "The Pen and the Sword: Writing and Conquest in Caesar's Gaul." *Classical Antiquity* 28(2009) 328–58.

Pelling, C. "Caesar's Battle-Descriptions and the Defeat of Ariovistus," *Latomus* 40(1981) 740–766.

Raaflaub, K., and J. T. Ramsey. "Reconstructing the Chronology of Caesar's Gallic Wars," *Histos* 11(2017) 1–74.

Rambaud, M. *L'Art de la déformation historique dans les Commentaires de César*. 1953.

Rice Holmes, T. *Caesar's Conquest of Gaul*. 2nd ed., 1911.

———. *Ancient Britain and the Invasions of Julius Caesar*. 1907.

———. *Commentarii rerum in Gallia gestarum VII; A. Hirti Commentarius VIII*. 1914.

Riggsby, A. *Caesar in Gaul and Rome: War in Words*. 2006.

Sahlins, M. *Apologies to Thucydides*. 2004. Provocative and useful for many reasons, not least for reminding us that the one who gets to name a war gets to create the war. Caesar created his "Gallic War" as Thucydides had created his Peloponnesian one. The struggle over names for the American war of 1861–65 illustrates the same principle.

Seager. R. *Pompey*. 2nd ed., 2002.

Shatzman, I. "Caesar: an economic biography and its political significance," *Scripta Hierosolymitana* 23(1972) 28–51.

Stevens, C. E. "The 'Bellum Gallicum' as a work of propaganda," *Latomus* 11(1952) 3–17, 165–79.

Syme, R. *The Roman Revolution*. 1939.

———. *Sallust*. 1964.

Ulrich, R. B. "Julius Caesar and the Creation of the Forum Iulium," *AJA* 97(1993) 49–80. "The Forum Iulium . . . reflected the impudence and even recklessness of its patron."

Weinstock, S. *Divus Julius*. 1971.

Welch, K. *Julius Caesar as Artful Reporter: the war commentaries as political instruments*. 1998.

Wiseman, T. P., and A. Wiseman *Battle for Gaul: Julius Caesar: a new translation.* 1980.

Wiseman, T. P. *Julius Caesar.* 2016.

———. *The Roman Audience.* 2015.

Woolf, G. *Becoming Roman: The Origins of Provincial Civilization in Gaul.* 2000.

* * * *

Two good books appeared too recently for me to use: K. Raaflaub et al., *The Landmark Julius Caesar* (2017) and L. Grillo and C. B. Krebs, eds., *The Cambridge Companion to the Writings of Julius Caesar* (2018). The nonscholarly reader can enjoy entering Caesar's (and Cicero's) world through the novels of Robert Harris, *Imperium, Lustrum,* and *Dictator,* or through the *Roma sub rosa* detective novels of Steven Saylor (eleven novels in the main sequence, plus some prequels and short stories).

Brief Index of Key Terms

9 780691 216690